Analog Interfacing to Embedded Microprocessor Systems

Analog Interfacing to Embedded Microprocessor Systems

Stuart R. Ball

AMSTERDAM • BOSTON • HEIDELBERG • LONDON
NEW YORK • OXFORD • PARIS • SAN DIEGO
SAN FRANCISCO • SINGAPORE • SYDNEY • TOKYO

Newnes is an imprint of Elsevier

ELSEVIER

Newnes

Newnes is an imprint of Elsevier.

 Recognizing the importance of preserving what has been written, Elsevier
prints its books on acid-free paper whenever possible.

Library of Congress Cataloging-in-Publication Data
Ball, Stuart R., 1956–
    Analog interfacing to embedded microprocessor systems / Stuart R. Ball.—2nd ed.
      p.   cm. — (Embedded technology series)
    Rev. ed. of: Analog inter-facing to embedded microprocessors. 2001.
    Includes index.
    ISBN 0-7506-7723-6
    1. Embedded computer systems—Design and construction.   I. Ball, Stuart R., 1956-
Analog inter-facing to embedded microprocessors. II. Title. III. Series.
TK7895.E42B33 2003
004.16—dc21   2003044211

British Library Cataloguing-in-Publication Data
A catalogue record for this book is available from the British Library.

The publisher offers special discounts on bulk orders of this book.
For information, please contact:

Manager of Special Sales
Elsevier
200 Wheeler Road, Sixth Floor
Burlington, MA 01803
Tel: 781-313-4700
Fax: 781-313-4882

For information on all Newnes publications available, contact our World Wide Web
home page at: http://www.newnespress.com

10 9 8 7 6 5 4 3 2 1

Printed in the United States of America

Contents

1 System Design   1

Dynamic Range   1
Calibration   2
Bandwidth   5
Processor Throughput   6
Avoiding Excess Speed   7
Other System Considerations   8
Sample Rate and Aliasing   11

2 Analog-to-Digital Converters   13

ADCs   15
Types of ADCs   17
ADC Comparison   25
Sample and Hold   26
Real Parts   29
Microprocessor Interfacing   30
Clocked Interfaces   35
Serial Interfaces   36
Multichannel ADCs   41
Internal Microcontroller ADCs   42
Codecs   43
Interrupt Rates   44
Dual-Function Pins on Microcontrollers   44
Design Checklist   46

3 Sensors   **47**

Temperature Sensors   47
Optical Sensors   59
CCDs   71
Magnetic Sensors   82
Motion/Acceleration Sensors   86
Strain Gauges   89

4 Time-Based Measurements   **91**

Measuring Period versus Frequency   94
Mixing   96
Voltage-to-Frequency Converters   98
Clock Resolution and Range   100
Extending Accuracy with Limited Resolution   102

5 Output Control Methods   **107**

Open-Loop Control   107
Negative Feedback and Control   107
Microprocessor-Based Systems   108
On-Off Control   109
Overshoot   112
Proportional Control   112
Proportional, Integral, Derivative Control   116
Motor Control   127
Predictive Control   133
Measuring and Analyzing Control Loops   134
PID Software Examples   138
Things to Remember in Control Design   143

6 Solenoids, Relays, and Other Analog Outputs   **145**

Solenoids   145
Heaters   149
Coolers   155
LEDs   157
DACs   162
Digital Potentiometers   163
Analog Switches   166

7 Motors   **171**

Stepper Motors   171
DC Motors   190
Tradeoffs between Motors   206
Power-Up Issues   207
Motor Torque   208
A Real-World Stepper Application   209

8 Electromagnetic Interference   **215**

Ground Loops   215
Electrostatic Discharge   220

9 High-Precision Applications   **225**

Input Offset Voltage   227
Input Resistance   228
Frequency Characteristics   229
Temperature Effects in Resistors   230
Voltage References   231
Temperature Effects in General   233
Noise and Grounding   234
Printed Circuit Board Layout   236
Statistical Tolerancing   239
Supply-Based References   240
Summary   241

10 Standard Interfaces   **243**

IEEE 1451.2   243
4–20 ma Current Loop   244
Fieldbus   245

11 Analog Toolbox   **247**

Microcontroller Supply and Reference   247
Resistor Networks   249
Multiple Input Control   250
AC Control   252
Voltage Monitors and Supervisory Circuits   254

Driving Bipolar Transistors   254
Driving MOSFETs   257
Reading Negative Voltages   261
Example Control System   262

Appendix A Opamp Basics   275

Opamp Configurations   275
General Opamp Design Equations   279
Nonresistive Elements   280
Reversing the Inputs   281
Comparators   281
Hysteresis   283
Instrumentation Amplifiers   285

Appendix B Pulse Width Modulation   287

Why PWM?   287
Real Parts   292
Frequency Limitations   292
Resolution Limitations   293
Power-Supply Considerations   294
PWM and EMI   294
Audio Applications   295
PWM Hardware   296
PWM Software   297

Appendix C Useful URLs   299

Semiconductors   299
Motors   299
Other   300

Appendix D Python Code for Chapter 11;   301
Excel Data for Chapter 4

Glossary   307

Index   311

Preface

There often seems to be a division between the analog and digital worlds. Digital designers usually do not like to delve into analog, and analog designers tend to avoid the digital realm. The two groups often do not even use the same buzzwords.

Even though microprocessors have become increasingly faster and more capable, the real world remains analog in nature. The digital designers who attempt to control or measure the real world must somehow connect this analog environment to their digital machines. There are books about analog design and books about microprocessor design. This book attempts to get at the issues involved in connecting the two together.

Someone said about my first book, *Embedded Microprocessor Systems: Real World Design*, that it needed more analog interfacing information. I felt that adding this material to that book would cause the book to lose focus. However, the more I thought about it, the more I thought that a book aimed at interfacing the real world to microprocessors could prove valuable. This book is the result. I hope it proves useful.

Introduction

Modern electronic systems are increasingly digital: digital microprocessors, digital logic, digital interfaces. Digital logic is easier to design and understand, and it is much more flexible than the equivalent analog circuitry would be. As an example, imagine trying to implement any kind of sophisticated microprocessor with analog parts. Digital electronics lets the PC on your desk execute different programs at different times, perform complex calculations, and communicate by the World Wide Web.

The electronic world is nearly all digital, but the real world is not. The temperature in your office is not just hot or cold, but varies over a wide range. You can use a thermometer to determine what the temperature is, but how do you convert the temperature to a digital value for use in a microprocessor-controlled thermostat? The ignition control microprocessor in your car has to measure the engine speed to generate a spark at the right time. A microprocessor-controlled machining tool has to position the cutting bit in the right place to cut a piece of steel.

This book provides coverage of practical control applications and gives some opamp examples; however, its focus is neither control theory nor opamp theory. Primarily, its coverage includes measurement and control of analog quantities in embedded systems that are required to interface with the real world. Whether measuring a signal from a satellite or the temperature of a toaster, embedded systems must measure, analyze, and control analog values. That's what this book is about—connecting analog input and output devices to microprocessors for embedded applications

System Design   *1*

Most embedded microprocessor designs involve processing some kind of input to produce some kind of output, and one or both of these is usually analog. The digital portions of an analog system, such as the microprocessor-to-memory interface, are outside the scope of this book. However, there are some system considerations in any design that must interface to the real world, and these will be considered here.

Dynamic Range

Before a system can be designed, the dynamic range of the inputs and outputs must be known. The dynamic range defines the precision that must be applied to measuring the inputs or generating the outputs. This in turn drives other parts of the design, such as allowable noise and the precision that is required of the components.

A simple microprocessor-based system might read an analog input voltage and convert it to a digital value (how this happens will be examined in Chapter 2). Dynamic range is usually expressed in decibels (dB) because it is usually a measurement of relative power or voltage. However, this does not cover all the things that a microprocessor-based system might want to measure. In simplest terms, the dynamic range can be thought of as the largest value that must be measured compared to (or divided by) the smallest. In most cases, the essential number that needs to be known is the number of bits of precision required to measure or control something.

As an example, say that we want to measure temperatures between 0 °C and 100 °C. If we want to measure with 1 °C accuracy, we would need 100 discrete values to accomplish this. An 8-bit analog-to-digital converter (ADC) can divide an input voltage into 256 discrete values, so this system would need only 8 bits of precision. On the other hand, what if we want to measure the same temperature range with 0.1 °C accuracy? Now we need 100/.1, or 1000 discrete values, and that means a 10-bit ADC (which can produce 1024 discrete values).

Voltage Precision

The number of bits required to measure our example temperature range is dependent on the range of what we are measuring (temperature, voltage, light intensity, pressure, etc.) and not on a specific voltage range. In fact, our 0-to-100 °C range might be converted to a 0-to-5 volt swing or a 0-to-1 volt swing. In either case, the dynamic range that we have to measure is the same. However, the 0-to-5 V range uses 19.5 mV steps (5v/256) for 1 °C accuracy and 4.8 mV steps (5v/1024) for 0.1 °C accuracy. If we use a 0-to-1 V swing, we have step sizes of 3.9 mV and 976 µV. This affects the ADC choices, the selection of opamps, and other considerations. These will be examined in more detail in later chapters. The important point is that the dynamic range of the system determines how many bits of precision are needed to measure or control something; how that range is translated into analog and then into digital values further constrains the design.

Calibration

Dynamic range brings with it calibration issues. A certain dynamic range implies a certain number of bits of precision. But real parts that are used to measure real-world things have real tolerances. A 10 K resistor can be between 9900 and 10,100 ohms if it has a 1% tolerance, or between 9990 and 10,010 ohms if it has 0.1% tolerance. In addition, the resistance varies with temperature. All the other parts in the system, including the sensors themselves, have similar variations. These will be addressed in more detail in Chapter 9, but for now the important thing from a system point of view is this: how will the required accuracy be achieved?

For example, say we're still trying to measure that 0-to-100 °C temperature range. Measurement with 1 °C accuracy may be achievable without adjustments. However, you might find that the 0.1 °C figure requires some kind of calibration because you can't get a temperature sensor in your price range with that accuracy. You may have to include an adjustment in the design to compensate for this variation.

The need for a calibration step implies other things. Will the part of the system with the temperature sensor be part of the board that contains the compensation? If not, how do you keep the two parts together once calibration is performed? And what if the field engineer has to change the sensor in the field? Will the engineer be able to do the calibration? Will it really be cheaper, in production, to add a calibration step to the assembly procedure than to purchase a more accurate sensor?

In many cases in which an adjustment is needed, the resulting calibration parameters can be calculated in software and stored. For example, you might bring the system (or just the sensor) to a known temperature and measure the output. You know that an ideal sensor should produce an output voltage X for temperature T, but the real sensor produces an output voltage Y for temperature T. By measuring the output at several temperatures, you can build up a table of information that relates the output of that specific sensor to temperature. This information can be stored in the microprocessor's memory. When the microprocessor reads the sensor, it looks in the memory (or does a calculation) to determine the actual temperature.

You would want to look at storing this calibration with the sensor if it was not physically located with the microprocessor. That way, the sensor could be changed without recalibrating. Figure 1.1 shows three means of handling this calibration. In diagram A, a microprocessor connects to a remote sensor via a cable. The microprocessor stores the calibration information in its EEPROM or flash memory. The tradeoffs for this method are:

- Once the system is calibrated, the sensor has to stay with that microprocessor board. If either the sensor or the microprocessor is changed, the system has to be recalibrated.
- If the sensor or microprocessor is changed and recalibration is not performed, the results will be incorrect, but there is no way to know that the results are incorrect unless the microprocessor has a means to identify specific sensors.
- Data for all the sensors can be stored in one place, requiring less memory than other methods. In addition, if the calibration is performed by calculation instead of by table lookup, all sensors that are the same can use the same software routines, each sensor just having different calibration constants.

Diagram B in Figure 1.1 shows an alternative method of handling a remote sensor, in which the EEPROM that contains the calibration data is located on the board with the sensor. This EEPROM could be a small IC that is accessed with an I^2C or microwire interface (more about those in Chapter 2). The tradeoffs here are:

- Since each sensor carries its own calibration information, sensors and microprocessor boards can be interchanged at will without affecting results. Spare sensors can be calibrated and stocked without having to be matched to a specific system.
- More memories are required, one for each sensor that needs calibration.

Finally, diagram C in Figure 1.1 takes this concept a step further, adding a microcontroller to the sensor board, with the microcontroller performing the

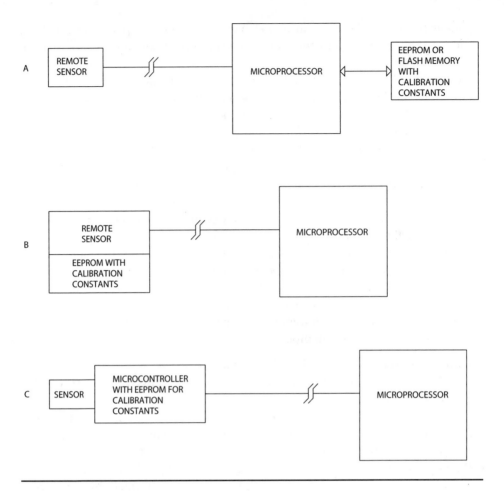

Figure 1.1
Sensor calibration methods.

calibration and storing calibration data in an internal EEPROM or flash memory. The tradeoffs here are:

- There are more processors and more firmware to maintain. In some applications with rigorous software documentation requirements (medical, military) this may be a significant development cost.
- No calibration effort is required by the main microprocessor. For a given real-world condition such as temperature it will always get the same value, regardless of the sensor output variation.
- If a sensor becomes unavailable or otherwise has to be changed in production, the change can be made transparent to the main microprocessor code, with all the new characteristics of the new sensor handled in the remote microcontroller.

Analog Interfacing to Embedded Microprocessor Systems

Another factor to consider in calibration is the human element. If a system requires calibration of a sensor in the field, does the field technician need arms twelve feet long to hold the calibration card in place and simultaneously reach the "ENTER" key on the keyboard? Should a switch be placed near the sensor so calibration can be accomplished without walking repeatedly around a table to hit a key or view the results on the display? Can the adjustment process be automated to minimize the number of manual steps required? The more manual adjustments that are needed, the more opportunities there are for mistakes.

Bandwidth

Several years ago, I worked on an imaging application. This system was to capture data using a charge coupled device (CCD) image sensor. We were capturing 1024 pixels per scan. We had to capture items moving 150 inches per second at a resolution of 200 pixels per inch. Each pixel was converted with an 8-bit ADC, resulting in 1 byte per pixel. The data rate was therefore $150 \times 1024 \times 200$, or 30,720,000 bytes per second.

We planned to use the VME bus as the basis for the system. Each scan from the CCD had to be read, normalized, filtered, and then converted to 1-bit-per-pixel monochrome. During the meetings that were held to establish the system architecture, one of the engineers insisted that we pass all the data through the VME bus. In those days, the VME bus had a maximum bandwidth specification of 40 megabytes per second, and very few systems could achieve the maximum theoretical bandwidth. The bandwidth we needed looked like this:

Read data from camera into system: 30.72 Mbytes/sec

Pass data to normalizer: 30.72 Mbytes/sec

Pass data to filter: 30.72 Mbytes/sec

Pass data to monochrome converter: 30.72 Mbytes/sec

Pass monochrome data to output: 3.84 Mbytes/sec

If you add all this up, you get 126.72 Mbytes/sec, well beyond even the theoretical capability of the VME bus back then. More recently, I worked on a similar imaging application that was implemented with digital signal processors (DSPs) and multiple PCI buses, and one of the PCI buses was near its maximum capability when all the features were added. The point is, know how much data you have to push around and what buses or data paths you are going to use. If you are using a standard interface such as Ethernet or Firewire, be sure it will support the total bandwidth required.

Processor Throughput

In many applications, the processor throughput is an important consideration. In the imaging example just mentioned, most of the functionality was performed in hardware because the available microprocessors could not keep up. As processor speeds increase, more functionality is pushed into the software. There are several key factors that you must consider to determine your throughput requirements.

Interrupts

How often must the interrupts occur, and how much processing must be performed in each interrupt service routine (ISR)? What is the maximum allowable latency for servicing an interrupt? Will interrupts need to be turned off for an extended length of time, and how will that affect the latency of other interrupts? You may find that you need two (or more) processors—one to handle high-speed interrupts with short latency requirements but low complexity processing needs, and another to handle low-rate interrupts with more complex processing requirements.

Interfaces

What must the system talk to? How will the data be passed around or get to the outside world? How much hardware support will there be for the interface and how much of the functionality will be performed in software? To take a simple example, an I^2C interface that is implemented on a microcontroller by flipping bits in software will impact overall throughput more than an I^2C interface that is implemented in hardware. This issue will likely be related to the interrupt considerations, because the interface will probably use interrupts. (If you don't know what I^2C is, it will be covered in Chapter 2.)

Hardware Support

An imaging application that has a direct memory access (DMA) controller to move large amounts of data around will not need as much processor horsepower as one that has to move the data in software. A processor that has to move the data in software but has some kind of block-move instruction in the hardware will probably be faster than one that has to have a series of instructions to construct a loop. Similarly, if the CPU has an on-chip floating point unit (FPU) coprocessor, then floating point operations will be much faster than they would be if they had to be executed in software.

Processing Requirements

If you are working on an imaging application, having a processor move the data from one process (such as the camera interface logic) to another (such as filtering logic) takes some degree of processing. If the processor has to actually implement the filtering algorithm in software, this takes a lot more processing horsepower. It is amazing how often systems are designed with little or no analysis of the amount of processing the CPU actually has to do.

Operating System Requirements

If you use an operating system (OS), how long will interrupts be turned off? Is this compatible with the interrupt latency requirements? What if the OS occasionally stops processing to spend a few seconds thrashing the hard disk? Will this cause data to be lost? Does the system have real-time requirements that will make a real-time operating system necessary?

Language/Compiler

If you plan to use an object-oriented language such as C++, what happens when the CPU has to do garbage collection on the memory? Will data be lost? Does choosing this approach mean you have to go from a 100 MHz processor to a 1 GHz processor just to keep the garbage collection interval short?

Avoiding Excess Speed

Choosing a bus architecture and a processor that are fast enough to do the job is important, but it can also be important to avoid too much speed. It may not seem logical that you wouldn't always want the fastest bus and the fastest microprocessor, but there are applications where that is exactly the case. There are two basic reasons for this: cost and electromagnetic compatibility (EMC).

Cost

The PC/104 standard defines mechanical and electrical characteristics of PC boards, optimized for embedded applications. PC/104 CPU boards come with the original PC/104 bus, which has electrical and timing characteristics similar to the ISA bus used in personal computers and is capable of data transfers in the 5 Mbytes/sec range. Many CPU boards also have the PC/104 Plus bus, which has characteristics similar to the much faster (133 Mbytes/sec) PCI bus. Although it might seem that the faster bus is always preferred, it is often less expensive to design a peripheral board for the PC/104 bus than for the PC/104 Plus. PC/104, due to the slower clock rates, allows longer traces and simpler logic. If you have a relatively large analog I/O board plugged into a PC/104 CPU board, the relaxed timing constraints of PC/104 may make layout easier. Many low-volume products simply do not sell enough units to justify the higher development costs associated with PC/104 Plus. Of course, this assumes that the PC/104 bus will support the necessary data rates. Similar considerations apply to other buses, such as PCI and Compact PCI.

EMC

Almost every microprocessor-based design will have to undergo EMC testing before it can be sold in the United States or Europe. EMC regulations limit the amount of energy the product can emit, to prevent interference with other equipment such as televisions and radios. Generally, the higher the clock rates are, the more emissions the equipment generates. Current EMC standards test radiated emissions in the frequency range between 30 MHz and 1 GHz. A processor running with a 6 MHz clock will not have any fundamental emissions in this range; the only frequencies in the test range will be those from the fifth and higher harmonics of the processor clock. The higher harmonics typically have less energy. On the other hand, a 33 MHz processor will produce energy in the test band from its fundamental frequency and higher. In addition, a faster processor clock rate means faster logic with faster edges and correspondingly higher energy in the harmonics. Although using a 6 MHz example in an era of 2 GHz Pentiums may seem archaic, it does illustrate the point. EMC concerns are a valid reason to limit bus and processor speeds only to what is actually needed for the application. The caution here is not to limit the design too much. If the processor can just barely keep up with the application, there is no margin left to fix problems or add enhancements.

Other System Considerations

Peripheral Hardware

An imaging system was having problems with lost data. This particular system buffered considerable image data on a hard disk drive. The problem was traced to the disk drive; the drive would just stop accepting data for a while and the image buffers would overflow. It turned out that this particular drive had a thermal compensation feature that required the on-drive CPU to "go away" for a few tens of milliseconds every so often. The application required continuous access to the drive. Be sure the peripheral hardware is compatible with your application and does not introduce problems.

Shared Interfaces

What is the impact of shared interfaces? For example, if you are continuously buffering data from two different image cameras on two disk drives, a single IDE interface may not be fast enough. You may need separate IDE interfaces for the two drives so they can operate independently, or you may need to go to an interface with higher performance. Similarly, will 10-baseT Ethernet handle all your data, or will you need 100-baseT? Look at all the data on all the interfaces and make sure the bandwidth you need is there.

Task Priorities

The IBM PC architecture has been used for all kinds of applications. It is a well-documented standard with an enormous number of compatible software packages available. But it has some drawbacks, including the non-real-time nature of the standard Windows operating system. You have probably experienced having your PC stop responding for a few seconds while it thrashes the hard disk for some unknown reason. If you are typing a document on a word processor, this is a minor annoyance—whatever you typed is captured (as long as it isn't too many characters) and shows up on the screen whenever the operating system gets back to processing the keyboard. What happens if you are getting a continuous stream of data from an audio or video device when this happens? If your system isn't constructed to permit your data stream to have a high priority, some data may be lost. If you are using a PC-like architecture, be sure the hardware and operating system software will support the things you need to do.

Hardware Requirements

Do you need a floating-point processor to do calculations on the data you will be processing? If so, you won't be able to use a simple 8-bit processor, you will need at least a 486-class machine. Does the data rate require a processor with a DMA controller to keep up? This limits your potential CPU selections to just a few. In some cases, you can make system adaptations that will lower hardware costs, as the following example will illustrate.

Imagine that you have a motor-driven wheel that produces an interrupt to your processor every 20° of rotation (see Figure 1.2). The motor runs at varying speeds and the processor has to schedule some event, such as activating a solenoid to open a valve, some number of degrees after the interrupt occurs. The 20°

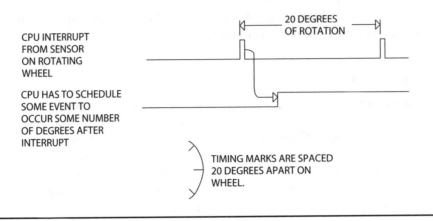

CPU INTERRUPT FROM SENSOR ON ROTATING WHEEL

20 DEGREES OF ROTATION

CPU HAS TO SCHEDULE SOME EVENT TO OCCUR SOME NUMBER OF DEGREES AFTER INTERRUPT

TIMING MARKS ARE SPACED 20 DEGREES APART ON WHEEL.

Figure 1.2
Rotating wheel timing.

interrupts will occur 3.3 ms apart if the wheel spins at 1000 rpm, and 666 μS apart if the wheel spins at 5000 rpm. If the processor uses a timer to measure the rotation speed (time between interrupts), and if the timer runs at 1 MHz, then the timer will increment 3300 counts between interrupts at 1000 rpm, and 666 counts at 5000 rpm.

Say that the CPU has to open our hypothetical solenoid when the wheel has rotated 5° past one of the interrupts, as shown in Figure 1.2. The formula for calculating the timer value (how much must be added to the current count for a 5° delay) looks like this:

$$\text{Timer increment value} = \frac{5 \text{ degrees delay}}{20 \text{ degrees/interrupt}} \times \begin{array}{l}\text{Number of}\\ \text{timer counts per interrupt}\end{array}$$

So at 1000 rpm, the 5° delay is 825 timer counts, and at 5000 rpm, the delay is 166 counts. The problem with this approach in an embedded system is the need to divide by 20 in the formula. Division is a time-consuming task to perform in software, and this approach might require that you choose a processor with hardware divide instruction.

If we change our measurement system so that the 20° divisions are divided into binary values, the math gets easier. Say that we decide to divide the 20° divisions into 32 equal parts, each part being 0.625 degrees. We'll call these increments units just so we have a name for them. The 5° increment is now 5/0.625 or 8 units. Now our formula looks like this:

$$\text{Timer increment value} = \frac{8 \text{ units}}{32 \text{ units per interrupt}} \times \begin{array}{l}\text{Number of}\\ \text{timer counts per interrupt}\end{array}$$

10

This gives us the same result as before (825 at 1000 rpm, 166 at 5000 rpm), but division by 32 can be performed with a simple shift operation instead of a complex software algorithm. A change like this may mean the difference between a simple 8-bit microcontroller and a more complex and expensive microprocessor. All we did was change from measuring degrees of rotation to measuring something that is easier to calculate.

Word Width

If you are connecting a processor to a 12-bit ADC, you will probably want a 16-bit processor instead of an 8-bit processor. While you can perform 16-bit operations on an 8-bit CPU, it usually requires multiple instructions and has other limitations. Unless the processor is simply passing the data on to some other part of the system, you will want to match the CPU to the devices with which it must interface. Similarly, if you will be performing calculations to 32-bit accuracy, you will want to consider a CPU with at least 16-bit and probably 32-bit word width to make computation easier and faster.

Interfaces

Be sure that interface conditions that are unusual but normal don't cause damage to any part of the system. For instance, a microprocessor board may connect to a motor control board with a cable. What happens if the service engineer leaves the cable unplugged and turns the system on? Will the motors remain stationary, or will they run out of control? Make sure that issues like this are addressed.

Sample Rate and Aliasing

Figure 1.3 shows a sinusoidal input signal and an ADC that is sampling at a slower rate than the signal is changing. If the system measuring this system assumed it was measuring a sinusoid of some frequency, it would conclude that it was measuring a sinusoid exactly half the frequency of the real input. This is called aliasing, and it can occur any time that the input frequency is a multiple of the sample frequency.

Also shown in Figure 1.3 is another input waveform that is not a sinusoid. In this case, the system doesn't assume it is sampling a sine, so it just stores the samples as they are read. As you can see, the resulting pattern of data values does not match the input at all.

Any system must be designed so that it can keep up with whatever it is measuring. This includes the speed at which the ADC can collect samples and

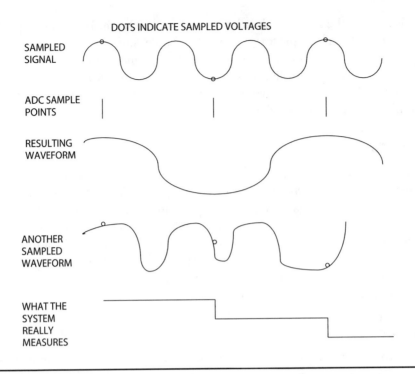

DOTS INDICATE SAMPLED VOLTAGES

SAMPLED SIGNAL

ADC SAMPLE POINTS

RESULTING WAVEFORM

ANOTHER SAMPLED WAVEFORM

WHAT THE SYSTEM REALLY MEASURES

Figure 1.3
Aliasing.

the speed at which the microprocessor can process them. If the input frequency will be greater than the measurement capability of the system, there are three ways to handle it:

1. Speed up the system to match the input.
2. Filter out high-frequency components with external hardware ahead of the ADC measuring the signal.
3. Filter out or ignore high-frequency components in software. This sounds silly—how do you filter something faster than you can measure? But if the valid input range is known, such as the number of cars entering a parking lot over any given time, then bogus inputs may be detectable. In this example, any input frequency greater than a couple per second can be assumed to be the result of noise or a faulty sensor—real cars don't enter parking lots that fast.

Good system design depends on choosing the right tradeoffs between processor speed, system cost, and ease of manufacture.

Analog-to-Digital Converters

## 2

Although this chapter is primarily about analog-to-digital converters (ADCs), an understanding of digital-to-analog converters (DACs) is important to understanding how ADCs work. Figure 2.1 shows a simple resistor ladder with three switches. The resistors are arranged in an R/2R configuration. The actual values of the resistors are unimportant; R could be 10 K or 100 K or almost any other value. Each switch, S0–S2, can switch one end of one 2R resistor between ground and the reference input voltage, VR. The Figure shows what happens when switch S2 is on (connected to VR) and S1 and S2 are OFF (connected to ground). By calculating the resulting series/parallel resistor network, the final output voltage (VO) turns out to be 0.5 × VR. If we similarly calculate VO for all the other switch combinations, we get this:

S2	S1	S0	Vo
OFF	OFF	OFF	0
OFF	OFF	ON	0.125 × VR (1/8 × VR)
OFF	ON	OFF	0.25 × VR (2/8 × VR)
OFF	ON	ON	0.375 × VR (3/8 × VR)
ON	OFF	OFF	0.5 × VR (4/8 × VR)
ON	OFF	ON	0.625 × VR (5/8 × VR)
ON	ON	OFF	0.75 × VR (6/8 × VR)
ON	ON	ON	0.875 × VR (7/8 × VR)

If the three switches are treated as a 3-bit digital word, then we can rewrite the table as follows (using ON = 1, OFF = 0):

S2	S1	S0	Equivalent Logic State			S0–S2 NUMERIC EQUIVALENT
			S2	S1	S0	
OFF	OFF	OFF	0	0	0	0
OFF	OFF	ON	0	0	1	1
OFF	ON	OFF	0	1	0	2
OFF	ON	ON	0	1	1	3
ON	OFF	OFF	1	0	0	4
ON	OFF	ON	1	0	1	5
ON	ON	OFF	1	1	0	6
ON	ON	ON	1	1	1	7

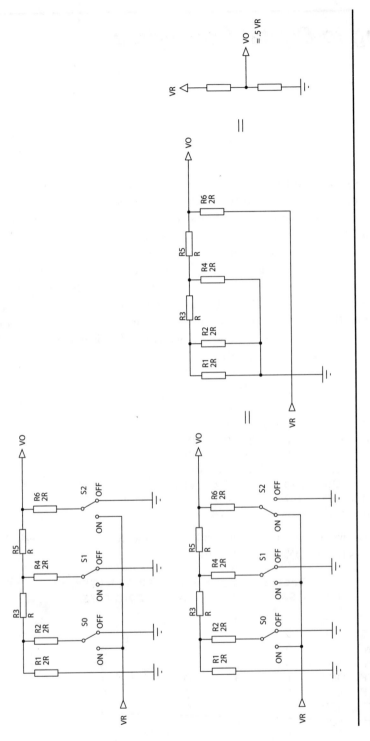

Figure 2.1
3-bit DAC.

Analog Interfacing to Embedded Microprocessor Systems

The output voltage is a representation of the switch value. Each additional table entry adds VR/8 to the total voltage. Or, put another way, the output voltage is equal to the binary, numeric value of S0–S2, times VR/8. This 3-switch DAC has 8 possible states and each voltage step is VR/8.

We could add another R/2R pair and another switch to the circuit, making a 4-switch circuit with 16 steps of VR/16 volts each. An 8-switch circuit would have 256 steps of VR/256 volts each. Finally, we can replace the mechanical switches in the schematic with electronic switches to make a true DAC.

ADCs

The usual method of bringing analog inputs into a microprocessor is to use an ADC. An ADC accepts an analog input, a voltage or a current, and converts it to a digital word that can be read by a microprocessor. Figure 2.2 shows a simple ADC. This hypothetical part has two inputs: a reference and the signal to be measured. It has one output, an 8-bit digital word that represents, in digital form, the input value. For the moment, ignore the problem of getting this digital word into the microprocessor.

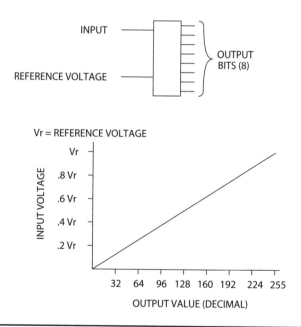

Figure 2.2
Simple ADC.

Reference Voltage

The reference voltage is the maximum value that the ADC can convert. Our example 8-bit ADC can convert values from 0 V to the reference voltage. This voltage range is divided into 256 values, or steps. The size of the step is given by:

$$\frac{\text{Reference Voltage}}{256} = \frac{5\,V}{256} = 0.0195\,V, \text{or } 19.5\,mv$$

This is the step size of the converter. It also defines the converter's resolution.

Output Word

Our 8-bit converter represents the analog input as a digital word. The most significant bit of this word indicates whether the input voltage is greater than half the reference (2.5 V, with a 5 V reference). Each succeeding bit represents half of the previous bit, like this:

Bit:	Bit 7	Bit 6	Bit 5	Bit 4	Bit 3	Bit 2	Bit 1	Bit 0
Volts:	2.5	1.25	0.625	0.3125	0.156	0.078	0.039	0.0195

So a digital word of 0010 1100 represents this:

Bit:	Bit 7	Bit 6	Bit 5	Bit 4	Bit 3	Bit 2	Bit 1	Bit 0
Volts:	2.5	1.25	0.625	0.3125	0.156	0.078	0.039	0.0195
Output Value	0	0	1	0	1	1	0	0

Adding the voltages corresponding to each bit, we get:

$$0.625 + 0.156 + 0.078 = 0.859\,\text{volts}$$

Resolution

The resolution of an ADC is determined by the reference input and the word width. The resolution defines the smallest voltage change that can be measured by the ADC. As mentioned earlier, the resolution is the same as the smallest step size, and can be calculated by dividing the reference voltage range by the number of possible conversion values.

For the example we've been using so far, an 8-bit ADC with a 5 V reference, the resolution is 0.0195 V (19.5 mv). This means that any input voltage below 19.5 mv will result in an output of 0. Input voltages between 19.5 and 39 mv will result in an output of 1. Between 39 mv and 58.6 mv, the output will be 2. Resolution can be improved by reducing the reference input. Changing from 5 V to 2.5 V gives a resolution of 2.5/256, or 9.7 mv. However, the maximum voltage that can be measured is now 2.5 V instead of 5 V.

The only way to increase resolution without changing the reference is to use an ADC with more bits. A 10-bit ADC using a 5 V reference has 2^{10}, or 1024 possible output codes. So the resolution is 5 V/1024, or 4.88 mv.

Types of ADCs

ADCs come in various speeds, use different interfaces, and provide differing degrees of accuracy. Three types of ADCs are illustrated in Figure 2.3.

Tracking ADC

The tracking ADC has a comparator, a counter, and a digital-to-analog converter. The comparator compares the input voltage to the DAC output voltage. If the input is higher than the DAC voltage, the counter counts up. If the input is lower than the DAC voltage, the counter counts down.

The DAC input is connected to the counter output. Say the reference voltage is 5 V. This would mean that the converter could convert voltages between 0 V and 5 V. If the most significant bit of the DAC input is "1," the output voltage is 2.5 V. If the next bit is "1," 1.25 V is added, making the result 3.75 V. Each successive bit adds half the voltage of the previous bit, so the DAC input bits correspond to the following voltages:

Bit:	Bit 7	Bit 6	Bit 5	Bit 4	Bit 3	Bit 2	Bit 1	Bit 0
Volts:	2.5	1.25	0.625	0.3125	0.156	0.078	0.039	0.0195

Figure 2.3 shows how the tracking ADC resolves an input voltage of 0.37 V. The counter starts at zero, so the comparator output will be high. The counter counts up once for every clock pulse, stepping the DAC output voltage up. When the counter passes the binary value that represents the input voltage, the comparator output will switch and the counter will count down. The counter will eventually oscillate around the value that represents the input voltage.

The primary drawback to the tracking ADC is speed—a conversion can take up to 256 clocks for an 8-bit output, 1024 clocks for a 10-bit value, and so on. In addition, the conversion speed varies with the input voltage. If the voltage in this example were 0.18 V, the conversion would take only half as many clocks as the 0.37 V example.

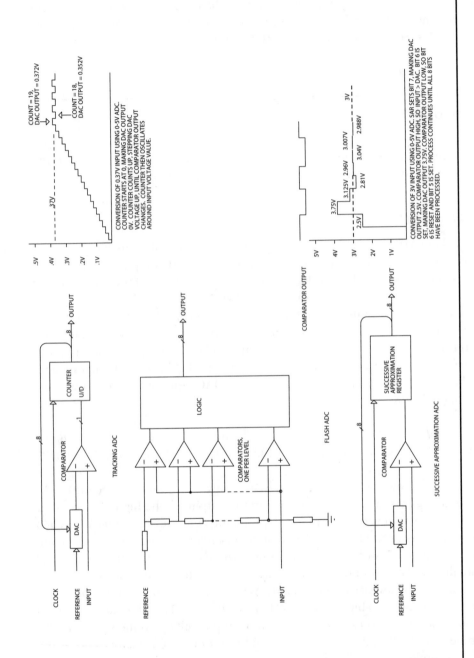

Figure 2.3
ADC types.

Analog Interfacing to Embedded Microprocessor Systems

The maximum clock speed of a tracking ADC depends on the propagation delay of the DAC and the comparator. After every clock, the counter output has to propagate through the DAC and appear at the output. The comparator then takes some amount of time to respond to the change in DAC voltage, producing a new up/down control input to the counter. Tracking ADCs are not commonly available; in looking at the parts available from Analog Devices, Maxim, and Burr-Brown (all three are manufacturers of ADC components), not one tracking ADC is shown. This only makes sense: a successive approximation ADC with the same number of bits is faster. However, there is one case where a tracking ADC can be useful; if the input signal changes slowly with respect to the sampling clock, a tracking ADC may produce an output in fewer clocks than a successive approximation ADC. However, since there are no commercial tracking ADCs available, a tracking ADC would have to be built from discrete hardware.

Flash ADC

The flash ADC is the fastest type available. A flash ADC has one comparator per voltage step. A 4-bit ADC will have 16 comparators, an 8-bit ADC will have 256 comparators. One input of all the comparators is connected to the input to be measured. The other input of each comparator is connected to one point in a string of resistors. As you move up the resistor string, each comparator trips at a higher voltage. All of the comparator outputs connect to a block of logic that determines the output based on which comparators are low and which are high.

The conversion speed of the flash ADC is the sum of the comparator delays and the logic delay (the logic delay is usually negligible). Flash ADCs are very fast, but take enormous amounts of IC real estate to implement. Because of the number of comparators required, they tend to be power hogs, drawing significant current. A 10-bit flash ADC IC may use half an amp.

Successive Approximation Converter

The successive approximation converter is similar to the tracking ADC in that a DAC/counter drives one side of a comparator and the input drives the other. The difference is that the successive approximation register performs a binary search instead of just counting up or down by one. As shown in Figure 2.3, say we start with an input of 3 V, using a 5 V reference. The successive approximation register would perform the conversion as follows:

```
Set MSB of SAR, DAC voltage = 2.5 V
    Comparator output high, so leave MSB set
    Result = 1000 0000
```

Set bit 6 of SAR, DAC voltage = 3.75 V (2.5 + 1.25)
  Comparator output low, reset bit 6
  Result = 1000 0000
Set bit 5 of SAR, DAC voltage = 3.125 V (2.5 + 0.625)
  Comparator output low, reset bit 5
  Result = 1000 0000
Set bit 4 of SAR, DAC voltage = 2.8125 V (2.5 + 0.3125)
  Comparator output high, leave bit 4 set
  Result = 1001 0000
Set bit 3 of SAR, DAC voltage = 2.968 V (2.8125 + 0.15625)
  Comparator output high, leave bit 3 set
  Result = 1001 1000
Set bit 2 of SAR, DAC voltage = 3.04 V (2.968 + 0.078125)
  Comparator output low, reset bit 2
  Result = 1001 1000
Set bit 1 of SAR, DAC voltage = 3.007 V (2.8125 + 0.039)
  Comparator output low, reset bit 1
  Result = 1001 1000
Set bit 0 of SAR, DAC voltage = 2.988 V (2.8125 + 0.0195)
  Comparator output high, leave bit 0 set
  Final result = 1001 1001

Using the 0-to-5 V, 8-bit DAC, this corresponds to:

$$2.5 + 0.3125 + 0.15625 + 0.0195 \text{ or } 2.988 \text{ volts}$$

This is not exactly 3 V, but it is as close as we can get with an 8-bit converter and a 5 V reference.

An 8-bit successive approximation ADC can do a conversion in 8 clocks, regardless of the input voltage. More logic is required than for the tracking ADC, but the conversion speed is consistent and usually faster.

Dual-Slope (Integrating) ADC

A dual-slope converter (Figure 2.4) uses an integrator followed by a comparator, followed by counting logic. The integrator input is first switched to the input signal, and the integrator output charges toward the input voltage. After a specified number of clock cycles, the integrator input is switched to a reference voltage (VREF1 in Figure 2.4) and the integrator charges down toward this value.

When the switch occurs to VREF1, a counter is started, and it counts using the same clock that determined the original integration time. When the integrator output falls past a second reference voltage (VREF2 in Figure 2.4), the compara-

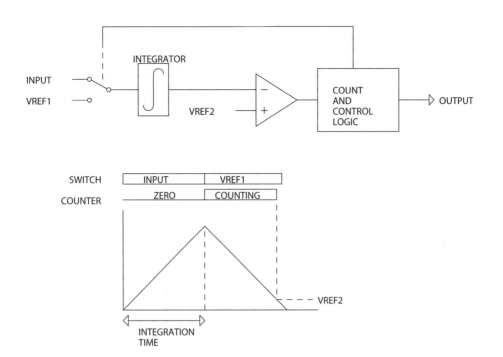

Figure 2.4
Dual-slope ADC.

tor output goes high, the counter stops, and the count represents the analog input voltage. Higher input voltages will allow the integrator to charge to a higher voltage during the input time, taking longer to charge down to VREF2, and resulting in a higher count at the output. Lower input voltages result in a lower integrator output and a smaller count.

A simpler integrating converter, the single-slope, runs the counter while charging up and stops counting when a reference voltage is reached (instead of charging for a specific time). However, the single-slope converter is affected by clock accuracy. The dual-slope design eliminates clock accuracy problems because the same clock is used for charging and incrementing the counter. Note that clock jitter or drift within a single conversion will affect accuracy. The dual-slope converter takes a relatively long time to perform a conversion, but the inherent filtering action of the integrator eliminates noise.

Sigma-Delta

Before describing the sigma-delta converter, we need to look at how oversampling works, because it is key to understanding the sigma-delta architecture.

Figure 2.5 shows a noisy 3 V signal, with 0.2 V peak-to-peak of noise. As shown in the Figure, we can sample this signal at regular intervals. Four samples are shown in the Figure; by averaging these we can filter out the noise:

$$(3.05\ V + 3.1\ V + 2.9\ V + 2.95\ V)/4 = 3\ V$$

Obviously this example is a little contrived, but it illustrates the point. If our system can sample the signal four times faster than data is actually needed, we can average four samples. If we can sample ten times faster, we can average ten samples for an even better result. The more samples we can average, the closer we get to the actual input value. The catch, of course, is that we have to run the ADC faster than we actually need the data, and must have software to do the averaging.

Figure 2.6 shows how a sigma-delta converter works. The input signal passes through one side of a differential amp, through a low-pass filter (integrator), and on to a comparator. The output of the comparator drives a digital filter and a 1-bit DAC. The DAC output can switch between $+V$ and $-V$. In the example shown in Figure 2.6, the $+V$ is 0.5 V, and the $-V$ is -0.5 V. The output of the DAC drives the other side of the differential amp, so the output of the differential amp is the difference between the input voltage and the DAC output. In the example shown, the input is 0.3 V, so the output of the differential amp is either 0.8 V (when the DAC output is -0.5 V) or -0.2 V (when the DAC output is 0.5 V).

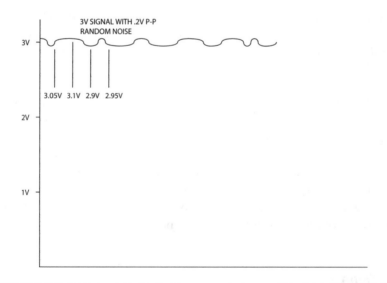

Figure 2.5
Oversampling.

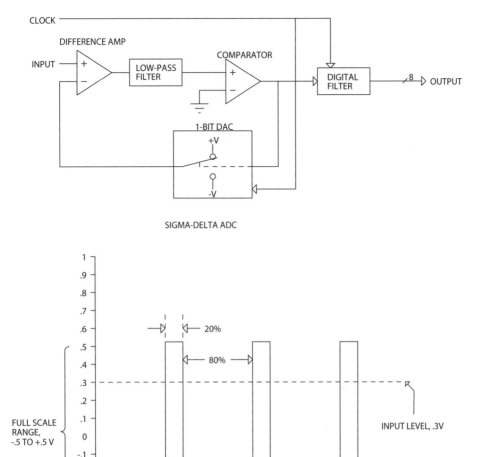

Figure 2.6
Sigma-delta ADC.

The output of the low-pass filter drives one side of the comparator, and the other side of the comparator is grounded. So any time the filter output is above ground, the comparator output will be high, and any time the filter output is below ground, the comparator output will be low. The thing to remember is that the circuit tries to keep the filter output at 0 V.

As shown in Figure 2.6, the duty cycle of the DAC output represents the input level; with an input of 0.3 V (80% of the −0.5 to 0.5 V range), the DAC output has a duty cycle of 80%. The digital filter converts this signal to a binary digital value.

The input range of the sigma-delta converter is the plus-and-minus DAC voltage. The example in Figure 2.6 uses 0.5 and −0.5 V for the DAC, so the input range is −0.5 V to 0.5 V, or 1 V total. For ±1 V DAC outputs, the range would be ±1 V, or 2 V total.

The primary advantage of the sigma-delta converter is high resolution. Because the duty cycle feedback can be adjusted with a resolution of one clock, the resolution is limited only by the clock rate. Faster clock equals higher resolution.

All of the other types of ADCs use some type of resistor ladder or string. In the flash ADC the resistor string provides a reference for each comparator. On the tracking and successive approximation ADCs, the ladder is part of the DAC in the feedback path. The problem with the resistor ladder is that the accuracy of the resistors directly affects the accuracy of the conversion result. Although modern ADCs use very precise, laser-trimmed resistor networks (or sometimes capacitor networks), there are still some inaccuracies in the resistor ladders. The sigma-delta converter does not have a resistor ladder; the DAC in the feedback path is a single-bit DAC, with the output swinging between the two reference endpoints. This provides a more accurate result.

The primary disadvantage of the sigma-delta converter is speed. Because the converter works by oversampling the input, the conversion takes many clocks. For a given clock rate, the sigma-delta converter is slower than other converter types. Or, to put it another way, for a given conversion rate, the sigma-delta converter requires a faster clock.

Another disadvantage of the sigma-delta converter is the complexity of the digital filter that converts the duty cycle information to a digital output word. Single-IC sigma-delta converters have become more commonly available with the ability to add a digital filter or DSP to the IC die.

Half-Flash

Figure 2.7 shows a block diagram of a half-flash converter. This example implements an 8-bit ADC with 32 comparators instead of 256. The half-flash converter has a 4-bit (16 comparators) flash converter to generate the MSB of the result. The output of this flash converter then drives a 4-bit DAC to generate the voltage represented by the 4-bit result. The output of the DAC is subtracted from the input signal, leaving a remainder that is converted by another 4-bit flash to produce the LS 4 bits of the result.

Analog Interfacing to Embedded Microprocessor Systems

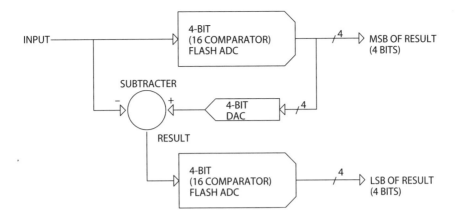

Figure 2.7
Half-flash converter.

If the converter shown in Figure 2.7 were a 0–5 V converter converting a 3.1 V input, then the conversion would look like this:

Upper flash converter output = 9

DAC output = 2.8125 V (9 × 16 × 19.53 mv)

Subtracter output = 3.1 V − 2.8125 V = 0.2875 V

Lower flash converter output = E (hex)

Final result = 9E (hex), 158 (decimal)

Half-flash converters can also use three stages instead of two; a 12-bit converter might have three stages of 4 bits each. The result of the MS 4 bits would be subtracted from the input voltage and applied to the middle 4-bit state. The result of the middle stage would be subtracted from its input and applied to the least significant 4-bit stage. A half-flash converter is slower than an equivalent flash converter, but uses fewer comparators, so it draws less current.

ADC Comparison

Figure 2.8 shows the range of resolutions available for integrating, sigma-delta, successive approximation, and flash converters. The maximum conversion speed for each type also is shown. As you can see, the speed of available sigma-delta ADCs reaches into the range of the SAR ADCs, but is not as fast as even the slowest flash ADCs. What these charts do not show is tradeoffs between speed and accuracy. For instance, although you can get SAR ADCs that range from 8 to 16

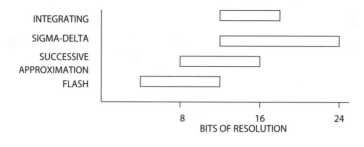

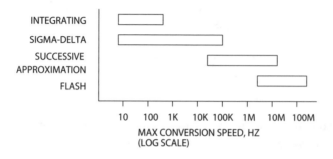

Figure 2.8
ADC comparison.

bits, you won't find the 16-bit version to be the fastest in a given family of parts. The fastest flash ADC won't be the 12-bit part, it will be a 6- or 8-bit part.

These charts are snapshots of the current state of the technology. As CMOS processes have improved, SAR conversion times have moved from tens of microseconds to microseconds to tens of nanoseconds. Not all technology improvements affect all types of converters; CMOS process improvements speed up all families of converters, but the ability to put increasingly sophisticated DSP functionality on the ADC chip doesn't improve SAR converters. It does improve sigma-delta types.

Sample and Hold

ADC operation is straightforward when a DC signal is being converted. What happens when the signal is changing? Figure 2.9 shows a successive-approximation ADC attempting to convert a changing input. When the ADC starts the conversion, the input voltage is 2.3 V. This should result in an output code of 117 (decimal) or 75 (hex). The SAR register sets the MSB, making the internal DAC voltage 2.5 V. Because the signal is below 2.5 V, the SAR resets bit 7 and sets

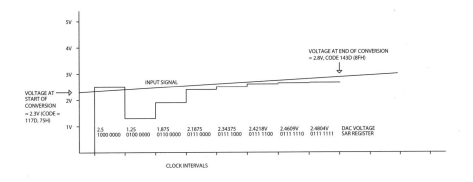

Figure 2.9
ADC inaccuracy caused by a changing input.

bit 6 on the next clock. The ADC "chases" the input signal, ending up with a final result of $127_{10}(7F_{16})$. The actual voltage at the end of the conversion is 2.8 V, corresponding to a code of $143_{10}(8F_{16})$.

The final code out of the ADC (127d) corresponds to a voltage of 2.48 V. This is neither the starting voltage (2.3 V) nor the ending voltage (2.8 V). This example used a relatively fast input to show the effect; a slowly changing input has the same effect, but the error will be smaller. One way to reduce these errors is to place a low-pass filter ahead of the ADC. The filter parameters are selected to ensure that the ADC input does not change appreciably within a conversion cycle.

Another way to handle changing inputs is to add a sample-and-hold (S/H) circuit ahead of the ADC. Figure 2.10 shows how a sample-and-hold circuit works. The S/H circuit has an analog (solid state) switch with a control input. When the switch is closed, the input signal is connected to the hold capacitor and the output of the buffer follows the input. When the switch is open, the input is disconnected from the capacitor.

Figure 2.10 shows the waveform for S/H operation. A slowly rising signal is connected to the S/H input. While the control signal is low (sample), the output follows the input. When the control signal goes high (hold), disconnecting the hold capacitor from the input, the output stays at the value the input had when the S/H switched to hold mode. When the switch closes again, the capacitor charges quickly and the output again follows the input. Typically, the S/H will be switched to hold mode just before the ADC conversion starts, and switched back to sample mode after the conversion is complete.

In a perfect world, the hold capacitor would have no leakage and the buffer amplifier would have infinite input impedance, so the output would remain stable forever. In the real world, the hold capacitor will leak and the buffer amplifier input impedance is finite, so the output level will slowly drift down toward ground as the capacitor discharges.

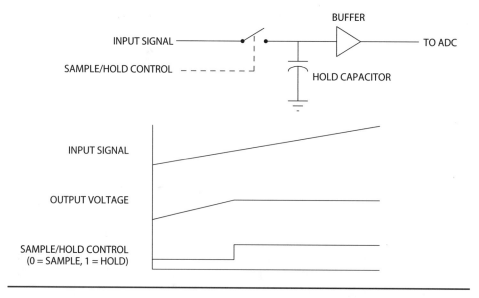

Figure 2.10
Sample-and-hold circuit.

The ability of an S/H to maintain the output in hold mode is dependent on the quality of the hold capacitor, the characteristics of the buffer amplifier (primarily input impedance), and the quality of the sample-and-hold switch (real electronic switches have some leakage when open). The amount of drift exhibited by the output when in hold mode is called the *droop rate*, and is specified in millivolts per second, microvolts per microsecond, or millivolts per microsecond.

A real S/H also has finite input impedance, because the electronic switch isn't perfect. This means that, in sample mode, the hold capacitor is charged through some resistance. This limits the speed with which the S/H can acquire an input. The time that the S/H must remain in sample mode in order to acquire a full-scale input is called the *acquisition time*, and is specified in nanoseconds or microseconds.

Because there is some impedance in series with the hold capacitor when sampling, the effect is the same as a low-pass R-C filter. This limits the maximum frequency the S/H can acquire. This is called the *full power bandwidth*, specified in kHz or MHz.

As mentioned, the electronic switch is imperfect and some of the input signal appears at the output, even in hold mode. This is called *feedthrough*, and is typically specified in dB.

The *output offset* is the voltage difference between the input and the output. S/H datasheets typically show a hold mode offset and sample mode offset, in millivolts.

Analog Interfacing to Embedded Microprocessor Systems

Real Parts

Real ADC ICs come with a few real-world limitations and some added features.

Input Levels

The examples so far have concentrated on ADCs with a 0–5 V input range. This is a common range for real ADCs, but many of them operate over a wider range of voltages. The Analog Devices AD570 has a 10 V input range. The part can be configured so that this 10 V range is either 0 to 10 V or −5 V to +5 V, using one pin. Of course, having a negative input voltage range implies that the ADC will need a negative voltage supply. Other common input voltage ranges are ±2.5 V and ±3 V.

With the trend toward lower-powered devices and small consumer equipment, the trend in ADC devices is to lower-voltage, single-supply operation. Traditional single-supply ADCs have operated from +5 V and had an input range between 0 V and 5 V. Newer parts often operate at 3.3 or 2.7 V, and have an input range somewhere between 0 V and the supply.

Internal Reference

Many ADCs provide an internal reference voltage. The Analog Devices AD872 is a typical device with an internal 2.5 V reference. The internal reference voltage is brought out to a pin and the reference input to the device is also connected to a pin. To use the internal reference, the two pins are connected together. To use your own external reference, connect it to the reference input instead of the internal reference.

Reference Bypassing

Although the reference input is usually high impedance with low DC current requirements, many ADCs will draw current from the reference briefly while a conversion is in process. This is especially true of successive approximation ADCs, which draw a momentary spike of current each time the analog switch network is changed. Consequently, most ADCs require that the reference input be bypassed with a capacitor of 0.1 µf or so.

Internal S/H

Many ADCs, such as the Maxim MAX191, include an internal S/H. An ADC with an internal S/H may have a separate pin that controls whether the S/H is in sample or hold mode, or the switch to hold mode may occur automatically when a conversion is started.

Microprocessor Interfacing

Output Coding

The examples used so far have been based on binary codes, where each bit in the result represents a voltage value and the sum of these voltages in the output word is the analog input voltage value. Some ADCs produce 2's complement outputs, where a negative voltage is represented by a negative 2's complement value. A few ADCs output values in BCD. Obviously this requires more bits for a given range; a 12-bit binary output can represent values from 0 to 4095, but a 12-bit BCD output can only represent values from 0 to 999.

Parallel Interfaces

ADCs come in a variety of interfaces, intended to operate with multiple processors. Some parts include more than one type of interface to make them compatible with as many processor families as possible.

The Maxim MAX151 is a typical 10-bit ADC with an 8-bit "universal" parallel interface. As shown in Figure 2.11, the processor interface on the MAX151 has 8 data bits, a chip select (–CS), a read strobe (–RD), and a –BUSY output. The MAX151 includes an internal S/H. On the falling edge of –RD and –CS, the S/H is placed into hold mode and a conversion is started. If –CS and –RD do not go low at the same time, the last falling edge starts a conversion. In most systems, –CS is connected to an address decode and will go low before –RD. As soon as the conversion starts, the ADC drives –BUSY low (active). –BUSY remains low until the conversion is complete.

In the first mode of operation, which Maxim calls Slow Memory Mode, the processor waits, holding –RD and –CS low, until the conversion is complete. In such a system, the –BUSY signal would typically be connected to the processor –RDY or –WAIT signal. This holds the processor in a wait state until the conversion is complete. The maximum conversion time for the MAX151 is 2.5 µs.

The second mode of operation is called ROM mode. In this mode the processor performs a read cycle, which places the S/H in hold mode and starts a conversion. During this read, the processor reads the results of the previous conversion. The –BUSY signal is not used to extend the read cycle. Instead, –BUSY is connected to an interrupt, or is polled by the processor to indicate when the conversion is complete. When –BUSY goes high, the processor does

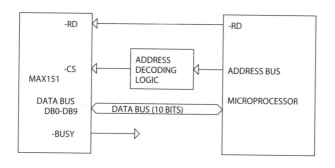

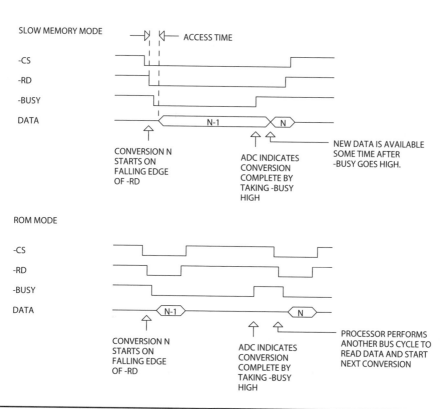

Figure 2.11
Maxim MAX151 interface.

another read to get the result and start another conversion. Although the data sheets refer to two different modes of operation, the ADC works the same way in both cases:

- Falling edge of –RD and –CS starts a conversion
- Current result is available on bus after read access time has elapsed

- As long as –RD and –CS stay low, current result remains available on bus
- When conversion completes, new conversion data is latched and available to the processor; if –RD and –CS are still low, this data replaces result of previous conversion on bus

The MAX151 is designed to interface to most microprocessors. Actually interfacing to a specific processor requires analysis of the MAX151 timing and how it relates to the microprocessor timing.

Data Access Time

The MAX151 specifies a maximum access time of 180 ns over the full temperature range (see Figure 2.12). This means that the result of a conversion will be available on the bus no more than 180 ns after the falling edge of –RD (assuming –CS is already low when –RD goes low). The processor will need the data to be stable some time before the rising edge of –RD. If there is a data bus buffer between the MAX151 and the processor, the propagation delay through the buffer must be included. This means that the processor bus cycle (the time that –RD is low) must be at least as long as the access time of the MAX151, plus the processor data setup time, plus any bus buffer delays.

–BUSY Output

The –BUSY output of the MAX151 goes low a maximum of 200 ns after the falling edge of –RD. This is too long for the signal to directly drive most microprocessors if you want to use the slow memory mode. Most microprocessors require that the RDY or –WAIT signal be driven low earlier than this in the bus cycle. Some require the wait request signal to be low one clock after –RD goes low. The only solution to this problem is to artificially insert wait states to the bus cycle until the –BUSY signal goes low. Some microprocessors, such as the 80188 family, have internal wait-state generators that can add wait states to a bus cycle. The 80188 wait-state generator can be programmed to add 0, 1, 2, or 3 wait states.

As shown in Figure 2.12, in Slow Memory mode the –BUSY signal goes high just before the new conversion result is available; according to the datasheet, this time is a maximum of 50 ns. For some processors, this means that the wait request must be held active for an additional clock cycle after –BUSY goes high to ensure that the correct data is read at the end of the bus cycle.

Bus Relinquish

The MAX151 has a maximum bus relinquish time of 100 ns. This means that the MAX151 can drive the data bus up to 100 ns after the –RD signal goes high. If the

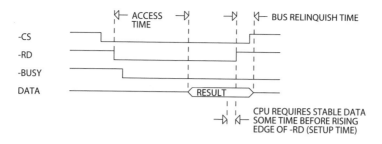

CPU REQUIRES STABLE DATA
SOME TIME BEFORE RISING
EDGE OF -RD (SETUP TIME)

ADDING A BUFFER TO REDUCE
BUS RELINQUISH TIME

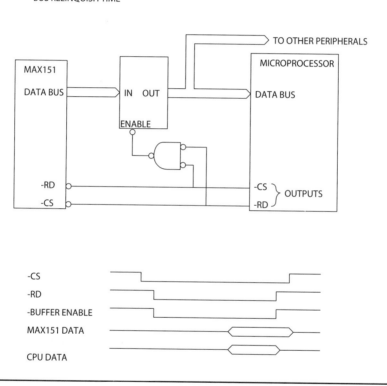

Figure 2.12
MAX151 data access and bus relinquish timing.

processor tries to start another cycle immediately after reading the MAX151 result, this may result in bus contention. A typical example would be the 80186 processor, which multiplexes the data bus with the address bus; at the start of a bus cycle the data bus is not tristated, but the processor drives the address onto the data bus. If the MAX151 is still driving the bus, this can result in an incorrect bus address being latched. The solution to this problem is to add a data bus buffer between the MAX151 and the processor. The buffer inputs are connected to the MAX151 data bus outputs, and the buffer outputs are connected to the processor data bus. The buffer is turned on when –RD and –CS are both low, and turned off when either goes high. Although the MAX151 will continue to drive the buffer inputs, the outputs will be tristated and so will not conflict with the processor data bus. A buffer may also be required if you are interfacing to a microprocessor that does not multiplex the data lines but does have a very high clock rate. In this case, the processor may start the next cycle before the MAX151 has relinquished the bus. A typical example would be a fast 80960-family processor, which we will look at later in the chapter.

Coupling

The MAX151 has an additional specification, not found on some ADCs, that involves coupling of the bus control signals into the ADC. Because modern ADCs are built as monolithic ICs, the analog and digital portions share some internal components such as the power supply pins and the substrate on which the IC die is constructed. It is sometimes difficult to keep the noise generated by the microprocessor data bus and control signals from coupling into the ADC and affecting the result of a conversion. To minimize the effect of coupling, the MAX151 has a specification that the –RD signal be no more than 300 ns wide when using ROM mode. This prevents the rising edge of –RD from affecting the conversion.

Delay between Conversions

When the MAX151 S/H is in sampling mode the hold capacitor is connected to the input. This capacitance is about 150 pf. When a conversion starts, this capacitor is disconnected from the input. When a conversion ends, the capacitor is again connected to the input, and it must charge up to the value of the input pin before another conversion can start. In addition, there is an internal 150 ohm resistor in series with the input capacitor. Consequently, the MAX151 specifies a delay between conversions of at least 500 ns if the source impedance driving the input is less than 50Ω. If the source impedance is more than 1 KΩ, the delay must be at least 1.5 μs. This delay is the time from the rising edge of –BUSY to the falling edge of –RD.

LSB Errors

In theory, of course, an infinite amount of time is required for the capacitor to charge up, because the charging curve is exponential and the capacitor never reaches the input voltage. In practice, the capacitor does stop charging. More important, the capacitor only has to charge to within 1 bit (called 1 LSB) of the input voltage; for a 10 V converter with a ±4 V input range, this is 8 V/1024, or 7.8 mv. This is an important concept that we will take a closer look at in Chapter 9. To simplify the concept, errors that fall within one bit of resolution have no effect on conversion accuracy. The other side of that coin is that the accumulation of errors (opamp offsets, gain errors, etc.) cannot exceed one bit of resolution or they *will* affect the result.

Clocked Interfaces

Interfacing the MAX151 to a clocked bus, such as that implemented on the Intel 80960 family, is shown in Figure 2.13. Processors such as the 960 use a clock-synchronized bus without a –RD strobe. Data is latched by the processor on a clock edge, rather than on the rising edge of a control signal such as –RD. These buses are often implemented on very fast processors and are usually capable of high-speed burst operation.

Shown in Figure 2.13 is a normal bus cycle without wait states. This bus cycle would be accessing a memory or peripheral able to operate at the full bus speed. The address and status information is provided on one clock, and the CPU reads the data on the next clock.

Following this cycle is an access to the MAX151. As can be seen, the MAX151 is much slower than the CPU, so the bus cycle must be extended with wait states (either internally or externally generated). This diagram is an example; the actual number of wait states that must be added depends on the processor clock rate. The bus relinquish time of the MAX151 will interfere with the next CPU cycle, so

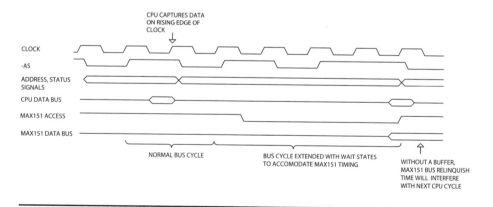

Figure 2.13
Interfacing to a clocked microprocessor bus.

a buffer is necessary. Finally, because the CPU does not generate a –RD signal, one must be synthesized by the logic that decodes the address bus and generates timing signals to memory and peripherals. The normal method of interfacing an ADC like this to a fast processor is to use the ROM mode. Slow Memory mode holds the CPU in a wait state for a long time—the 2.5 μs conversion time of the MAX151 would be 82 clocks on a 33 MHz 80960. This is time that could be spent executing code.

Serial Interfaces

Many ADCs use a serial interface to connect to the microprocessor. This has the advantage of providing a processor-independent interface that does not affect processor wait states, bus hold times, or clock rates. The primary disadvantage is speed, because the data must be transferred one bit at a time.

SPI/Microwire

SPI is a serial interface that uses a clock, chip select, data in, and data out bits. Data is read from a serial ADC a bit at a time (Figure 2.14). Each device on the SPI bus requires a separate –CS signal.

The Maxim MAX1242 is a typical SPI ADC. The MAX1242 is a 10-bit successive approximation ADC with an internal S/H, in an 8-pin package. Figure 2.15 shows the MAX1242 interface timing. The falling edge of -CS starts a conversion, which takes a maximum of 7.5 μs. When –CS goes low, the MAX1242 drives its data output pin low. After the conversion is complete, the MAX1242 drives the data output pin high. The processor can then read the data a bit at a time by toggling the clock line and monitoring the MAX1242 data output pin. After the 10 bits are read, the MAX1242 provides two sub-bits, S1 and S0. If further clock transitions occur after the 13 clocks, the MAX1242 outputs zeros.

Figure 2.15 shows how a MAX1242 would be connected to a microcontroller with an on-chip SPI/Microwire interface. The SCLK signal goes to the SPI

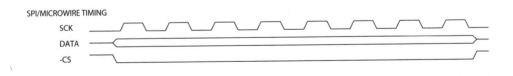

Figure 2.14
SPI bus.

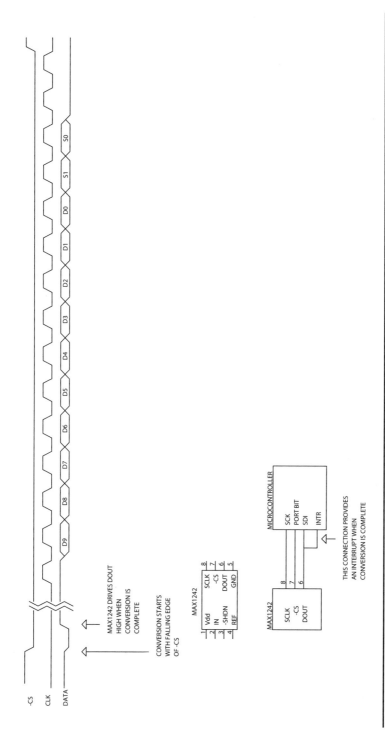

Figure 2.15
Maxim MAX1242 interface.

SCLK signal on the microcontroller, and the MAX1242 DOUT signal connects to the SPI data input pin on the microcontroller. One of the microcontroller port bits generates the –CS signal to the MAX1242. Note that the –CS signal starts the conversion and must remain low until the conversion is complete. This means that the SPI bus is unavailable for communicating with other peripherals until the conversion is finished and the result has been read. If there are interrupt service routines that communicate with SPI devices in the system, they must be disabled during the conversion. To avoid this problem, the MAX1242 could communicate with the microcontroller over a dedicated SPI bus. This would use three more pins on the microcontroller. Since most microcontrollers that have on-chip SPI have only one, the second port would have to be implemented in software.

Finally, it is possible to generate an interrupt to the microcontroller when the ADC conversion is complete. An extra connection is shown in Figure 2.15, from the MAX1242 DOUT pin to an interrupt on the microcontroller. When –CS is low and the conversion is completed, DOUT will go high, interrupting the microcontroller. To use this method, the firmware must disable or otherwise ignore the interrupt except when a conversion is in process.

Another ADC with an SPI-compatible interface is the Analog Devices AD7823. Like the MAX1242, the AD7823 uses three pins: SCLK, DOUT, and –CONVST. The AD7823 is an 8-bit successive approximation ADC with internal S/H. A conversion is started on the falling edge of –CONVST, and takes 5.5 μs. The rising edge of –CONVST enables the serial interface.

Unlike the MAX1242, the AD7823 does not drive the data pin until the microcontroller reads the result, so the SPI bus can be used to communicate with other devices while the conversion is in process. However, there is no indication to the microprocessor when the conversion is complete—the processor must start the conversion, then wait until the conversion has had time to complete before reading the result. One way to handle this is with a regular timer interrupt; on each interrupt, the result of the previous conversion is read and a new conversion is started.

I²C Bus

The I²C bus uses only two pins: SCL (SCLock) and SDA (SDAta). SCL is generated by the processor to clock data into and out of the peripheral device. SDA is a bidirectional line that serially transmits all data into and out of the peripheral. The SDA signal is open-collector, so several peripherals can share the same two-wire bus.

When sending data, the SDA signal is allowed to change only while SCL is in the low state. Transitions on the SDA line while SCL is high are interpreted as start and stop conditions. If SDA goes low while SCL is high, all peripherals on the bus will interpret this as a START condition. SDA going high while SCL is high is a STOP or END condition. Figure 2.16 illustrates a typical data transfer. The processor initiates the START condition and then sends the peripheral address, which is 7 bits long, and tells the devices on the bus which one is to be selected. This is followed by a read/write bit (1 for read, 0 for write).

After the read/write bit, the processor programs the I/O pin connected to the SDA bit to be an input and clocks an acknowledge bit in. The selected peripheral will drive the SDA line low to indicate that it has received the address and read/ write information.

After the acknowledge bit, the processor sends another address, which is the internal address within the peripheral that the processor wants to access. The length of this field varies with the peripheral. After this is another acknowledge; then the data is sent. For a write operation, the processor clocks out 8 data bits, and for a read operation, the processor treats the SDA pin as an input and clocks in 8 bits. After the data comes another acknowledge.

Some peripherals permit multiple bytes to be read or written in one transfer. The processor repeats the data/acknowledge sequence until all the bytes are transferred. The peripheral will increment its internal address after each transfer.

One drawback to the I^2C bus is speed—the clock rate is limited to about 100 KHz. A newer Fast-mode I^2C bus that operates to 400 Kbits/sec is also available, and a high-speed mode that goes to 3.4 Mbits/sec is also available. High speed and fast-mode buses both support a 10-bit address field so up to 1024 locations can be addressed. High-speed and fast-mode devices are capable of operating in the older system, but older peripherals are not useable in a higher-speed system. The faster interfaces have some limitations, such as the need for active pullups and limits on bus capacitance. Of course, the faster modes of operation require hardware support and are not suitable for a software-controlled implementation.

A typical ADC that uses I^2C is the Philips PCF8591. This part includes both an ADC and a DAC. Like many I^2C devices, the 8591 has three addressing pins: A0, A1, and A2. These can be connected to either "1" or "0" to select which address the device responds to. When the peripheral address is decoded, the PCF8591 will respond to address 1001xxx, where xxx matches the value of the A2, A1, and A0 pins. This allows up to eight PCF8591 devices to share a single I^2C bus.

SMBus

SMBus is a variation on I^2C, defined by Intel in 1995. I^2C is primarily defined by hardware and varies somewhat from one device to the next, but SMBus defines the bus as more of a network interface between a processor and its peripherals. The SMBus specification defines things such as powerdown operation of devices (no bus loading) and operating voltage range (3–5 V) that all devices must meet. The primary

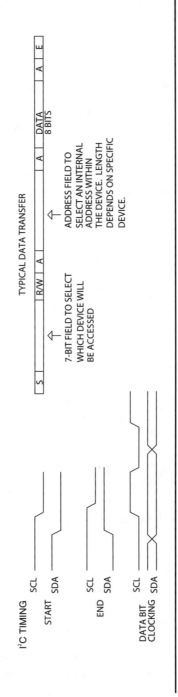

Figure 2.16
I²C timing.

Analog Interfacing to Embedded Microprocessor Systems

difference between SMBus and I^{2}C is that SMBus defines a standard set of read and write protocols, rather than leaving these specifics up to the IC manufacturers.

Proprietary Serial Interfaces

Some ADCs have proprietary interfaces. The Maxim MAX1101 is a typical device. This is an 8-bit ADC that is optimized for interfacing to CCDs. The MAX1101 uses four pins: MODE, LOAD, DATA, and SCLK. The MODE pin determines whether data is being written or read (1 = read, 0 = write). The DATA pin is a bidirectional signal, the SCLK signal clocks data into and out of the device, and the LOAD pin is used after a write to clock the write data into the internal registers. The clocked serial interface of the MAX1101 is similar to SPI, but because there is no chip select signal, multiple devices cannot share the same data/clock bus. Each MAX1101 (or similar device) needs four signals from the processor for the interface.

Many proprietary serial interfaces are intended for use with microcontrollers that have on-chip hardware to implement synchronous serial I/O. The 8031 family, for example, has a serial interface that can be configured as either an asynchronous interface or as a synchronous interface. Many ADCs can connect directly to these types of microprocessors. The problem with any serial interface on an ADC is that it limits conversion speed. In addition, the type of interface limits speed as well. Because every I^{2}C exchange involves at least 20 bits, an I^{2}C device will never be as fast as an equivalent SPI or proprietary device. For this reason, there are many more ADCs available with SPI/Microwire than with I^{2}C interfaces.

The required throughput of the serial interface drives the design. If you need a conversion speed of 100,000 8-bit samples per second and you plan to implement an SPI-type interface in software, then your processor will not be able to spend more than $1/(100,000 \times 8)$ or 1.25 μS transferring each bit. This may be impractical if the processor has any other tasks to perform, so you may want to use an ADC with a parallel interface or choose a processor with hardware support for the SPI.

As mentioned in Chapter 1, the bandwidth of the bus must be considered as well as the throughput of the processor. If there are multiple devices on the SPI bus, then you have to be sure the bus can support the total throughput required of all the devices. Of course, the processor has to keep up with the overall data rate as well.

Multichannel ADCs

Many ADCs are available with multiple channels—anywhere from two to eight. The Analog Devices AD7824 is a typical device, with eight channels. The AD7824 contains a single 8-bit ADC and an 8-channel analog multiplexer. The microprocessor interface to the AD7824 is similar to the Maxim MAX151, but with the addition of three address lines (A0–A2) to select which channel is to be converted. Like the MAX151, the AD7824 may be used in a mode in which the microprocessor starts a conversion and is placed into a wait state until the conversion is complete. The microprocessor can also start a conversion on any channel (by reading data from that channel), then wait for the conversion to complete and perform another read to get the result. The AD7824 also provides an interrupt output that indicates when a conversion is complete.

Internal Microcontroller ADCs

Many microcontrollers contain on-chip ADCs. Typical devices include the Microchip PIC167C7xx family and the Atmel AT90S4434. Most microcontroller ADCs are successive approximation because this gives the best tradeoff between speed and IC real estate on the microcontroller die.

The PIC16C7xx microcontrollers contain an 8-bit successive approximation ADC with analog input multiplexers. The microcontrollers in this family have from four to eight channels. Internal registers control which channel is selected, start of conversion, and so on. Once an input is selected, there is a settling time that must elapse to allow the S/H capacitor to charge before the A/D conversion can start. The software must ensure that this delay takes place.

Reference Voltage

The Microchip devices allow you to use one input pin as a reference voltage. This is normally tied to some kind of precision reference. The value read from the A/D converter after a conversion is:

$$\text{Digital word} = (\text{Vin}/\text{Vref}) \times 256$$

The Microchip parts also permit the reference voltage to be internally set to the supply voltage, which permits the reference input pin to be another analog input. In a 5 V system, this means that Vref is 5 V. So measuring a 3.2 V signal would produce the following result:

$$\text{Result} = \frac{\text{Vin} \times 256}{\text{Vref}} = \frac{3.2\,\text{V} \times 256}{5\,\text{V}} = 163_{10} = \text{A3}_{16}$$

However, the result is dependent on the value of the 5 V supply. If the supply voltage is high by 1%, it has a value of 5.05 V. Now the value of the A/D conversion will be:

$$\frac{3.2\,\text{V} \times 256}{5.05\,\text{V}} = 162_{10} = \text{A2}_{16}$$

So a 1% change in the supply voltage causes the conversion result to change by one count. Typical power supplies can vary by 2 or 3%, so power supply variations can have a significant effect on the results. The power supply output can vary with loading, temperature, AC input variations, and from one supply to the next.

This brings up an issue that affects all ADC designs: the accuracy of the reference. The Maxim MAX1242, which we have already looked at, uses an internal reference. The part can convert inputs from 0 V to the reference voltage. The reference is nominally 2.5 V, but it can vary between 2.47 V and 2.53 V. Converting a 2 V input at the extremes of the reference ranges gives the following result:

$$\text{At Vref} = 2.47\,\text{V}, \text{Result} = \frac{2\,\text{V} \times 1024}{2.47} = 829_{10}$$

$$\text{At Vref} = 2.53\,\text{V}, \text{Result} = \frac{2\,\text{V} \times 1024}{2.53} = 809_{10}$$

(Note: Multiplier is 1024 because the MAX1242 is a 10-bit converter.)

So the variation in the reference voltage from part to part can result in an output variation of 20 counts.

Codecs

The term *codec* has two meanings: it is short for compressor/decompressor, or for coder/decoder. In general, a codec (either type) will have two-way operation; it can turn analog signals into digital and vice-versa, or it can convert to and from some compression standard.

The National Semiconductor LM4546 is an audio codec intended to implement the sound system in a personal computer. It contains an internal 18-bit ADC and DAC. It also includes much of the audio-processing circuitry needed for 3D PC sound. The LM4546 uses a serial interface to communicate with its host processor.

The National TP3054 is a telecom-type codec, and includes ADC, DAC, filtering, and companding circuitry. The TP3054 also has a serial interface.

Interrupt Rates

The MAX151 can perform a conversion every 3.3 µs, or 300,000 conversions per second. Even a 33 MHz processor operating at one instruction per clock cycle can execute only 110 instructions in that time. The interrupt overhead of saving and restoring registers can be a significant portion of those instructions.

In some applications, the processor does not need to process every conversion. An example would be a design in which the processor takes four samples, averages them, and then does something with the average. In cases like this, using a processor with DMA capability can reduce the interrupt overhead. The DMA controller is programmed to read the ADC at regular intervals, based on a timer (the ADC has to be a type that starts a new conversion as soon as the previous result is read). After all the conversions are complete, the DMA controller interrupts the processor. The accumulated ADC data is processed and the DMA controller is programmed to start the sequence over. Processors that include on-chip DMA controllers include the 80186 and the 386EX.

Dual-Function Pins on Microcontrollers

If you work with microcontrollers, you sometimes find that you need more I/O pins than your microcontroller has. This is most often a problem when working with smaller devices, such as the 8-pin Atmel ATtiny parts, or the 20- and 28-pin Atmel AVR and Microchip PIC devices. In some cases, you can make an analog input double as an output or make it handle two inputs. Figure 2.17A shows how an analog input can also control two outputs. In this case, the analog input is connected to a 2.5 V reference diode. A typical use for this design would be in an application where you are using the 5 V supply as the ADC reference, but you want to correct the readings for the actual supply value. A precise 2.5 V reference permits you to do this, because you know that the value of the reference should read as 80 (hex) if the power supply is exactly 5 V.

The pin on the microcontroller is also tied to the inputs of two comparators. A voltage divider sets the noninverting input of comparator A at 3 V, and the inverting input of comparator B at 2 V. By configuring the pin as an analog input, the reference value can be read. If the pin is then configured as a digital output and set low, the output of comparator A will go low. If the pin is configured as a digital output and set high, the output of comparator B will go low. Of course, this scheme works only if the comparator outputs drive signals that never need to both be low at the same time. The resistor values must be large

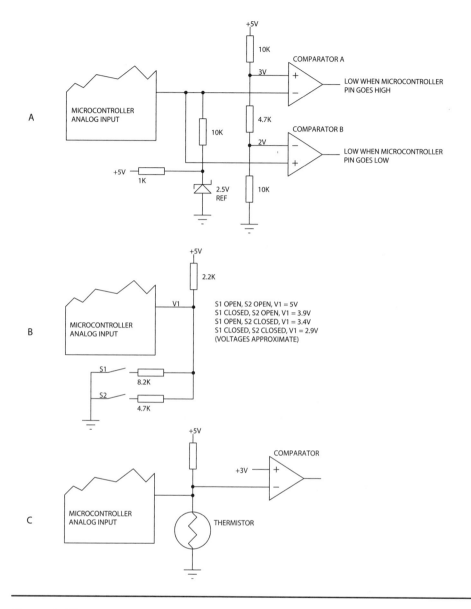

Figure 2.17
Dual-function pins.

enough that the microcontroller can source enough current to drive the pin high. This technique will also work for a digital-only I/O pin; instead of a 2.5 V reference, a pair of resistors is used to hold the pin at 2.5 V when it is configured as an input.

Figure 2.17B shows how a single analog input can be used to read two switches. When both switches are open, the analog input will read 5 V. When switch S1 is closed, the analog input will read 3.9 V. When switch S2 is closed, the input will read 3.4 V, and when both switches are closed, the input will read 2.9 V. Instead of switches, you could also use this technique to read the state of open-collector or open-drain digital signals.

Figure 2.17C shows how a thermistor or other variable-resistance sensor can be combined with an output. The microcontroller pin is programmed as an analog input to read the temperature. When the pin is programmed as an output and driven high, the comparator output will go low. To make this work, the operating temperature range must be such that the voltage divider created by the thermistor and the pullup resistor never brings the analog input above 3 V. Like the example shown in 2.17A, this circuit works best if the output is something that periodically changes state, so the software has a regular opportunity to read the analog input.

Design Checklist

- Be sure ADC bus interface is compatible with microprocessor timing. Pay particular attention to bus setup, hold, and min/max pulse width timings.
- If using SPI and an ADC that requires the bus to be inactive during conversion, ensure that the system will work with this limitation or provide a separate SPI bus for the ADC.
- If using an ADC that does not indicate when conversion is complete, ensure that software allows conversion to complete before reading result.
- Be sure reference accuracy meets requirements of the design.
- Bypass reference input as recommended by ADC manufacturer.
- Be sure the processor can keep up with the conversion rate.

Sensors

## 3

Sensors provide the window through which a microprocessor system can see what is happening in the real world. In this chapter we will take a look at various sensors, their applications, and how they interface to microprocessors.

Temperature Sensors

Temperature is one of the most common real-world characteristics that needs to be measured. Many industrial processes, from steel manufacturing to semiconductor fabrication, depend on temperature. Some electronics products need to measure their own temperature, such as computers that monitor the temperature of the CPU or motor controllers that must know the temperature of the power driver IC.

Thermistors

A thermistor is a temperature-sensitive resistor. Most thermistors have a negative temperature coefficient (NTC), meaning that the resistance goes up as the temperature goes down. Of all passive temperature measurement sensors, thermistors have the highest sensitivity (resistance change per degree of temperature change). Thermistors do not have a linear temperature/resistance curve.

Thermistor characteristics are dependent on the manufacturing process and materials used. Often, many thermistors in a family will have similar characteristics and identical curves. The resistance of the thermistors may vary by 10:1 or 100:1, but the curves are the same. Such thermistors are typically characterized by the manufacturer in a table that shows the ratio of resistance at a given temperature to the resistance at 25 °C. Data for a typical NTC thermistor family is shown in the following table.

Typical NTC Thermistor Data

Temp °C	R/R_{25}	Temp °C	R/R_{25}
−50	39.03	30	0.8276
−40	21.47	40	0.6406
−30	12.28	50	0.5758
−20	7.28	60	0.4086
−10	4.46	70	0.2954
0	2.81	80	0.2172
10	1.82	90	0.1622
20	1.21	100	0.1229
25	1	110	0.09446

This data is for a Dale thermistor, but it is typical for NTC thermistors in general. The resistance is given as a ratio (R/R_{25}). A thermistor from this family with a resistance at 25 °C (R_{25}) of 10,000 ohms would have a resistance of 28.1 K at 0 °C and a resistance of 4.086 K at 60 °C. Similarly, a thermistor with R_{25} of 5 K would have a resistance of 14,050 ohms (5000 × 2.81) at 0 °C.

Figure 3.1 shows how this thermistor curve looks graphically. As mentioned, the resistance/temperature curve is not linear. The data for this thermistor is given in 10° increments. Some thermistor tables have 5° or even 1° increments.

In some cases, you need to know the temperature between two points on the table. You can estimate this by using the curve, or you can calculate the resistance directly. The formula for resistance looks like this:

$$\frac{Rt}{R_{25}} = \exp\left(A + \frac{B}{T} + \frac{C}{T^2} + \frac{D}{T^3}\right)$$

Where T = temperature in degrees Kelvin, and A, B, C, and D are constants that depend on the characteristics of the thermistor. These parameters must be supplied by the thermistor manufacturer.

Thermistors have a tolerance that limits their repeatability from one sample to the next. This tolerance typically ranges from 1% to 10%, depending on the specific part used. Some thermistors are designed to be interchangeable in applications where it is impractical to have an adjustment. Such an application might include an instrument in which the user or a field engineer has to replace the thermistor and has no independent means to calibrate it. These thermistors are available with accuracy around 0.2 °C.

Figure 3.2 shows a typical circuit that could be used to allow a microprocessor to measure temperature using a thermistor. A resistor (R1) pulls the thermistor

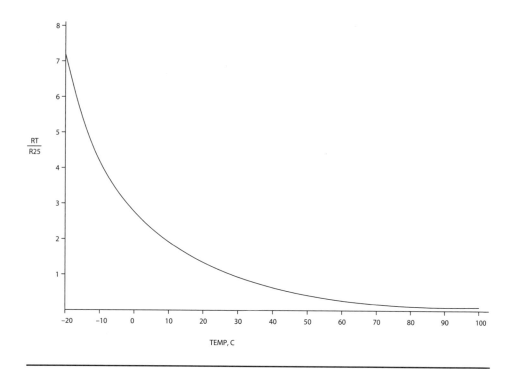

Figure 3.1
Thermistor resistance/temperature curve.

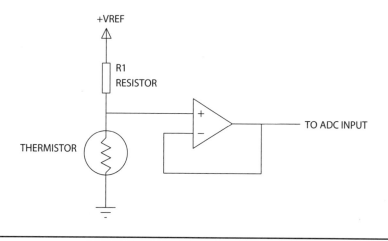

Figure 3.2
Thermistor circuit.

up to a reference voltage. This is typically the same as the ADC reference, so Vref would be 2.5 V if the ADC reference was 2.5 V. The thermistor/resistor combination makes a voltage divider, and the varying thermistor resistance results in a varying voltage at the junction. The accuracy of this circuit is dependent on the thermistor tolerance, resistor tolerance, and reference accuracy.

Because a thermistor is a resistor, passing current through it will generate heat. This is called self-heating. The circuit designer must ensure that the pullup resistor (R1 in the diagram) is large enough to prevent excessive self-heating, or the system will end up measuring the thermistor dissipation instead of the temperature of whatever the thermistor is attached to.

The amount of power that the thermistor has to dissipate to affect the temperature is called the dissipation constant (D.C.), and is usually expressed in milliwatts. The D.C. varies with the package the thermistor is provided in, the lead gauge (if a leaded device), type of encapsulating material (if the thermistor is encapsulated), and other factors. The D.C. is the number of milliwatts needed to raise the thermistor temperature 1 °C above ambient. The amount of self-heating allowed, and therefore the size of the limiting resistor, is dependent on the measurement accuracy needed. A system that is only measuring with an accuracy of ± 5 °C can tolerate more thermistor self-heating than a system that must be accurate to ± 0.1 °C. The formula for calculating the amount of self-heating dissipation allowed for a design is:

$$P = D.C. \times \text{Required accuracy, in } °C$$

For instance, if the D.C. for our example thermistor was 2 mw/°C, and we needed to measure temperature with an accuracy of 0.5 °C, then the maximum allowable dissipation would be:

$$2 \, \text{mw}/°C \times 0.5 \, °C = 1 \, \text{mw}$$

Because there are other errors and tolerances in the system, we would probably want a little margin, so we might divide this by 2, giving 0.5 mw as the maximum self-heating dissipation. Note that this is the maximum self-heating dissipation we want to allow over the measurement temperature range. Say we are using our example thermistor, with an R_{25} of 10 K, and we want to measure temperatures from 0 °C to 25 °C. At 25 °C, the thermistor resistance is 10 K. To limit dissipation to 0.5 mw using a 2.5 V Vref, the pullup resistor (R1 in Figure 3.2) can be calculated as follows:

$$\text{Thermistor dissipation} = 0.5 \, \text{mw at } 10 \, \text{K}$$

Thermistor voltage drop at this dissipation : $\left(P = \dfrac{E^2}{R}\right)$; $\sqrt{0.0005 \times 10,000} = 2.23\,\text{V}$

Current through thermistor $= 2.23\,\text{V}/10\,\text{K} = 223\,\mu\text{a}$

Voltage across pullup $= 2.5 - 2.23 = 0.27\,\text{V}$

Pullup (minimum value) $= 0.27\,\text{V}/223\,\mu\text{a} = 1210\,\Omega$

Now, suppose that we want to use this thermistor from $0\,°\text{C}$ to $50\,°\text{C}$. The thermistor resistance (from the table) at $50\,°\text{C}$ is $5758\,\Omega$. Repeating the preceding calculation for this resistance results in a minimum pullup resistance of 2725 ohms. Because the thermistor resistance is lower at higher temperatures, the original 1210 ohm value would cause too much dissipation at those temperatures.

Scaling

Sometimes it is necessary to shift an analog signal to put it in the right range for an A/D converter to use. Figure 3.3 shows such a situation. Here we have a thermistor that is interfaced to an 8-bit, 0-to-5 V A/D converter, such as that found on the Microchip 16C7x parts. We'll use the same thermistor we've been using. The formula for the voltage V1 is:

$$V1 = \frac{2.5 \times \text{Rth}}{\text{Rth} + \text{R1}}$$

In Figure 3.3, R1 = 10 K. Using this equation and the resistance/temperature table for the thermistor, we can calculate the value of V1 for the temperature range we are interested in:

Temp °C	Rth	V1
−10	44.6 K	2.04 V
0	28.1 K	1.84 V
10	18.2 K	1.61 V
25	10 K	1.25 V
30	8.276 K	1.13 V
40	6.406 K	0.976 V
50	4.08 K	0.7244 V
70	2.954 K	0.569 V
100	1229 Ω	0.273 V

Now, say that we want to measure temperature between 10° and 40° with an accuracy of at least three A/D steps per degree (or 0.333 °C

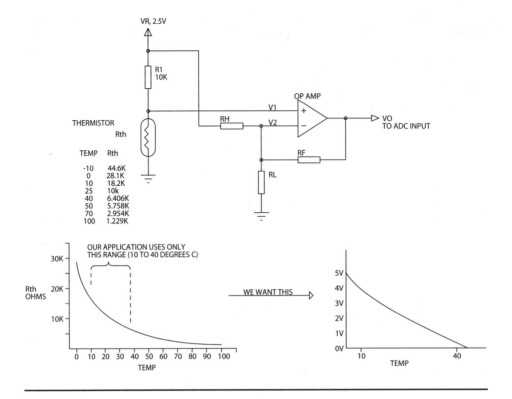

Figure 3.3
Thermistor scaling.

per ADC step). If we convert the range in the table to ADC values, we get this:

$$10 \text{ degrees: digital word} = \frac{1.61}{5} \times 256 = 82$$

$$40 \text{ degrees: digital word} = \frac{0.976}{5} \times 256 = 49$$

$$82 - 49 = 33 \text{ ADC counts}, 40\,°C - 10\,°C = 30\,°C \text{ (span)}$$

$$\frac{33 \text{ counts}}{30 \text{ degrees}} = 1.1 \text{ ADC steps per degree}$$

This is less than the resolution we wanted, so we have to scale the output. This involves amplifying the signal so that the 10-to-40 degree range we're interested in spans the ADC voltage range. In this example, the 10-to-40 span ranges from 0.976 to 1.61 volts, a span of 0.634 V (1.61 – 0.976). We could make this a 5 V span by multiplying it by 5 V/0.634 V, or 7.88. The result of such a multiplication would be to make the 10-to-40 degree voltage range between 7.67 and 12.67 volts. This is a 5 V span, but it is outside the 0-to-5 volt range of the ADC. What is needed is both multiplication and scaling, which amplifies the signal and shifts it down to the ADC input range.

The schematic in Figure 3.3 shows how an opamp can be configured to perform this function. We can calculate the output voltage of the opamp as follows: Writing equations for V2:

$$\frac{Vo - V2}{Rf} + \frac{Vr - V2}{Rh} = \frac{V2}{RL}$$

As long as the opamp is operating in the linear range, $V1 = V2$. So we can rewrite the preceding equation like this:

$$\frac{Vo - V1}{Rf} + \frac{Vr - V1}{Rh} = \frac{V1}{RL}$$

If we solve this equation for Vo, we get the following:

$$Vo = V1\left(1 + \frac{Rf}{RL} + \frac{Rf}{Rh}\right) - \frac{VrRf}{Rh}$$

$V1\left(1 + \dfrac{Rf}{RL} + \dfrac{Rf}{Rh}\right)$ is the gain and $\dfrac{VrRf}{Rh}$ is the offset

Now we can apply this to the thermistor we've been using as an example. Say that we want the 10-to-40 degree range to fall between 0.5 V and 4.5 V at the ADC. This gives a little margin to accommodate the need to use standard resistor values. This scaling will give an ADC range of 204 counts over a range of 30 degrees, or 6.8 counts per degree. So the 0.634 V swing of the output must translate into a swing of 4.5–0.5, or 4 V. This is a gain of 4/0.634 or 6.3. We can write this in equation form as:

$$6.3 = 1 + \frac{Rf}{RL} + \frac{Rf}{Rh}$$

If we just multiply V1 by 6.3, we get outputs of

$$0.976 \times 6.3 = 6.14 \text{ V}$$
$$1.61 \times 6.3 = 10.143 \text{ V}$$

So the span $(10.14 - 6.14 = 4 \text{ V})$ is right, but now we need the offset. The offset is found by subtracting either of these voltages from the corresponding desired voltage:

$$6.14 - 0.5 = 5.64 \text{ V, or } 10.14 - 4.5 = 5.64 \text{ V}$$

(Both have to give the same result or something is wrong in the earlier calculations.)

The offset is given by Vr Rf/Rh, so we can write another equation:

$$5.64 = \frac{\text{Vr} \times \text{Rf}}{\text{Rh}}$$

Now we can solve the simultaneous equations for gain $(6.3 = 1 + \text{Rh/RL} + \text{Rf/Rh})$ and offset $(5.64 = \text{VrRf/Rh})$ for resistor values. The example circuit uses a reference voltage, Vr, of 2.5 V, as shown on the schematic. Note that this is the reference voltage only for the thermistor and opamp circuit; the ADC still uses a 5 V reference. We have two equations and three resistors, so we have to choose the value of one resistor. Selecting 100 K for Rf, we have:

$$6.3 = 1 + \frac{100 \text{ K}}{\text{RL}} + \frac{100 \text{ K}}{\text{Rh}}; \quad 5.64 = \text{Vr} \frac{100 \text{ K}}{\text{Rh}}$$

Since $\text{Vr} = 2.5$, then the second equation is: $5.64 = \frac{250 \text{ K}}{\text{Rh}}$

Solving these simultaneous equations we get:

$$\text{Rh} = 44.32 \text{ K}$$
$$\text{RL} = 32.85 \text{ K}$$

The next step is to choose standard resistor values; the nearest 1% values are 44.2 K and 33.2 K. Plugging these values into the equation for Vo, we get a gain of 6.27 and an offset of 5.65 V. We can make a chart showing the actual ADC result for each temperature in the range:

Temp °C	Rth	Opamp Output	(Decimal)
10	18.2 K	4.44 V	227
25	10 K	2.18 V	111
30	8.276 K	1.44 V	74
40	6.406 K	0.467 V	23

You need the chart because the thermistor isn't linear, so the software needs to know what ADC value to expect for a given temperature. If this were a real application, we would probably calculate the chart in 1-degree increments. For this specific example, the opamp has to swing almost all the way between 5 V and ground, so it must either operate from positive and negative voltages, or else a single-supply, 5 V-only opamp with rail-to-rail output capability would be needed. The accuracy of this circuit is $(227 - 23)/30\,°\text{C} = 6.8$ ADC steps per °C.

Tolerance Stackup

In any opamp application, there are gain variations caused by the tolerances of the components. In the thermistor scaling application we just looked at, we selected standard 1% resistor values to produce the gain and scaling factors we wanted, then calculated the actual ADC values that would result from that circuit. But 1% resistors have a 1% tolerance, so they can vary by 1%. What happens in that case? We can calculate this for our example as follows.

Result if Rh is 1% High (44.642 K Instead of 44.2 K)

Temp	Rth	Rh = 44.2 K		Rh = 44.64 K	
		Vo	ADC Result	Vo	ADC Result
10	18.2 K	4.44 V	227	4.48	229
25	10 K	2.18 V	111	2.21	113
30	8.276 K	1.44 V	74	1.47	75
40	6.406 K	0.467 V	23	0.50	25

What happens if Rh is high by 1% ($= 44.64$ K) and RL is low by 1% ($= 32.868$)?

Result if Rh is 1% High and RL is 1% Low

Temp	Rth	Rh, RL normal		Rh high, RL low	
		Vo	ADC Result	Vo	ADC Result
10	18.2 K	4.44 V	227	4.47	229
25	10 K	2.18 V	111	2.19	112
30	8.276 K	1.44 V	74	1.45	74
40	6.406 K	0.467 V	23	0.478	24

In a real application, you could use a spreadsheet to calculate the effects of all the resistors, including the thermistor itself. In this simple application, just varying Rh and RL by 1% throws the result off by 5 counts at 10 °C. This may or may not be a problem, depending on the accuracy required. In a real application, you would probably want to use at least 0.1% resistors. This would give the following result.

Result if Rh is 0.1% High, R1 and RL are 0.1% Low

Temp	Rth	Rh, RL normal		Rh high, RL low	
		Vo	ADC Result	Vo	ADC Result
10	18.2 K	4.44 V	227	4.47	229
25	10 K	2.18 V	111	2.19	112
30	8.276 K	1.44 V	74	1.45	74
40	6.406 K	0.467 V	23	0.478	24

This is much closer to the ideal result. Other factors that would need to be included in a real application would be the tolerance of the voltage reference and the tolerance of the thermistor itself.

Another way to get this kind of accuracy is to calibrate the system after it is built. In many applications, this is not an option because the circuit boards and/or thermistor must be field replaceable. However, in cases where the equipment is not field replaceable, or where the field technicians have an independent means to monitor the temperature, it is possible to let the software build a table of temperature-versus-ADC values. There must be some means to input the actual temperature (measured with the independent tool) so the software can construct the table.

Resistance Temperature Detectors

A resistance temperature detector (RTD) is just a wire that changes resistance with temperature. Typical RTD materials include copper, platinum, nickel, and nickel/iron alloy. An RTD element can be a wire or a film, plated or sprayed onto a substrate such as ceramic.

RTD resistance is specified at 0 °C. A typical platinum RTD with 100 Ω resistance at 0 °C would have a resistance of 100.39 Ω at 1 °C and a resistance of 119.4 Ω at 50 °C. The tolerance of RTDs is better than thermistors. Typical tolerance for RTDs looks like this:

- Platinum: 0.01% to 0.03%
- Copper: 0.2%
- Nickel and nickel/iron: 0.5%

Aside from better tolerance and overall lower resistance, the interface to an RTD is similar to that for a thermistor.

Thermocouples

A thermocouple is made by joining two dissimilar metals. Thomas Seebeck discovered in 1821 that when such a junction is heated, it generates a tiny voltage. The amount of voltage is dependent on which two metals are joined. Three common thermocouple combinations are iron-constantan (Type J), copper-constantan (Type T), and chromel-alumel (Type K).

The voltage produced by a thermocouple junction is very small, typically only a few millivolts. A type K thermocouple changes only about $40\,\mu V$ per °C change in temperature; to measure temperature with 0.1 °C accuracy, the measurement system must be able to measure a $4\,\mu V$ change. Because any two dissimilar metals will produce a thermocouple junction when joined, the connection point of the thermocouple to the measurement system will also act as a thermocouple. Figure 3.4 shows this effect, where a thermocouple is connected to a board using copper. The wires leading to the amplifier could be either copper wires or the copper traces on a PCB.

As shown in Figure 3.4, this effect can be minimized by placing the connections on an isothermal block, which is a good conductor of heat. This minimizes the temperature difference between the connection points and minimizes the error introduced by the connection junctions. A common method of compensating for the temperature of the connection block is to place a diode or other semiconductor on the isothermal block and measure the (temperature-sensitive) drop across the semiconductor junction.

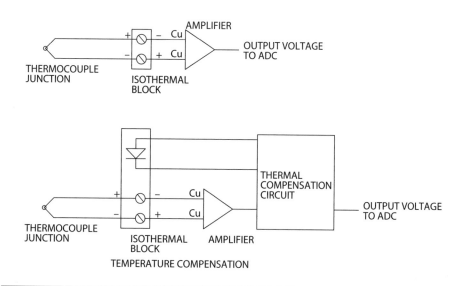

Figure 3.4
Thermocouple.

The amplifier used to increase the signal level from the thermocouple is usually an instrumentation amp. The gain required to measure a thermocouple is typically in the range of 100 to 300, and any noise picked up by the thermocouple will be amplified by the same amount. An instrumentation amplifier rejects the common mode noise in the thermocouple wiring.

Analog Devices makes a thermocouple signal conditioner, the AD594/595, which is specifically intended for interfacing to a thermocouple. The AD594/595 does not use an external semiconductor junction to compensate for connection temperature; instead the part includes an internal junction that is expected to be the same temperature as the connection. Consequently, the thermocouple connection must be made on the PC board, close to the AD595/595 package.

The amplified thermocouple signal may need scaling, just like a thermistor, to place it in a useable range for an ADC. Thermocouples are relatively linear over a limited range of temperatures, but if the range of measurement is wide, the software will need to compensate for nonlinearities. The formula for thermocouple voltage is a polynomial, just like thermistor resistance formula.

Solid State

The simplest semiconductor temperature sensor is a PN junction, such as a signal diode or the base-emitter junction of a transistor. If the current through the forward-biased silicon PN junction is held constant, the forward drop decreases about 1.8 mv per °C. The Maxim MAX1617 is an IC that measures temperature using an external transistor, such as a 2N3904, as a temperature-sensing element. The transistor can be a discrete part, or it can be embedded in the die of an IC to measure the IC temperature. The MAX1617 has a serial SMBus output.

The LM335 (Figure 3.5) from National Semiconductor produces an output voltage proportional to temperature. The LM135 produces 10 mv per degree Kelvin. At 0 °C, the output is 2.73 V, and at 100 °C the output is 3.73 V. The LM335 operates with input current from 400 μa to 5 ma.

The National LM34 and LM35 sensors operate from supply voltages between 4 V and 20 V, and produce a voltage output that directly corresponds to voltage. The LM35 produces a voltage of 500 mv at 50 °C, with an additional 10 mv for every additional °C increase. The LM34 is calibrated for Fahrenheit temperatures, and the LM35 for Centigrade. The outputs of the LM34/LM35 can be connected directly to an ADC or to a comparator.

The National LM74 measures temperatures between −55 °C and +150 °C and communicates with a microprocessor via the serial SPI/Microwire interface. The LM74 output is a 13-bit signed value. The part contains a temperature sensor and a sigma-delta converter. It is available in 3.3 V or 5 V versions and comes in an 8-pin SMT package. The National LM75 is similar to the LM74, but uses the I²C interface. The LM75 has a narrower operating temperature range: −55 °C to

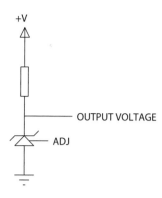

Figure 3.5
LM335.

+125 °C. The LM75 produces a 9-bit output and includes a comparator that can indicate when the temperature exceeds a limit. The limit temperature can be programmed via the I^{2}C bus.

Optical Sensors

Slotted Switches

Figure 3.6 shows a slotted optical switch. An LED is mounted in a plastic housing, facing a phototransistor. A gap separates the two, so if something moves into the gap, it blocks the light path between the LED and the phototransistor. Slotted switches are often used to detect motor speed by placing a slotted wheel on the motor shaft; as the shaft rotates, it alternately blocks and unblocks the light path. Another use for slotted switches is as indicators when a door or hood is open or closed. A flag on the door drops into the slot and blocks the light when the door is closed. A mechanical computer mouse uses slotted optical switches as well (an optical mouse uses a different method of sensing motion).

Reflective Sensors

Figure 3.7 shows a reflective sensor. A reflective sensor works the same way as a slotted switch, except that the phototransistor picks up reflected light from whatever is in front of the switch. Most reflective sensors have a focal length, the optimum distance at which the object to be measured should be placed, typically between 0.1 and 0.5 inches. A typical use for a reflective sensor is to detect motor motion by painting or anodizing the motor shaft black, then having a strip of

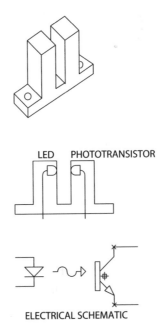

LED   PHOTOTRANSISTOR

ELECTRICAL SCHEMATIC

Figure 3.6
Slotted optical switch.

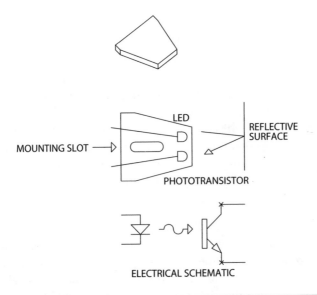

REFLECTIVE
SURFACE

MOUNTING SLOT

LED

PHOTOTRANSISTOR

ELECTRICAL SCHEMATIC

Figure 3.7
Reflective optical sensor.

Analog Interfacing to Embedded Microprocessor Systems

reflective material on the shaft. As the shaft rotates, the sensor sees no reflection from the part of the shaft that is black, then high reflection from the reflective strip.

Both types of optical sensors have some common characteristics that must be taken into account when designing a system that uses them, as detailed in the following sections.

Speed   The phototransistor in any optical switch is fairly slow. This limits the maximum speed that can be detected. Typical numbers are 8 µs turn-on time and 50 µs turn-off time. This time is driven by the speed of the base-emitter junction.

Gain   The LED and phototransistor pair have a limited gain, usually less than 1. The amount of current generated in the phototransistor collector for a given current through the LED is called the current transfer ratio (CTR). A typical CTR for a slotted switch is 0.1. This means that 10 ma of current in the LED will result in 1 ma of current in the collector. The CTR is sometimes specified as a ratio, and sometimes specified in a table that shows the collector current for various values of LED current. The CTR is dependent on the LED and phototransistor characteristics, and can vary widely from one device to the next.

The current transfer ratio has several implications when you want to interface a switch to a microprocessor system. First, if you want to connect the switch directly to a digital input (Figure 3.8), the transistor output has to swing between valid logic levels. To ensure that the phototransistor saturates, the value of the pullup resistor is limited. For example, if you are driving the LED with 10 ma and the CTR has a minimum value of 0.1, then the pullup resistor will be around 5000 ohms. A smaller resistor would provide better noise immunity (lower impedance) and possibly faster speed, but wouldn't work with all devices because the transistor would not be able to sink enough current to ensure a valid logic low level. To use a smaller pullup, you could use an optical switch with a higher CTR, or drive the LED with more current.

Optical switches are available with darlington transistor outputs, and these often have a CTR higher than 1. However, they are typically only 20% as fast as a single transistor output and have a higher saturation voltage.

Reflective sensors also have a CTR. Because the sensor depends on reflected light, the CTR is dependent on the type of surface used for testing and the distance of that surface from the sensor. The CTR of a reflective sensor is normally established with a standard reflective surface, placed at the specified focal length from the sensor. For example, the QT optoelectronics reflective sensors include the following statement: "Measured using an Eastman Kodak neutral white test card with 90% diffused reflectance as a reflecting surface."

The CTR of a reflective sensor varies from device to device, but also with your application. If your sensor is aimed at a surface that switches between gray and

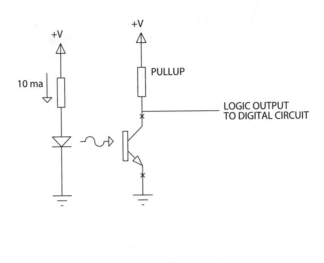

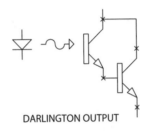

DARLINGTON OUTPUT

Figure 3.8
Optical switch digital output.

black, you will not get the same CTR you get with the white reference used by the manufacturer. Your design has to accommodate the actual CTR resulting from your application of the sensor. One way to determine the range of CTR is to measure the CTR in your application, then compare that to the CTR of the same sensor using the same white reference used by the sensor manufacturer. This will give you an idea of the CTR range you can expect to see.

Because the CTR of an optical sensor has a wide range, you may want to connect the output of the sensor to an ADC. This allows the system to look for changes in the output level, rather than depending on the ability of the part to generate digital logic levels. The price for this capability, of course, is the cost of adding an ADC and the slower speed caused by the time needed for ADC sampling. A comparator can also be used; it does not provide the flexibility of the ADC, but is faster and cheaper. The threshold of the comparator can be adjusted to compensate for circuit limitations, such as the relatively high saturation voltage of a darlington output. In addition, a comparator permits the use of

Analog Interfacing to Embedded Microprocessor Systems

hysteresis (see Appendix A) to avoid a noisy output caused by the slow speed of the phototransistor.

IR Problems

Most slotted and reflective sensors use IR LEDs and phototransistors. This means that the response of the part may not be the same as it would be for something in the visible spectrum. Specifically, objects that are good at reflecting or blocking visible light may be less effective at IR wavelengths. IR is also susceptible to interference from fluorescent lights and sunlight.

Figure 3.9 shows how driving the LED with a square wave signal can be combined with a filter to eliminate this type of interference. In this example, a source of ambient light causes the phototransistor to have a constant DC offset, and the signal is superimposed on a 60 Hz signal from fluorescent lighting. By passing the output of the transistor through a filter that is tuned to the original modulation frequency, these components can be removed and the signal converted to digital. The filter can be implemented in hardware or software. The IR method used in television remote control uses a 40 kHz modulation technique (a high-speed photodiode is used in the receiver to get this kind of speed).

Filtering such as this has some drawbacks. The first is speed. Due to the turn-on and turn-off times of the phototransistor, there is a maximum modulation

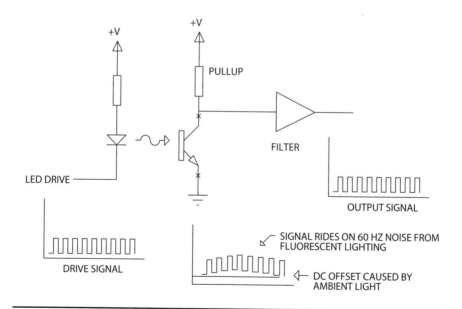

Figure 3.9
Optical sensor filtering.

frequency that will work—typically around 10 kHz. Because filtering the signal takes some time, it takes several cycles for a mechanical change in whatever is being measured to show up at the output. So, while the *sensor* may be able to operate at 10 kHz, the *system* may be able to handle a rate of only 1000 Hz or so. In the example shown, if the ambient light causes so much DC offset that the phototransistor saturates, no amount of filtering will recover the signal.

Mechanical Instability

Mechanical jitter can cause strange results with reflective sensors. I saw a system once that used a reflective sensor to look at a shiny strip on a flat black motor shaft to count rotations. The output of the sensor circuit generated an interrupt to a microprocessor. Occasionally, the motor would stop with the shiny strip right at the edge of the detection area for the sensor. Machine vibration would then generate enormous numbers of interrupts to the processor, effectively shutting it down. You could envision a similar situation with a slotted sensor, if the flag that interrupted the light path only partially obscured the phototransistor. This could leave the phototransistor halfway on, causing an ambiguous output.

Reflective sensors have some additional considerations. Reflective sensors are frequently used to sense objects of differing types. A good example would be paper moving down a high-speed sorting mechanism. The paper has varying quality, color, and reflective properties. The sensor system must be designed to handle all the types of material used. What if someone runs a flat black document down the transport? Does your system have to detect it?

Even when the mechanical system being measured doesn't change, reflective sensors can cause problems. Imagine that a sensor is measuring motor speed by looking at a reflective strip on a flat black motor shaft, as described in the preceding paragraphs. What happens if there is a scratch on the shaft, making another tiny reflector? Will this confuse the system? Suppose a film of oil builds up on the shaft, diffusing light from the reflective strip or increasing the reflectivity of the black part. These types of questions have to be answered.

In some cases, you may have to add hardware and/or software to detect unusual conditions. In the example already mentioned, in which a reflective sensor generated excessive interrupts, the software might have a timer that keeps track of the time between interrupts. If the sensor ISR is exited and immediately reentered, the ISR could disable the interrupt and set a flag to tell the rest of the system that something is wrong.

Open Sensors

In systems where safety is an issue, be sure that a failed sensor doesn't cause the system to operate in an unsafe manner. A typical example would be a safety hood that must be closed before the machine can start. The idea is that all the dangerous moving parts are under the hood, so if the hood is closed you know the operator's hands are out of the way. You could use a slotted optical switch and a flag that blocks the light path when the hood is closed. You then connect the phototransistor emitter to ground and pull the collector up with a resistor. When the flag is blocking the sensor, the transistor is off and the output is high.

The problem with this approach is that an open or disconnected LED would appear the same to the system as a closed hood. The system might then try to start with the hood open. In a case like this, use a flag that *unblocks* the sensor when the hood is closed. A bad LED then looks like an open hood and everything is safe.

An even safer method would be to use two sensors, one that is blocked when the hood is open and one that is blocked when the hood is closed. The machine isn't allowed to start unless both sensors are in the correct (safe) state. For the ultimate safety, use a flag that has an opaque strip and a translucent strip. When the hood is closed, the opaque strip passes through the sensor first, but when the hood is closed all the way, the translucent strip is blocking the sensor. The system looks for the signal to be completely blocked by the opaque strip, providing an "opaque reference" level. Then it looks for the translucent strip, which only blocks part of the light, giving a partial output. As soon as the signal changes to indicate either the opaque strip or no flag at all, the system assumes that the hood is open. This protects against unsafe conditions even if the phototransistor is shorted or if someone tries to defeat the interlocks.

Multiple Sensors

In some systems, it is possible to control multiple sensors with a single ADC or digital input. In Figure 3.10, four optical sensors use one input on the microprocessor. Each sensor LED is connected to a separate output. This can be a port output bit on the microprocessor or a separate register. Figure 3.10 shows an 8-bit register, with 4 bits used. All of the phototransistor emitters are grounded, and the collectors are tied together, with a common pullup resistor.

To use this circuit, the LED for each optical sensor is turned on one at a time, then the common input is read (if an ADC is used, a conversion is performed and the result is read). After each read, the LED is turned off and the next LED is turned on. This approach has some restrictions:

- The LEDs must be left on long enough for the phototransistor to settle before the input is read.
- When an LED is turned off, the next reading must not be performed until the corresponding phototransistor has had time to turn off. However, the next LED can be turned on as soon as the current result is read. It is not a problem to

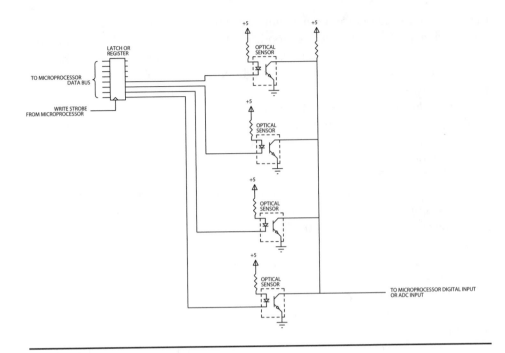

Figure 3.10
Multiple optical sensors with a single output.

have two LEDs and their corresponding phototransistors on at the same time, as long as no readings are taken in that state.
- There is a limit to the number of transistors that can be paralleled this way, due to the leakage of the phototransistors.
- Finally, this scheme depends on the fact that only one phototransistor is on at a time (because only one LED is on at a time). If ambient light causes other phototransistors to be partially on, the results will be ambiguous.

You occasionally need to know if an LED in a sensor has failed. An example would be a situation in which you use a slotted switch to determine if a motor is turning. If the motor appears to stop, you might need to know whether the motor is jammed or the sensor LED has failed (or been disconnected) so you can put the correct diagnostic message on the operator panel. Figure 3.11 illustrates a simple way to detect a failed LED. A comparator senses the voltage at the LED anode. When the LED is on, it will have a voltage drop of around 1.2 V (typical), so the comparator output will be high. If the LED opens, the voltage at the anode will rise to V+. (For this to work, V+ must be greater than 3 V.) The circuit as shown is for an LED that is on all the time. You can also use this method for a switched LED, but take the voltage drop across the switching transistor into account when

Analog Interfacing to Embedded Microprocessor Systems

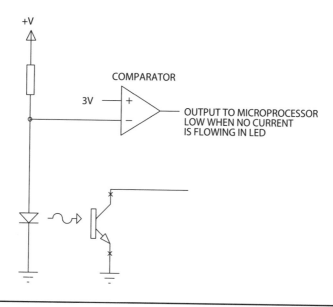

Figure 3.11
Detecting an open LED.

selecting the reference voltage. Of course, the comparator output is valid only when the LED is turned on.

Although a disconnected LED is much more likely than a shorted LED, you can add a second comparator to detect that condition. The reference voltage would be around 0.6 V and the software would declare an error if the voltage dropped below the reference.

Optical Isolators

Figure 3.12 shows an optical isolator. The optical isolator (called an optoisolator or optocoupler) houses an LED and a phototransistor in a package like an IC. The optical isolator is sealed—there is no way to break the light path. The optical isolator is not used to detect mechanical motion, but to provide electrical isolation between two circuits. A common use for optical isolators is to isolate a high-voltage circuit from the microprocessor that controls it. Musical Instrument Digital Interface (MIDI) uses optical isolation to connect synthesizers, computers, and other electronic musical instruments. In this application, the use of optical isolators prevents problems caused by different ground potentials.

Figure 3.12 shows how an optoisolator can be used to pass signals from one system to another. The ground and power connections for the system may be completely separate. Even in a single system where the grounds are nominally the same, an optoisolator may be used to prevent current from flowing from one

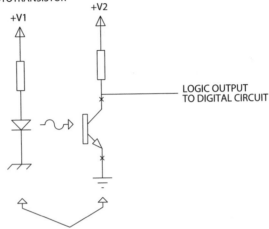

V1 IS REFERENCED TO THE GROUND FOR THE LED,
V2 IS REFERENCED TO THE GROUND FOR THE
PHOTOTRANSISTOR

+V2

+V1

LOGIC OUTPUT
TO DIGITAL CIRCUIT

THESE TWO GROUNDS MAY BE AT DIFFERENT
POTENTIALS. THEY CAN BE SEPARATED BY
HUNDREDS OF VOLTS

Figure 3.12
Optoisolator.

ground to the other. If one ground is particularly noisy, such as the ground for a pulse-width modulated (PWM) motor system, an optoisolator may be used to keep the motor noise out of the logic ground.

Some optoisolators are available with logic outputs instead of phototransistor outputs. These devices typically place a logic gate inside the IC to convert the analog output into a digital level. Optoisolators have the same speed and gain issues that optical sensors have. The CTR of an optoisolator can be higher, typically in the 20% to 100% range, because the LED is closer to the phototransistor base. The speed of an optoisolator is usually better than for an optical switch. The common 4N35 optoisolator has turn-on and turn-off times of 10 µs each, so it can pass signals over 10 Khz. However, as signals approach the limits of the optoisolator speed, the output signal looks less like the input. For high-speed isolation, a fast optoisolator is normally used. The 6N136 (Figure 3.13) is capable of speeds up to about 1 MHz. This part uses a photodiode coupled to a transistor to achieve high speed.

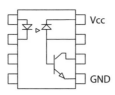

Figure 3.13
6N136.

Discrete Optical Sensors

A design occasionally calls for the use of discrete optical parts: an LED and a phototransistor. These are usually infrared parts, like those in packaged optical switches. They are normally used to detect when an object is blocking the light between the LED and phototransistor, but in places where the distance or width is too large for an optical switch.

Discrete parts are connected and used the same way as an optical switch or optoisolator, but there are a few additional considerations. Because the distance between sensor and phototransistor is usually larger, the CTR is lower. The circuit often needs an adjustment for LED current or sensing threshold for reliable and repeatable operation. In some cases, a lens may be required on one of the parts to focus the light.

Focusing is often a problem with discrete parts. This is especially true if the LED and phototransistor are on separate mechanical assemblies—the mechanical tolerance stackup can cause the LED and transistor to be misaligned.

In a packaged optical switch, the LED and phototransistor are matched to the same IR wavelength. Although most IR phototransistors and LEDs will work together, these parts do operate at different peak wavelengths in the IR range. When using discrete parts, it is best to select an LED and phototransistor that are designed for the same IR range. If the parts have different ranges, then an LED at one end of its range and a phototransistor at the other end of its range may result in a system with significantly lower CTR.

Figure 3.14 summarizes the three basic methods of interfacing an optical sensor to a microprocessor. All of these show the LED always on with a current limiting resistor, and the phototransistor using a grounded emitter and a pullup on the collector. All three methods will also work with other LED drive methods, such as using a microprocessor to turn the LED on and off. They will also work with other phototransistor configurations, such as connecting the collector to the positive supply and sensing the voltage across a resistor connected from the emitter to ground.

Figure 3.15 shows how optoisolators can be used to isolate a bidirectional signal between two systems. In the figure, an SPI device has a common I/O pin,

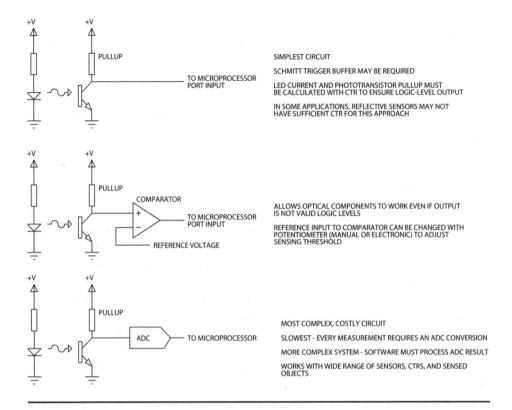

Figure 3.14
Interfacing optical sensors to a microprocessor.

but the design calls for this device to be DC isolated from the microprocessor. Two optoisolators are used to provide the required isolation. The SPI output is buffered (to provide the required LED drive current) and the output of optoisolator U1 produces an isolated, low output when the SPI device drives the I/O pin low. The output of U1 would be connected to an input pin or port bit on a microprocessor or microcontroller.

The second optoisolator (U2) drives the common I/O pin low when the microprocessor drives its LED low. When the microprocessor is not driving data onto the I/O pin, it must leave this LED in the OFF state so that the SPI device can drive the pin. When the microprocessor drives the I/O pin low, the output optoisolator will follow the signal, so the microprocessor must ignore transitions on the output while it is driving the SPI device. Or, the return signal can be used to verify that the data is being correctly passed through to the SPI device. Although not shown in Figure 3.15, a second optocoupler and another microprocessor port pin would be needed to drive the SPI clock signal.

Analog Interfacing to Embedded Microprocessor Systems

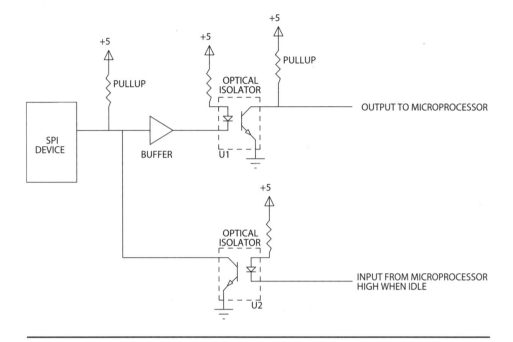

Figure 3.15
Bidirectional signal buffering with optoisolators.

Driving a bidirectional pin in this manner requires that the controlling micro-processor use two port pins (one input, one output), but it allows DC isolation of the peripheral device or system. In most cases, you will want to use high-speed optoisolators for an application like this. Either a diode/transistor or logic output optoisolators may be used, but optoisolator U2, which connects directly to the bidirectional pin, must have an open-collector output. The pullup resistor on the bidirectional pin should be chosen to provide sufficient speed (avoiding excessive rise time) without exceeding the drive capability of the pin. If optoisolator U2 is a diode/transistor device, it must be driven with sufficient LED current to ensure that the output can pull the bidirectional pin to a logic low.

CCDs

CCDs directly convert light intensity to an electrical value. CCDs are used in handheld camcorders, surveillance cameras, bar code readers, imaging systems, and any other place where a representation of an image is needed.

CCD Basics

A CCD operates by accumulating charge on a semiconductor area. When photons fall on a CCD pixel array, the energy from the photons is absorbed by the silicon, causing an electron-hole pair to be formed. The number of electron-hole pairs is directly related to the number of photons that were absorbed, and so is directly related to the amount of light. The longer that charge is allowed to accumulate, the more electron-hole pairs will be formed. The process of allowing light to fall on a CCD array for a particular time to accumulate charge is called *integration*, and the amount of time that charge is allowed to accumulate is called the *integration time*.

The accumulated charge represents an electrostatic potential. It can be moved by applying voltages to the clock pins of the CCD, creating changing potential voltages that can push the electrostatic charge around. There are a number of mechanisms to generate the needed voltages, all with different numbers of clock inputs and timing requirements. The essential point is that the CCD is configured as an analog shift register that passes the charges in one direction, from one cell to the next. At the end of the shift register is a sense node that converts the electrostatic charge to a voltage. Figure 3.16 illustrates the CCD process.

The sense node is constructed using a floating gate. The output of the sense node is directly proportional to the charge on this gate. To measure charge, the gate must first be drained of existing charge, which is performed with a reset transistor.

The functions that must be performed in any CCD-based system consist of the following:

- Provide phase clocks to control movement of the charges along the CCD shift register. This may require up to four input pins on the CCD, each with a clock signal of a different phase.
- Reset the output node prior to each measurement.
- Read the analog output voltage and convert it to a digital value using an ADC.

Exposure Control

What happens if too much light is accumulated on the CCD pixels? The result is saturation: all the pixels come out as full white. This happens if the light source that is illuminating the object to be scanned is too bright, or if the integration time is too long. Most modern CCDs provide exposure control, which is an input pin that allows the charge to be dumped into the device substrate, preventing it from accumulating in the CCD.

Analog Interfacing to Embedded Microprocessor Systems

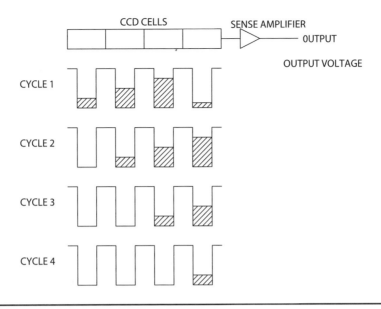

CCD CELLS   SENSE AMPLIFIER

OUTPUT

OUTPUT VOLTAGE

CYCLE 1

CYCLE 2

CYCLE 3

CYCLE 4

Figure 3.16
CCD operation.

Linear CCDs

Linear (or line-scan) CCDs have a single line of pixels. They are used in applications in which the object to be scanned is moving. The CCD scans a single row of pixels. When the target moves one pixel's width, the CCD scans another row of pixels. By assembling the rows of pixels, an image of the object may be built in memory. Typical applications include any kind of imaging that involves moving objects along a track, such as packages on a conveyor belt or documents moving down a transport. Figure 3.17 illustrates this process. To keep this figure simple, an array of only 24 elements is shown; a real array typically has 512 to 4096 elements. Linear CCDs can also be used where the object is motionless and the CCD array moves. Most computer scanners work this way. A motor moves the CCD array and the light source across the paper.

In most applications, a lens is used to translate the image to the CCD array. For instance, in a document imaging application, you might use an array that is 1 inch long and contains 1024 elements. If you are building a machine that a bank would use to scan checks, you might want to image documents up to 5 inches in width. The lens would have to perform a 5:1 reduction to scale the 5-inch document width down to the 1-inch array length. This would provide a resolution of 1024 pixels/5 inches, or 204.8 pixels per inch. If you wanted higher resolution (more pixels per inch), you would have to either limit the application to shorter documents or use an array with more elements.

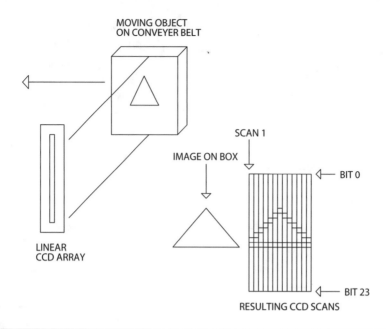

MOVING OBJECT
ON CONVEYER BELT

SCAN 1

IMAGE ON BOX

BIT 0

LINEAR
CCD ARRAY

BIT 23

RESULTING CCD SCANS

Figure 3.17
Linear CCD imaging.

Linear arrays are typically made with one, two, or four outputs. Multi-output arrays provide higher speeds by providing more than one data channel at a time. If the 1024-element array that we just looked at had two outputs, pixels 0–511 might be output on channel 1, and pixels 512–1023 on channel 2. Or, all the even pixels (0, 2, 4, ... 1022) might be output on channel 1 and the odd pixels (1, 3, 5, ... 1023) on channel 2. If a single-channel array were capable of operation to 15 MHz, an equivalent 2-channel array would be able to output data at the same rate on each channel, for twice the total data rate.

The required data rate of a CCD array depends on the application. In our document imaging example, if the documents are going by at 100 inches per second, then the array will have to take a full scan (1024 pixels) 204.8 times per inch. This works out to 204.8 × 100, or 20,480 scans per second. Because there are 1024 pixels per scan, the output rate is 20,480 × 1024, or 20.971 MHz. The ADCs and analog buffers have to operate at this rate. The 20,480 scans/sec rate means that the integration time is 48.8 µs. The CCD and lighting system must be selected to provide sufficient image quality at that speed. Of course, a 2-output array would cut the required processing rate in half, but would require twice as many ADCs.

Most linear arrays have a "storage" area to which the charge is transferred after integration is complete. Once the charge has been transferred to this storage area, further light integration will not affect the stored charge (but will affect the "capture" array that is exposed to the light). This mechanism prevents the data from changing while it is being shifted to the sense node.

Color

CCDs are not color sensors. They produce an output that is proportional to the amount of light that strikes the array. The CCD does not detect the color of the light, and CCDs do not typically respond to all colors equally. Color processing is normally performed by using three color filters, usually red, green, and blue. Figure 3.18 shows a linear array with a slide that has three color filters. To take a color image, a scan is made with the red filter in place, then one with the green filter, then one with the blue. Of course, the data rate for a color image is three times the data rate for a monochrome image, and the software has to control a motor or other actuator to move the correct filter into position for the current scan.

An alternative to using a single CCD and three filters for color applications is to use three CCDs with three filters, as shown in Figure 3.19. A beam splitter provides the same image to three CCDs. The problems with this approach are that three CCDs are needed, with their associated drivers and ADCs and the resulting difficulty in aligning the system.

Trilinear CCDs

There are newer linear CCDs called trilinear CCDs that are designed for color (Figure 3.20). A trilinear CCD has three CCD elements on one CCD die, and each element has a filter. This three-element array eliminates the alignment problems

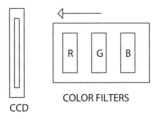

Figure 3.18
Color imaging with filters.

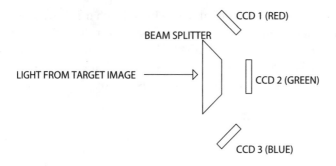

Figure 3.19
Color imaging with a beam splitter.

of the beam-splitter approach, and a single CCD with three arrays is less expensive than three single-line arrays of equivalent characteristics. Typical trilinear CCDs include the Kodak KLI series and the Sony ILX series.

A trilinear array solves the alignment problem of using three individual CCDs, but still has three individual outputs that require three ADCs. The three arrays in

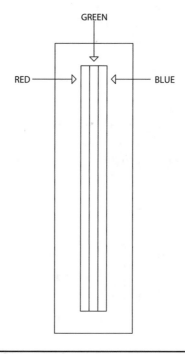

Figure 3.20
Trilinear color CCD array.

a trilinear part are side by side, but separated by some distance (Figure 3.21). In the Kodak KLI-2113 and the Sony ILX724, the pixel arrays are separated by a distance of 8 pixels. As shown in Figure 3.21, a given point on the image appears at one array in the CCD first (blue, in the Figure), at the middle array second, and finally at the last array. However, all three outputs of the CCD are active the entire time, meaning that the data is skewed in time.

This problem can be fixed in software by taking the data from the buffers in an offset fashion; data from scan 0 of the blue buffer is combined with data from scan 8 of the green buffer and scan 16 of the red buffer. Remember that one scan is many bytes; for an array that is 1024 pixels long, each scan is separated by 1024 bytes in memory.

Another way to handle this problem, in hardware, is to buffer the data in first in, first out memory (FIFO) and throw away the first 16 scans from the blue buffer and the first 8 scans from the green buffer. This ensures that the actual data is aligned and reduces the software overhead.

This problem also has ramifications for the motion part of the system. If the speed of motion is not well controlled, the scans won't align in the buffers because

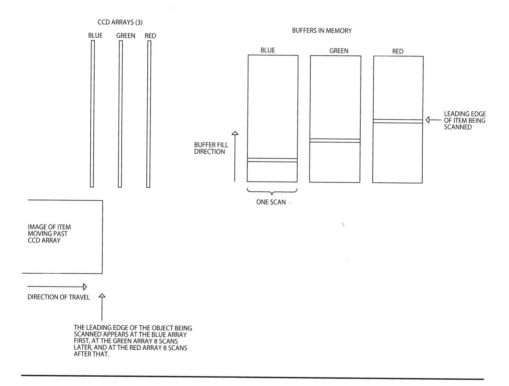

Figure 3.21
Trilinear data alignment.

the actual position of the object with respect to the CCD won't be what it should be. This is only a problem, of course, in systems that require all the scans to be well aligned.

Color Processing

The concepts of color processing are beyond the scope of this book. However, it is safe to say that most applications that need color have to perform some processing to get from raw CCD data to the actual image. In a monochrome application, all the information needed to manipulate or store the image is contained in the raw data. A monochrome image is just a black-and-white image of the object. The data from a color system has to have the three single-color data values combined to get the monochrome information. For instance, a color CCD system that is looking at something blue might produce a large value from the blue CCD, a smaller value from the green CCD, and zero from the red CCD. To get a monochrome (light/dark) representation, the data from the three CCDs has to be averaged or summed. To get color information, the software has to calculate the actual color of the target from the relative intensities of the three CCD outputs. In short, a color system will produce three times as much data as an equivalent monochrome system, but may require more than three times as much processing capability.

Area CCDs

An area CCD is typically used where neither the target nor the CCD is moved to take an image. As the name implies, an area CCD images a square or rectangular area. Area CCDs are used in camcorders and surveillance cameras, or in any imaging application where a "snapshot" is required of a stationary object. An area CCD could also be used in a motion system in which the motion isn't linear or isn't regular.

A trilinear CCD is three linear CCD arrays side by side. An area CCD can be thought of as a lot more linear arrays side by side. A 512×512 area CCD would have 512 linear arrays of 512 pixels each.

Unlike the trilinear CCD, the area CCD does not have one output per linear CCD array. Instead, data is shifted a row at a time into an output array and then shifted out a bit at a time. Obviously, the bit-at-a-time output limits the rate at which the array can capture images.

Some area arrays do not have the output "storage" area of the linear CCD, so the light must be turned off, or a mechanical shutter must be used to prevent continuous integration from occurring while the data is being read. Like the linear CCD, area CCDs are available with color outputs, and the mechanism works the same, with adjacent pixels picking up different colors that then have to be mixed by the software.

Dark Reference

One problem with CCDs is that the pixels will accumulate charge even in the dark. This has the effect of adding an offset to the output of the CCD. Most CCDs include a few pixels at each end that are not used for imaging. These pixels are identical to the imaging pixel elements, but are shielded from light. The output from these elements is a result only of the non-light-induced charge accumulation in the device. In most systems, this is subtracted from the values of the light-gathering pixels to eliminate unwanted offsets in the result. The subtraction can be accomplished either by software or by capturing the dark value in a sample-and-hold and performing the subtraction before the ADC.

Correlated Double Sampling

One way to reduce the noise in the CCD result is to use correlated double sampling (CDS). As shown in Figure 3.22, CDS uses two sample-and-hold circuits. One S/H captures the CCD output immediately after reset, when the CCD output is at the reset level. The other S/H captures the CCD output when the charge value is present. A differential amplifier provides the difference between the two levels to the ADC. Of course, the timing logic that generates the CCD clocks must ensure that the two S/H circuits take samples at the appropriate times.

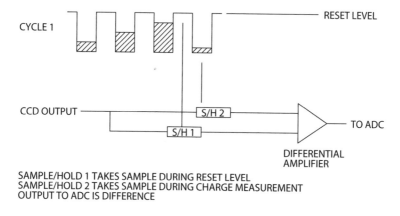

Figure 3.22
Correlated double sampling.

Another method to implement CDS is to couple the CCD output to the ADC input with a capacitor and use a clamp. The clamping circuit clamps the input to a fixed reference voltage when activated. This causes the capacitor to develop a DC bias that is equal to the difference between the reference voltage and the input signal (which is at the reset level). When the clamp is released, the ADC input will follow the CCD output, but with the offset added (until the charge bleeds off the capacitor). Typically, the signal will be clamped just before each pixel is read, restoring the DC offset on the capacitor.

Nonuniformity

Nonuniformity is the amount of variation between pixels in an array when they are exposed to the same light. In a linear array, it can result in bars of lighter or darker areas across the reconstructed image. There are several sources of non-uniformity inside the CCD, as well as lighting variations in a typical system. Lighting variations can be caused by an uneven light source or by things that affect the light path, such as reflections off a shiny object adjacent to the path that the target image takes.

One way of minimizing the effect of nonuniformity is to normalize this output. As shown in Figure 3.23, this process consists of passing the output of the CCD through an ADC, then passing the output of the ADC through a programmable read-only memory (PROM) before passing it to the microprocessor. The PROM contains normalization information for each pixel position. The pixel data from the ADC comprises the high-order PROM address bits and the row number is the low address bits. The PROM contents consist of values that multiply the ADC output by the value needed to make the output uniform. If a given pixel has an output that is 85% of nominal, then the values for that pixel will be multiplied by 1/85%, or 1.176. If the value out of the ADC is 25, then the value out of the PROM will be 29 (25 × 1.176).

The data in the PROM comes from calibrating the system with a known target. In a document-processing application, the calibration might be done with a white document of known, uniform characteristics. Of course, if the CCD or the lighting

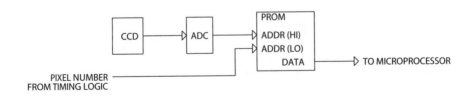

Figure 3.23
CCD normalization.

is changed, the system has to be recalibrated. The PROM has to be as big as the number of CCD pixels times the ADC resolution. A 1024-element CCD followed by an 8-bit ADC would require a PROM $256 \times 1024 \times 8$ bits wide. The timing logic has to be sure that the low address (pixel number) corresponds to the correct high address (converted pixel output).

A PROM was used in Figure 3.23 to illustrate the principle; in practice you would normally want this table to be stored in RAM or flash memory so the microprocessor could modify it. You can implement the same normalization technique in software if the microprocessor can keep up with the data rate. The microprocessor has to have a lookup table the same size as the PROM. For each sample, the pixel value is shifted to the left by however many bits are needed for the pixel number (10 for a 1024-element array), added to the pixel number, and then the result is used as an offset into the normalization lookup table. Of course, the table can be rearranged so that the pixel number is the high address and the pixel value is the low address.

Driving CCDs

One final note about CCDs; many CCDs have unusual voltage requirements for the clocks, such as 6.5 V for a logic "1" and less than 0.1 V for a logic "0." Even inputs that are apparently CMOS logic levels may have very tight requirements, requiring the driver to operate very close to the supply rails. In addition, the CCD clock inputs have very high capacitance, often over 2000 pf.

Because of these characteristics, the clock and reset inputs on most CCDs cannot be driven with standard logic. Many CCD manufacturers supply reference designs that indicate the types of drivers that are suitable. In many cases, drivers intended for driving high-power MOSFETs are suitable, because they are capable of delivering considerable current into a large capacitance. Another possibility is to use a logic driver with multiple sections and parallel the individual gates to obtain more drive.

CCD ADCs

A number of manufacturers make ADCs that are optimized for interfacing to CCDs. These often contain clamping circuitry to implement CDS and some of these parts include three channels for interfacing to trilinear or other color arrays. Typical parts include the 3-channel Fairchild TMC1103, the TI VSP 2000 and VST 3000 series, and the Maxim MAX1101.

Magnetic Sensors

Hall Effect Sensors

Probably the simplest magnetic sensor to use in an embedded application is a Hall effect sensor. Dr. Edwin Hall discovered the Hall effect in 1879. He discovered that if a magnetic field was placed perpendicular to one face of a thin gold sheet in which a current was flowing, a voltage would appear across the sheet (Figure 3.24). This voltage is proportional to the current flowing in the sheet and the magnetic flux density. A Hall effect sensor is made from silicon, and the Hall voltage produced in silicon is only a few microvolts per volt per gauss. Consequently, a high-gain amplifier is required to bring the signal from the Hall element to a useable range. Hall effect sensors integrate the amplifier into the same package as the sensor element.

Hall effect sensors are available as sensors that produce an output proportional to the magnetic field, or as switches that change state when the magnetic field exceeds a certain level. Analog Hall effect sensors are suited to applications in which you need to know how close a magnet is to the sensor—such as sensing whether an oscillating arm is really moving. Hall effect switches are best for applications in which you just need to know if a magnet is near the sensor, such as sensing whether a safety hood is closed or open.

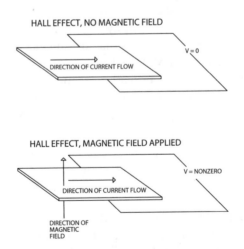

Figure 3.24
The Hall effect.

The output of an analog Hall effect sensor can be connected to a comparator or ADC like any other voltage-output sensor. One caution: some analog output sensors provide an output that is proportional to the supply voltage. For an accurate, noise-free output you must power the sensor from a noise-free, well-regulated supply.

A typical analog Hall effect sensor will produce an output that is halfway between the supply voltage and ground when no magnetic field is present. When a north pole is near the sensor, the voltage moves toward ground, and when a south pole is near the sensor the voltage moves toward the positive supply.

Hall effect switches produce a digital output to indicate the presence of a magnetic field. They drive the output active when a certain magnetic strength (the operate point) is sensed, then drive the output inactive when the magnetic field drops below a certain level (the release point). There is some hysteresis in the range, where the release point is less than the operate value.

Hall effect switches come in two varieties: unipolar and bipolar, which are sometimes called nonlatching and latching. Bipolar switches have a positive (south pole) operate point and a negative (north pole) release point. Unipolar switches have a positive (south pole) operate point and a less-positive release point. The operate and release points vary with temperature. Both bipolar and unipolar switches typically have an open-collector output that has to be pulled up with an external resistor.

Hall effect sensors are commonly available in three-lead packages similar to the TO-92 transistor package and in surface-mount packaging. The three leads are power, ground, and output. Typical supply voltages are 5 to 10 V, although some sensors operate up to 30 V or more. When using a Hall effect sensor, remember to account for stray magnetic fields. If using a magnet on, say, a rotating shaft, be sure that the magnet doesn't excessively magnetize the shaft itself, or this will affect the output of the sensor.

Remember that the magnetic field falls off with the approximate square of the distance (approximate because the size and shape of the magnet, as well as surrounding magnetizable objects, affect the result). In any event, the output of an analog Hall effect sensor may be linear with respect to the strength of the magnetic field, but it will not be linear with respect to distance.

Geartooth Hall effect sensors include a magnet and Hall effect sensor in one package. They are designed to measure rotation of a geared device by placing the sensor near the gear teeth (Figure 3.25). As each gear tooth moves past the sensor, it affects the magnetic field between the magnet and the Hall effect sensor, causing an output pulse to be generated.

Clarostat makes a Hall effect potentiometer. This device produces an output voltage that is proportional to the amount of rotation of the shaft. It is ideal for applications where a control knob is required, but where the reliability of a resistive potentiometer is inadequate.

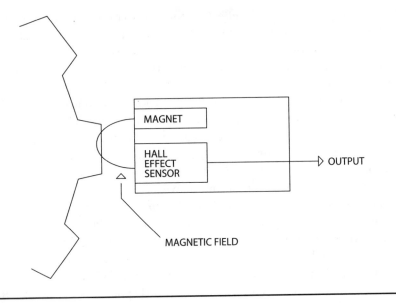

Figure 3.25
Geartooth Hall effect sensor.

Linear Variable Differential Transformers

The linear variable differential transformer (LVDT) consists of an excitation coil, two pickup coils, and a movable, magnetic core (Figure 3.26). The core provides coupling between the coils. The two pickup coils are connected in series opposed such that their fields oppose each other. When an AC signal is applied to the excitation coil, voltages are induced in the other two coils. If the movable core is centered, the two pickup coils will produce equal but opposite voltages, and the resulting output is zero.

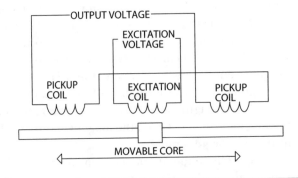

Figure 3.26
LVDT.

If the core is displaced toward one end, then one pickup coil will have more coupling with the excitation coil and will produce a larger output voltage.

Variable Reluctance Sensors

The variable reluctance sensor (VRS) consists of a coil and a magnet (Figure 3.27). When a shaft-mounted geartooth wheel moves past the sensor, the magnetic field from the magnet is disturbed, inducing a signal in the coil and permitting shaft speed to be measured. The VRS allows the speed of the geartooth wheel to be measured without requiring any power to the sensor. In addition, no semiconductor components are required, allowing the VRS to be used in places where the temperature is too high for a Hall effect sensor, such as in an automobile engine block.

In some applications, a tooth is left off the geartooth wheel, and the microprocessor software detects this condition to determine the reference position of the wheel. In other applications, a second geartooth wheel, mounted on the same

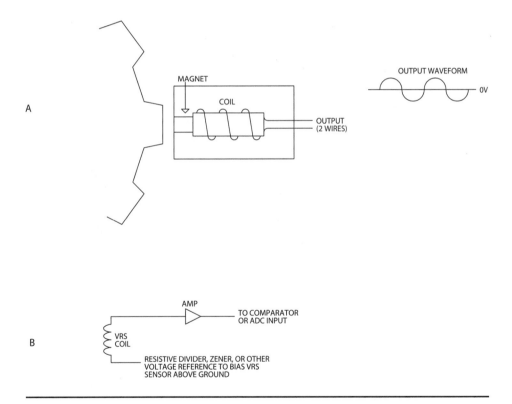

Figure 3.27
VRS.

shaft but having a different pattern or with a single tooth, can be used to identify the reference position.

The output of the VRS is typically amplified and passed to the microprocessor through a comparator or directly to an ADC input. The output amplitude from the VRS increases as the shaft speed goes up. For systems with a wide range of shaft speeds, it may be necessary to limit the voltage at the input amplifier with a zener or with diodes to the supply rails.

The VRS produces a bipolar output, with a negative component. Single-supply systems should bias the VRS to half the supply voltage (Figure 3.27B) before amplifying the signal. Note that the bias point must be a low impedance at all the frequencies at which the VRS will operate, or the overall gain of the system will be reduced. This may mean that a fairly large bypass capacitor is needed if the shaft can turn at low speeds and a resistive divider is used to provide the bias.

Motion/Acceleration Sensors

Sometimes you need to measure acceleration or tilt or other motion. The obvious application is airbag deployment in a car. However, there are other applications, such as sensing vibration that could indicate excessive bearing wear or an unbalanced load in a motor-driven application.

Solid-state acceleration sensors use internal capacitors to measure this force (Figure 3.28). A micromachined movable beam and two fixed plates are used. The movable beam has a spring that keeps it centered between the two fixed plates when there is no acceleration. The two fixed plates are driven with a signal from an oscillator. The two plates get the same signal, but 180° out of phase with each other. The resulting voltage at the movable beam is zero. When force is applied to the beam, it moves closer to one of the fixed plates. This causes the capacitance between the movable beam and that plate to be higher, and the capacitance between the beam and the other plate to be lower. The result is that the closer plate couples more signal into the beam and the farther plate couples less. The output voltage is a function of the distance the beam was deflected.

The Analog Devices ADXL202 is a typical acceleration sensor. The ADXL202 is a 2-axis sensor that provides a digital output instead of a voltage, suitable for connection to a microprocessor. The output of the ADXL202 is a high period followed by a low period. The duty cycle of the output indicates the acceleration. With 0g acceleration, the duty cycle is approximately 50%. The ADXL202 can measure acceleration from $-2\,g$ to $+2\,g$ and the duty cycle of the outputs varies about 12% per g. External resistors set the frequency of the outputs and external capacitors provide filtering.

Tilt can be measured with an acceleration sensor, as indicated in Figure 3.29.

Analog Interfacing to Embedded Microprocessor Systems

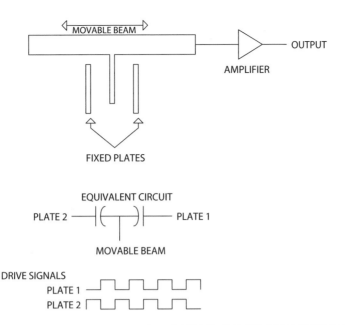

Figure 3.28
Solid-state acceleration sensor.

Switches

Switches come in various types, including magnetically activated reed switches, interlock switches on doors, and pushbutton switches for people to use. Switches may seem too simple to include here. They are either closed or open, right? The answer, as with many things, is: it depends.

Figure 3.30 illustrates a common way to connect a switch to a microprocessor. A pullup resistor takes the input high when the switch is open, and the switch grounds the input when it is closed. Also shown in the figure is the waveform produced at the input when the switch opens and closes. A mechanical switch will typically "bounce," making and breaking contact many times when opening and closing. This interval usually lasts several milliseconds.

If the switch is used as a safety interlock on a door, the bounce may not be a problem. The software may simply check the state of the switch when the user tries to start the instrument, and if the switch happens to be open, it won't let the motors start. If the operator has to close the door before being able to reach the start button, then the switch will have stopped bouncing when the software checks.

On the other hand, the switch might be used in an application in which you need to detect each time the switch is pressed. In this case, the contact bounce will

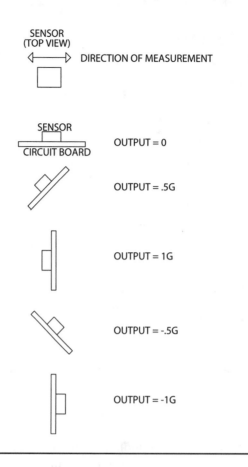

SENSOR
(TOP VIEW)

DIRECTION OF MEASUREMENT

SENSOR
CIRCUIT BOARD
OUTPUT = 0

OUTPUT = .5G

OUTPUT = 1G

OUTPUT = -.5G

OUTPUT = -1G

Figure 3.29
Measuring tilt with an acceleration sensor.

look like multiple switch presses to the software, and they must be filtered out. The algorithm usually looks like this:

Detect switch closure.
Wait 10–30 ms.
If switch still closed, then it was a valid closure. Otherwise, ignore it.

The delay can be implemented with a delay loop or as part of a regular timer routine. When developing the delay, don't make it just barely enough for the sample switch. The contact bounce time will vary from switch to switch and as the switch ages.

Switch contact resistance also can change with age. Switches with gold-plated contacts have low contact resistance, but the gold plating wears off eventually.

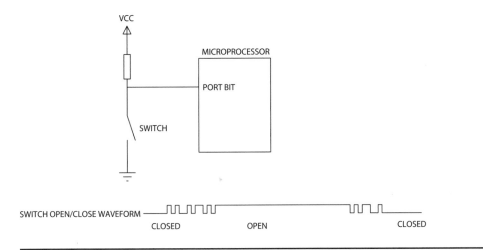

VCC

MICROPROCESSOR

PORT BIT

SWITCH

SWITCH OPEN/CLOSE WAVEFORM

CLOSED   OPEN   CLOSED

Figure 3.30
Switch bounce.

Increased contact resistance means higher voltage when the switch is closed, especially if the value of the pullup resistor is small.

Strain Gauges

A strain gauge (Figure 3.31) consists of a conductor, such as a copper trace printed on an insulator. The resistance of the conductor is determined by its dimensions. If the insulator holding the conductor is compressed or stretched, the conductor will change its shape slightly and its resistance will change. Strain gauges are characterized by very small resistance and even smaller resistance changes. The advantage of a strain gauge is that it can be used to measure force (such as the weight of a truck on a scale) without any "moving" parts. The strain gauge is part of the structure of the scale, and while it flexes under load, it does not have any rotating or sliding parts to wear out or break. Note that the flexible element may be a printed circuit substrate or even an aluminum support, as long as the strain gauge element itself is insulated.

As shown in Figure 3.31, a strain gauge is typically sensed using a bridge circuit. In this example, the ratio R1/R2 is the same as R3/Rs (Rs is the strain gauge resistance) when the strain gauge is unloaded. In this condition, the output voltage, VOUT, is zero. If the strain gauge is deformed and its resistance changes, the bridge becomes unbalanced, the ratio of R1/R2 is no longer the same as R3/Rs

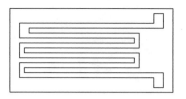

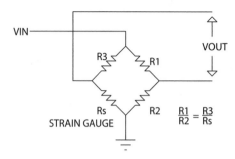

$$\frac{R1}{R2} = \frac{R3}{Rs}$$

Figure 3.31
Strain gauge.

(Rs changed), and the output voltage is nonzero. This voltage can be amplified and measured. The advantage of a bridge circuit like this one is that it filters out any noise (such as AC line ripple) on the input voltage. The output voltage is dependent on the input voltage, but variations in the input voltage don't affect the output.

Due to the extremely low resistance of the strain gauge, the voltage out of the bridge must be amplified by a significant amount before it is measured. A typical strain gauge might have a resistance of around 100 ohms, and in a practical application it might be necessary to sense resistance changes of 0.0002% of the nominal value. Strain gauges in various configurations are used to measure weight, force, and pressure.

Semiconductor strain gauges with micromachined resistance elements etched into silicon also are available. The advantage of these parts is that the signal conditioning and amplification can be included on the part.

Time-Based Measurements

4

In many microprocessor systems, it is preferable to use frequency to make measurements, instead of measuring voltage or current with an ADC. Reasons for using frequency measurement include the following:

- In systems with ground offsets, signals can be capacitively coupled or optically isolated to eliminate ground loops and other detrimental effects.
- Noise that would be introduced on an analog signal sent down a long cable may be eliminated by transmitting a logic-level frequency signal instead.
- Measuring frequency instead of analog values may allow a simpler microprocessor to be used, because an ADC is not required.

In many cases, you can convert an analog input, such as temperature, to a time-based signal that can be measured with a microprocessor. One IC that can do this is the Maxim MAX6576 (and a related part, the MAX6577). The MAX6576 is a 6-pin surface-mount (SOT-23) device that converts temperature to a square-wave output. The period of the output signal is proportional to temperature. The MAX6576 has two pins that are tied high or low to select an output range of 10, 40, 160, or 640 μs per °K.

Using frequency in this way permits a microprocessor to measure temperature with a single pin. The microprocessor software can perform this measurement in several ways. In a microprocessor with capture capability, such as the microchip PIC16C6x series, the sensor output can be connected to the microprocessor input that is used for pulse capture. A simplified block diagram of such a capture system is shown in Figure 4.1. Here, a free-running, 16-bit counter is captured by a 16-bit register when the input frequency changes from the low to high state. At the same time, a short pulse is generated to reset the counter.

In the example shown in Figure 4.1, one period of the input is 90 μs and the second is 100 μs. In this case, the counter will count up 90 (decimal) counts for the first period and 100 (decimal) counts for the second period. The count is read by the microprocessor to determine the period and therefore the temperature.

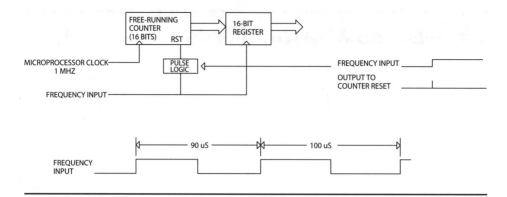

Figure 4.1
Frequency-based measurement system.

In some microcontrollers, the timer cannot be reset when an input capture occurs. In that case, the counter keeps running between interrupts. For instance, if a regular signal is applied to the capture input and it has a period equal to 100 timer counts, then the first interrupt will result in a capture value of 100, the second will result in 200, the third will be 300, and so on. The firmware has to subtract the current count from the previous count to find the number of counts that occurred since the last interrupt. The code also has to adjust the count when the capture counter rolls over from its maximum value to zero.

The code to implement a capture counter in this way would consist of setup code, interrupt service routine (ISR), and non-ISR code. The code has to perform the following functions:

Setup

Program timer as input capture

Program timer prescaler (if used)

Program input capture edge (rising edge in this example)

Program timer to generate interrupt on capture

Capture interrupt logic (if the counter resets after capture)

Read captured count from timer capture register

Convert time to temperature (table lookup or algorithm)

Capture interrupt logic (if the counter does not reset after capture)

Read captured count from timer capture register

Analog Interfacing to Embedded Microprocessor Systems

Subtract previous count from new count

If result negative, subtract previous count from new count $+10000\,H$

Convert result to temperature (table lookup or algorithm) Store new count as previous count for next interrupt

Note: This code assumes a 16-bit counter. If the counter is wider, the constant used to adjust a negative result is equal to the maximum count value plus 1. For example, a 20-bit timer would use $100,000\,H$ instead of $10,000\,H$.

Another way to handle the negative result situation is to program the microcontroller so that the timer also generates an interrupt on rollover. The code for the timer rollover interrupt sets a flag. When the next capture interrupt occurs, the interrupt code reads the rollover flag, adjusts the calculated time, then resets the rollover flag.

Microprocessors that do not have a capture capability can perform a similar measurement by letting a counter free-run and connecting the frequency signal to an interrupt input. The counter can be an external IC or an internal counter that is clocked from a derivative of the microprocessor clock. When the interrupt occurs, the software reads and resets the counter. This method is slightly less accurate than the capture method, due to variable interrupt latency. In a system in which you don't want other interrupts to affect latency of the measurement, and where the microprocessor has an non-maskable interrupt (NMI) input, you can use that for the frequency input.

If the microcontroller has timers that can be incremented with an external signal, the frequency input can be connected to one of those timer inputs. The microprocessor can then read the timer on a regular basis (based on a second timer running from the microprocessor clock) to get the number of counts that occurred in the measurement period.

Interrupt latency issues can be minimized by connecting a period-based signal to a counter that runs from the microprocessor clock, but only counts when the input is high (some microcontroller counters can be operated in this mode). The counter will count up while the input is high and hold the count while the input is low. The microprocessor can read the count any time the count is low. As long as the microprocessor reads the count before the input goes high again, the count will be accurate (Figure 4.2).

Analog Devices makes a pair of temperature sensors, the TMP03 and TMP04, that convert temperature to a time-based output. These devices generate an output with a fixed high time and a low time that varies with temperature. In other words, both the period and frequency vary with temperature. Temperature is measured by calculating the ratio of the high to low periods. (The ratio is used to compensate for frequency variations caused by temperature.)

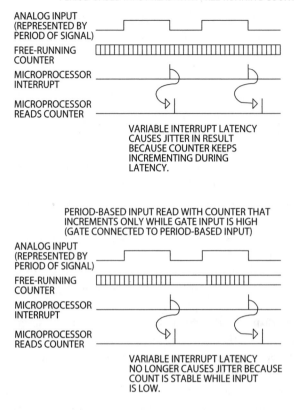

Figure 4.2
Measuring period-based inputs with a free-running counter.

Measuring Period versus Frequency

I worked on one system in which an analog value was converted to frequency. The sensor circuit converted a mechanical change to a slight frequency shift in an RF signal. The frequency value for several sensors was captured using a PLD and then read by a microprocessor. A block diagram of the capture system is shown in Figure 4.3. A counter was incremented by the frequency input. Once every sample period, the count was captured in a register and read by the microprocessor. In this case, the counter was never reset, but was allowed to roll over from FFFF to 0000; the microprocessor took care of calculating the correct count when this happened.

Analog Interfacing to Embedded Microprocessor Systems

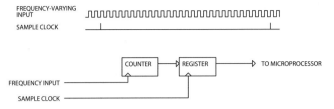

FREQUENCY-BASED MEASUREMENT

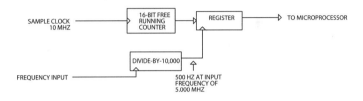

PERIOD-BASED MEASUREMENT

Figure 4.3
Frequency versus period measurement.

In this system, we needed to detect frequency changes fairly quickly—on the order of 2 ms. Walking through an example, say that the frequency changes from 5 MHz to 5.005 MHz, and the sample interval is 2 ms. The results look like this:

$$\text{At } 5.00 \text{ MHz} : \text{Count read by processor} = \frac{2 \text{ ms}}{200 \text{ ns}} = 10,000 \text{ counts}$$

$$\text{At } 5.005 \text{ MHz} : \text{ Count read by processor} = \frac{2 \text{ ms}}{199.8 \text{ ns}} = 10,010 \text{ counts}$$

So this change produces a change of 10 counts in the result. Getting more resolution (the ability to measure smaller frequency changes) requires going to a longer sampling period, or changing the circuit that generates the input frequency.

Figure 4.3 also shows an alternative method for making the same measurement. Here, the input is divided by 10,000, producing a 500 Hz signal (at 5.000 MHz input). This signal clocks a register with the contents of a free-running 16-bit counter. The counter is incremented by a regular clock—10 MHz in this example. Again, counter rollover is handled in software. Measuring the same frequency shift gives the following results:

$$\text{At } 5.00\,\text{MHz}: \text{Count read by processor} = \frac{10\,\text{MHz}}{500\,\text{Hz}} = 20,000$$

$$\text{At } 5.005\,\text{MHz}: \text{Count read by processor} = \frac{10\,\text{MHz}}{500.5\,\text{Hz}} = 19,980$$

These results amount to a 20-count difference. This approach requires more hardware and a higher frequency sampling clock. The sampling rate is not fixed, but is dependent on the input frequency. However, this approach allows higher resolution without changing the sampling interval. More resolution is obtainable simply by increasing the sampling clock. In this case, going from 10 MHz to 20 MHz would double the number of counts for the same frequency change without changing the sample interval. Of course, you would need a larger counter to hold the result.

Mixing

Figure 4.4 shows a variation on this approach that provides a greater output frequency shift for a given input change. The input frequency is passed through a frequency mixer with a 7 MHz offset frequency. The mixer produces as an output the two original frequencies, and the sum and difference frequencies. In this case,

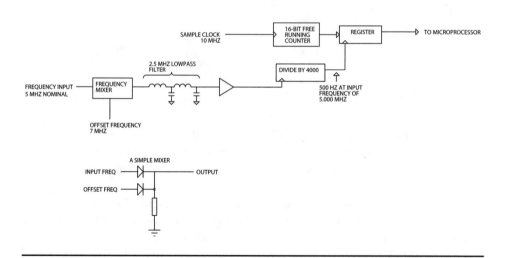

Figure 4.4
Using a frequency mixer to increase frequency shift.

Analog Interfacing to Embedded Microprocessor Systems

the mixer outputs will be 5 MHz, 7 MHz (the input frequencies), 12 MHz (the sum), and 2 MHz (the difference). This output is passed through a 2.5 MHz low-pass filter to remove everything but the 2 MHz difference frequency. This result is amplified and divided by 4000 to produce the same 500 Hz signal to the rest of the period-measurement logic.

Now if the 5 MHz input shifts to 5.005 MHz, the difference will be 7–5.005 or 1.995 MHz. Divided by 4000, this is 498.75 Hz. If we measure the period with the same 10 MHz reference, we get this:

$$\text{At 5.000 MHz : Count read by processor} = \frac{10\,\text{MHz}}{500\,\text{Hz}} = 20,000$$

$$\text{At 5.005 MHz : Count read by processor} = \frac{10\,\text{MHz}}{498.75\,\text{Hz}} = 20,050$$

Now instead of a 20-count difference we have a 50-count difference. Note that the frequency shift into the divide-by-4000 circuit is negative, where the original frequency shift was positive. This is due to the fact that the circuit uses *high-side injection*, mixing the 5 MHz input frequency with a higher 7 MHz frequency. If we had mixed the 5 MHz with 4 MHz, to get a 1 MHz difference, then the output frequency shift would have moved in the same direction as the original input. The reason for using high-side injection in this example is because it makes the low-pass filter simpler. The farther the unwanted mixer frequencies are from the desired frequency, the easier they are to filter out.

Although mixer theory and design are beyond the scope of this book, Figure 4.4 shows a simple mixer that uses two diodes and could be used for two logic-level signals. Nearly any nonlinear device will work as a mixer to one degree or another. Off-the-shelf mixers are available, such as the Philips NE612.

This example used a two-stage L/C low-pass filter. In some applications, you might want to use a more sophisticated filter or a bandpass filter. You could even use a DSP to perform the filtering in software, although that is a significant increase in overall complexity.

Although the mixer approach does multiply the frequency shift, making measurement easier, it also has some drawbacks:

- The mixer approach multiplies the frequency shift you want to measure, but also any other frequency shift. This includes drift caused by component heating, noise, and so forth.
- The input frequency range has to be limited or it will end up being filtered out. If the 5 MHz input in Figure 4.4 shifted down to 4.5 MHz, the difference frequency would then be 2.5 MHz and would be filtered out by the low-pass filter.

- The design of the mixer and low-pass filter can be complicated. It is made worse if the amplitude of the input signal varies as well as the frequency.
- Finally, the addition of another frequency (the injection frequency for mixing) complicates the circuit and may produce additional EMI.

Voltage-to-Frequency Converters

One means of converting an analog input to a time value is to use a voltage-to-frequency (V-F) converter. The block diagram of a V-F converter is shown in Figure 4.5. A comparator drives a one-shot, which produces an output pulse of a fixed width when triggered. On one side of the comparator, a capacitor is charged through a constant current source or discharged through a resistor, depending on the position of the (solid-state) switch.

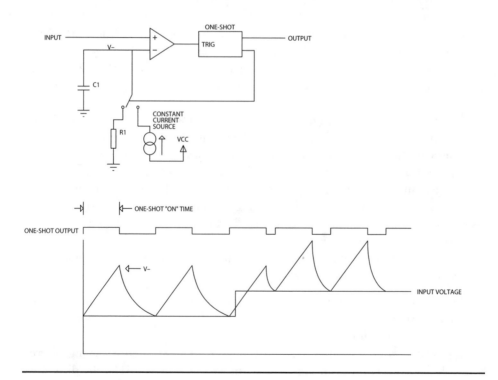

Figure 4.5
Voltage-to-frequency converter operation.

Analog Interfacing to Embedded Microprocessor Systems

Figure 4.5 also shows the waveform for operation of the V-F converter. With the input at some voltage, the capacitor is charged by the constant current source (providing a linear charging ramp) until the one-shot times out. The capacitor then discharges through resistor R1 until V- equals the input voltage. The comparator output will then go low, triggering the one-shot again. The charge time is always equal to the one-shot "on" time. When the input voltage changes level, the capacitor will charge up the same way as before, but now it discharges only down to the new voltage level. The next charge cycle pushes V- above the new input level, and the capacitor discharges down to this level. However, the discharge is through the resistor, which is an exponential curve, and it is discharging toward ground. Consequently, the discharge time at the new voltage is less than it was for the original voltage, and the resulting output LOW time is shorter, making the frequency higher.

The accuracy of a V-F is dependent on the accuracy of the current source, the accuracy of the one-shot timing, and the accuracy of capacitor C1. The one-shot "on" time is controlled by a resistor/capacitor combination, so these components are extremely important. Likewise, capacitor C1 and resistor R1 determine the output frequency. It is typical to use precision resistors and Teflon, polystyrene, or polypropylene capacitors in V-F circuits. On startup, the capacitor has to be charged from 0 V to the input voltage. The one-shot "on" time may be too short to ensure that this happens. Typically, the switch is left in the charge mode until V- reaches the input voltage.

The LM231 from National Semiconductor is a typical V-F converter. This part uses an internal voltage reference to set the charging current; a resistor from an external pin to ground determines the current. The LM231 is capable of operation from 1 Hz to 100 kHz.

So far, we have looked at asynchronous V-F converters. Synchronous V-F converters work the same way, except that an external clock determines the "on" time that charges the capacitor. This makes the V-F characteristics independent of the resistor-capacitor combination in the asynchronous V-F one-shot. The same techniques described for other time-based inputs can be used to read the output of a V-F converter.

Applications

One application for a V-F converter is in cases where a sensor is operating from a different reference. For instance, a microprocessor system in one building might be monitoring the temperature of a process in a building some distance away. The grounds of the two buildings might be far enough apart to make a digital interface impractical. Instead of using an ADC, a voltage could be monitored with a V-F converter and an optocoupler could be used to isolate the sensor circuit from the microprocessor circuit (Figure 4.6). Only two wires are needed to

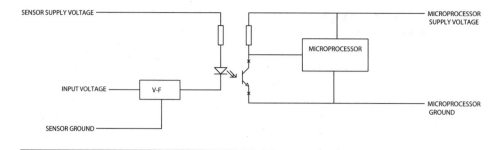

Figure 4.6
Using a V-F converter to interface a remote sensor.

transfer the analog value to the microprocessor. Of course, the optocoupler has to be capable of operating at the maximum frequency the V-F will generate.

A V-F converter is also useful any time an analog signal needs to be transmitted over a wire that is electrically noisy. As long as the noise levels aren't large enough to affect the switching point (thereby affecting the frequency measured at the receiving end), the receiver will be able to extract valid data.

Filtering

Using a divider with a V-F converter (Figure 4.7) provides an automatic filtering function. Figure 4.7 shows a V-F connected to a microprocessor through a divide-by-16 counter. The resulting frequency to the microprocessor will be the sum of 16 cycles from the V-F. If the V-F input voltage is varying slightly, this will effectively filter the result. Of course, the filtering could also be performed in software.

Clock Resolution and Range

All of the methods we've looked at have one limitation: the sampling clock used to measure the period or frequency. If you have a sensor that can convert an analog signal to a period with an accuracy of 100 ns, but you're measuring the period with a 2 MHz (500 ns) clock, then 500 ns is all the accuracy you will ever get from the overall system.

Figure 4.7
V-F filtering with a divider.

Analog Interfacing to Embedded Microprocessor Systems

Resolution and range are related. As an example, say that the MAX6576 temperature sensor mentioned at the beginning of this chapter is used with a range of 10 μs per °K. The temp sensor is connected to the interrupt pin of a microcontroller, and a free-running counter is used to measure the temperature (Figure 4.8). When an interrupt occurs, the microcontroller reads the count and calculates the temperature. If the MAX6576 is being used to measure temperature from −30 °C to +100 °C, the output of the MAX6576 will range from about 2400 microseconds to 3730 microseconds. Using a 5 MHz clock in the microcontroller counter, when the interrupt occurs the microcontroller will read a counter value that ranges from 12,000 counts to 18,650 counts. For this example, assume that the microcontroller does not have an input capture feature; it has to read the count and subtract the result from the previous value to get the number of clocks that have occurred since the last interrupt.

In an application like this, the microcontroller may have other interrupts or may have to disable interrupts for some functions. This will result in a varying latency from the time when the MAX6576 interrupt occurs until it is serviced. If the microcontroller has a maximum interrupt latency of 10 microseconds, the inaccuracy of the overall system is the inaccuracy of the MAX6576 (ranging from 3.5 to 7.5 degrees over its temperature range) plus the microcontroller latency (1 degree).

Say that a decision is made that the interrupt rate from the MAX6576 is too high or that the interrupt latency adds too much error to the system. As a result, the MAX6576 is configured for 40 microseconds per °K. Now the 10 μs interrupt latency of the microcontroller only affects the accuracy by 0.25 degrees. However, this change has two other effects.

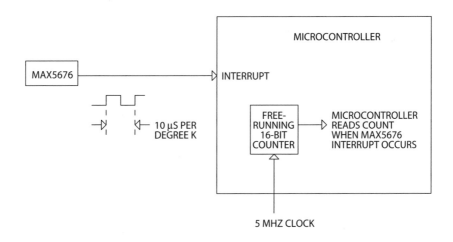

Figure 4.8
MAX6576 application.

First, the value read from the counter now ranges from 48,000 to 74,600. Because the counter is only 16 bits wide (maximum value 65,535), higher temperatures will cause the counter to overflow. The software will need to detect this condition, probably by programming the timer to generate an interrupt on rollover and setting a flag when this interrupt occurs. This approach does, however, add to the overall interrupt processing latency of the system.

The second effect of changing the period of the MAX6576 output is the time required to get a result. At the new setting, temperature readings can be made only once every 9.6 ms (at $-30\,^\circ$C) to 14.9 ms (at $100\,^\circ$C). If the MAX6576 were configured for the slowest rate of 640 µs per $^\circ$K, the time between readings would range from 0.15 seconds to 0.24 seconds. This may or may not be a problem, depending on your application.

The clock resolution has to be matched to the frequency and resolution of the input signal. This may place some limits on your choice of microprocessors. For instance, some microcontrollers have an input capture capability that can only run at a submultiple of the processor clock—say, 1/4 or 1/8 of the processor clock rate. So an 8 MHz processor of this type could measure an input period with an accuracy of only 500 ns or 1 µs. This may be insufficient for your application.

As mentioned in Chapter 1, range and resolution are important in any analog system. When measuring analog quantities using time or period, the smallest interval that can be accurately measured is equivalent to the resolution, and the largest period that can be measured is equivalent to the range. An analysis of the measurement accuracy and range is needed any time that frequency or period is used to measure analog values.

Extending Accuracy with Limited Resolution

Any time you measure the period of an event with a microprocessor, there is always a measurement inaccuracy of plus or minus one clock. With normal measurement techniques, you need many measurement clocks per event to get an accurate measurement. Events that last only a few measurement clocks cannot be measured accurately. An example is shown in Figure 4.9, where an event that lasts for 2.5 interrupt periods is measured by a microprocessor. In this case, the microprocessor would make the measurement by counting the number of interrupts that occur between the start and end of the event. As shown in the figure, the number of interrupts that would occur ranges between 2 and 3, depending on when the event starts. It is impossible to tell what the actual length of the event is using a single measurement. The figure shows the measurement being made by counting interrupts from a regular timer; the same principle applies if the measurement is made by reading the contents of a free-running timer.

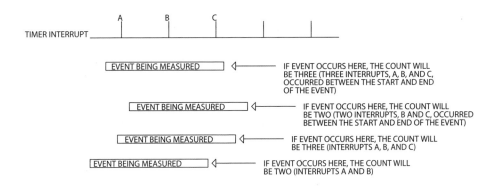

Figure 4.9
One clock ambiguity in measuring an event.

Cases like this typically occur under conditions such as the following:

- A very short event has to be measured using a timer with limited resolution. On many PCs and PC-compatible single-board computers, the fastest clock available for making such measurements is about 122 μs.
- The event being measured is so short that measuring it accurately would require a very fast interrupt, using an excessive percentage of the CPU throughput.
- The system has a timer capable of operating with a faster clock, but it is needed for another function and cannot be operated at a high enough clock rate to make accurate measurements.

It is possible to make accurate measurements in such circumstances. Each measurement in Figure 4.9 will vary between 2 and 3 timer interrupts. If a large number of measurements are made, the average value will represent the actual time for the event. For this example, about 50% of the measurements will be 2 and about 50% will be 3. If the length of the event was 2.75 timer interrupt periods instead of 2.5, the percentage of values for 2 and 3 would be 25% and 75%, respectively. To make an accurate measurement of a short event, you can take 100 measurements, add them together, and then divide the result by 100 (the number of measurements). The result will be very close to 2.5. Interestingly, this measurement method also works if the event duration is less than one clock period.

Of course, this requires floating point math to calculate such a result. However, you could divide by 10 instead of 100 and get a result of 25. As long as an accuracy of one decimal position is adequate for your application, this approach would work. If you need more accuracy but don't want to use floating-point math, you could use a 16-bit integer to hold the number, leaving anywhere from four to eight bits for the fractional portion of the result.

To explain why this method works, it is probably easiest to use a value shorter than the measurement clock. Say that the event is a square wave signal from a time-based sensor, and that the period of the signal is 400 µs. If it's being measured with a 1 ms interrupt, then the period of the event is 40% of the interrupt period. If the leading edge of the sensor signal starts at some random time, there is a 40% chance that one measurement clock will occur between the start and end of the sensor signal. There may not be an interrupt during the sensor signal the first time that it is measured, so the interrupt count would be zero. However, if enough samples are taken, 40% of them will have a count of 1 because one interrupt will occur during the sensor signal period.

With an event duration longer than the clock period, the same principle applies. Using the 2.5 clock event mentioned earlier as an example, there is a 100% chance that two clocks will occur during the event. There is a 50% chance that three clocks will occur. Again, if you average a large number of samples, the result will be very close to the actual value.

The more samples you take with this method, the more accurate the result will be. Table 4.1 is a table of values showing the relationship between the number of samples, the percentage of values, and the result calculated using this method.

The data in Table 4.1 was generated using the random number function in Microsoft Excel (details are in Appendix D). As you can see, going from 100 to 1000 samples greatly increases the accuracy. Although this method allows you to make time-based measurements with better accuracy than the measurement clock would normally allow, there are some restrictions on making measurements this way.

- The event being measured cannot be synchronized in any way to the measurement clock. This technique works only if the start time of the event with respect to the measurement clock is random. However, the event can be a repetitive event, such as a regular square wave. The event can also be started and stopped in software, as long as the start and stop are not synchronized to the measurement clock.

Table 4.1
Statistical Sampling Method Using 100 and 1000 Samples.

Value	Number of Samples	Number of Samples Where Count = 2	Number of Samples Where Count = 3	Calculated Result; Total of All Values Number of Samples
2.25	100	67	33	2.33
2.25	1000	740	260	2.26
2.5	100	55	45	2.45
2.5	1000	507	493	2.49
2.8	100	13	87	2.87
2.8	1000	188	812	2.81

Analog Interfacing to Embedded Microprocessor Systems

- The system must be capable of doing division, although that can be simplified by using a binary number of samples (128, 1024, etc.). This allows the division to be a simple shift operation.
- The duration of the event being measured must not change appreciably over the entire measurement interval.
- The overall accuracy is limited by the number of samples taken, the repeatability of the event being measured, and the accuracy of the measurement clock. For example, if you are making this type of measurement by counting interrupts, variations in interrupt latency will affect overall accuracy.
- The measurement time is equal to the event period times the number of measurements. When the event period increases, the measurement time will go up by the amount of the increase times the total number of measurements.

Figure 4.10 shows two repetitive waveforms measured using this method. Both are square wave signals, such as might be produced by the MAX6576, so an event is defined as the time period from one rising edge to the next. For both waveforms, the number of interrupts counted during the event period is noted below the event in the figure. Again, this example measures the event by counting interrupts; the same result would be obtained by reading a free-running timer.

The frequency of the first waveform is 1.2 times the interrupt period. If you add up the number of interrupts detected (11) and divide by the number of events (9), you get 1.22. This is a reasonably accurate measure of the event period, given that only 9 events are averaged.

The frequency of the second waveform is 60% of the interrupt period. Adding up the number of interrupts detected (11) and dividing by the number of events (19) yields 0.578. Again, this is a reasonable approximation of the actual value. More samples would produce a more accurate result.

A typical application where this might be useful would be a refrigerator that measures temperature using a device such as the MAX6576. In a refrigerator, the

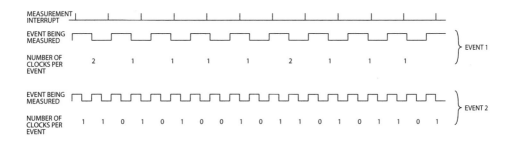

Figure 4.10
Using averaging to measure repetitive events.

temperature typically does not change rapidly, so taking 100 or 1000 measurements to get an accurate reading is not an unreasonable thing to do.

To implement this measurement in software, you could either bring the signal representing the event into the processor as an edge-sensitive interrupt or poll it. If you are measuring the event using a timer interrupt, the timer interrupt ISR will typically increment a counter. The event interrupt ISR interrupt would reset the counter at the start of the event and read it at the end of an event. For a repetitive event, where the end of one event is the start of the next, the event code would reset the counter immediately after reading it. The value in the counter is the number of timer interrupts that occurred since the start of the event interrupt.

If you are making the measurement using a free-running counter, the event ISR would read the timer at the start and end of the event, subtracting the starting value from the ending value (accounting for rollover, if any) to calculate the period.

As mentioned earlier, you can avoid complicated division by making the number of samples a multiple of two. In many applications, you could avoid division altogether, using just the summed measurement values. For example, if you are using a sensor where 0.6 measurement clocks equals 25 degrees, you could instead take 64 samples, sum the values, and structure the software to interpret the sum ($0.6 \times 64 = 38$) as 25 degrees.

Finally, for repetitive events, such as a sensor with a regular, frequency-based output, you do not need to count how many interrupts occur per event. You can instead count how many interrupts occur over a number of events. You can connect the external event signal so that it increments (or decrements) a hardware counter, and then program the counter to generate an interrupt when a specific count has expired. This minimizes the number of event interrupts that must be serviced, which is particularly useful if the event is very fast compared to the processor ISR service time.

Output Control Methods   **5**

Open-Loop Control

The simplest form of control mechanism is an open-loop output. *Open loop* means that there is no feedback from the controlled device back to whatever is controlling it. There is no indication of whether the device being controlled is actually doing what it is told to do. An example would be the vibrating motor in a pager or cell phone. Neither the user nor the instrument cares if the motor speed varies by 10% or 20%. So the microprocessor can just send an on/off signal to the motor— no feedback about the actual speed is needed. The actual motor speed will depend on the motor friction, battery voltage, and the condition of the motor brushes. Unlike this example motor, where actual speed is unimportant, most microprocessor control applications will measure whatever is being controlled to ensure that the control action actually did what was expected. This requires feedback from the controlled device to the microprocessor. The remainder of this chapter will address feedback control systems.

Negative Feedback and Control

Figure 5.1 shows a simple control system—an opamp. The opamp has very high gain, and by connecting the output to the inverting input, we introduce negative feedback. The opamp amplifies the difference between the inverting and non-inverting inputs. Say that the input and output are at 2 V. The difference between the input and the output is 0 V, so the difference between the inverting and

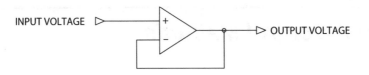

INPUT VOLTAGE ▷————————————————————▷ OUTPUT VOLTAGE

Figure 5.1
Simple control system: an opamp.

noninverting inputs is also 0 V. The opamp, which amplifies this difference, has no difference to amplify.

Now, if the input changes suddenly from 2 V to 2.1 V, there will be a difference between the two inputs—the noninverting input is at 2.1 V, and the inverting input, still connected to the output, is at 2 V. The 0.1 V difference is amplified by the opamp, which starts to move the output toward a more positive voltage as soon as the output reaches 2.1 V, the difference between the two inputs is again 0, and the output stays at that voltage.

If the temperature changes and the opamp output transistors change characteristics slightly, they might drift to a new voltage level. However, as soon as that happens, the opamp inputs see a difference, amplify it, and the output stabilizes at the input voltage again. The gain of an ideal opamp is just a very large integer. A real opamp, of course, has frequency limitations and other deviations from the ideal.

Microprocessor-Based Systems

Microprocessor-based control systems work the same way as the opamp. They control some real-world device, such as a heater or a motor, that attempts to make something (position, temperature, etc.) match a desired value. The magic, of course, is in the gain function. Unlike our simple opamp example, a digital control system can produce an output that is a much more complex function of the input. The microprocessor can provide a control signal that is a function not only of the input and output, but of the history of the output, the rate of change, the type of load, and so on.

One fact that sets microprocessor-based control systems apart from linear systems is that the microprocessor system is always a sampled system. This means that the microprocessor samples the output of the sensors at regular intervals. Any changes that happen between samples are lost. The sampling rate must be high enough to ensure that no information crucial to operation of the system falls between samples. This speed depends on the system, of course, and may range

Analog Interfacing to Embedded Microprocessor Systems

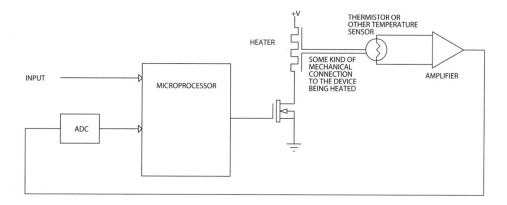

Figure 5.2
Simple microprocessor control system.

from seconds or minutes for a slow system to tens of thousands of samples per second for something faster.

Figure 5.2 shows a simple control system. Here, a microprocessor turns a heater on and off via a MOSFET transistor. A thermistor is used to measure the temperature of whatever the system is heating. The microprocessor reads the temperature and turns the heater on or off to maintain the correct temperature. The desired temperature is an input to the system. For now, we won't worry about where that input comes from.

On-Off Control

The simplest control system is on-off control, sometimes called bang-bang control. The microprocessor reads the temperature. If the temperature is low, the heater is turned on. If the temperature is high, the heater is turned off. Figure 5.3 shows the equivalent control system using a comparator. The figure also shows what the typical response of such a system is. When the system starts, the heater is cool. The microprocessor turns the heater on until the temperature measured at the thermistor reaches the desired point. It then turns the heater off. When the temperature drops below the setpoint, the heater is turned on again and the heater temperature goes back up. The temperature oscillates around the setpoint.

Figure 5.3 shows the actual temperature of the heater and the temperature of the thermistor. As you can see, they don't quite match, either in time or in amplitude. When the heater is first turned on, it overshoots the setpoint by some amount, then oscillates around the desired temperature. The key reasons for this are:

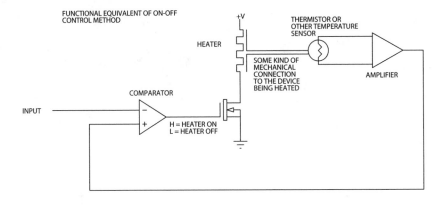

FUNCTIONAL EQUIVALENT OF ON-OFF
CONTROL METHOD

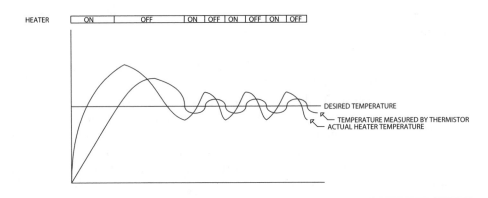

Figure 5.3
On-off control system.

- The coupling between the heater and the heated object is not perfect. The heater temperature must be higher than the object it is heating to be able to transfer heat into it.
- The object being heated has some thermal mass, so it doesn't heat up or cool down instantly.
- There is a time lag between the object reaching the setpoint temperature and the resistance of the thermistor changing to match. This is because the coupling between the thermistor and whatever it is measuring is imperfect, and because the thermistor has a thermal mass (usually small, but not zero) and cannot change temperature instantly.
- There is a time lag between the point when the heater is turned on and the point where it actually heats up. When power to the heater is turned off, there is another time lag while the heater cools down.

Analog Interfacing to Embedded Microprocessor Systems

The temperature profile shown in Figure 5.3 is similar to that for a real system that I worked on once. The heater control circuit could put significant energy into the heater—much more than was needed to heat the object in question. The object being heated had fairly low mass, almost as low as the heater itself, so it heated quickly. In fact, the object being heated changed temperature faster than the thermistor responded to temperature changes. In the actual system, when the heater was turned on, it would overshoot the desired setpoint in just a few seconds, then stay off for 10 or 20 seconds while the temperature came back down. After that, the oscillation around the setpoint was fairly large. I picked a particularly bad example to illustrate these concepts, but on-off control is not necessarily a bad means of controlling something if it is matched to the requirements. On-off control works best in a situation where:

- The object being controlled does not respond quickly to changes in the controlling signal.
- The sensor that measures the state of the controlled object responds to changes much faster than the controlled object does.

For the heater example, this would translate into a heater that is heating a relatively large thermal mass (large compared to the available energy from the heater) and a thermistor that is well coupled to the heated object and that responds quickly to temperature changes. The placement of the thermistor can have significant impact on the performance. In the actual system I just described, the thermistor was in contact with the heater on one side and with the heated object on the other (due to space constraints). This means that the output was somewhere between the two temperatures. On a system where the heated object has a large mass, this could mean that the setpoint temperature might never be reached because the thermistor was reading a temperature higher than the actual temperature of the mass.

The furnace in your house is a good example of on-off control that works well. The furnace is either on or off (in most houses). The air in the house has a fairly large thermal mass, so the furnace can't change the temperature quickly. The thermostat, while slow compared to microprocessor speeds, closely follows the actual air temperature in the house.

The disadvantage to this system is that the furnace is sized to the house and has limited ability to raise the temperature. If the furnace has been off all day while the outside temperature dropped, then it will take some time to raise the temperature to a comfortable level once the furnace is turned on. There is no way to quickly add energy to the system. You could buy a furnace that is several times too big for the house so the house would heat quickly, but then you would have more overshoot and oscillation around the desired temperature.

Some on-off control systems have a "dead band" where the output will not change. This prevents excessive switching of the control mechanism. For example, a temperature control system might have a 1° deadband, where the output is not changed if the temperature is within 1° of the setpoint. If the heater is on, it won't go off until the temperature is 1° above the setpoint. The heater won't go back on until the temperature is 1° below the setpoint. In some systems, a dead band is part of the basic physics. For example, the thermostat in most houses lags the actual temperature slightly, so the thermostat will sense the temperature continuing to rise after it has reached setpoint and turned the heater off. In actuality, the thermostat is just catching up with the actual room temperature.

Overshoot

The heater example in Figure 5.3 had significant overshoot in the waveform. Not all systems will exhibit overshoot, and not all will exhibit it to the same degree. Typically, overshoot is a result of inertia or momentum in the system. In the heater example, the heater would continue to heat the load for some time after power was removed. In addition, because the heater was large with respect to the load and there was a lot of power applied to the heater, the heating time was much faster than the cooldown time. Some systems do not exhibit significant overshoot, or exhibit it in one direction only (while heating but not while cooling, for example). In addition to heaters, motors often exhibit overshoot when they are driving loads that have significant momentum.

Proportional Control

The next step up in complexity from an on-off design is proportional control. The concept behind proportional control is that you vary the amount of control signal, based on the size of the difference between the actual condition and the desired condition. The difference between the actual and the desired value is called the *error*. The formula for calculating the control output of a proportional controller is:

$$\text{Output} = G \times e$$

where G = gain, e = error (setpoint—actual value). To go back to the opamp analogy, the proportional control system is like using an opamp with limited gain as the control mechanism instead of a comparator (which is represented by very

Analog Interfacing to Embedded Microprocessor Systems

large gain). The actual control mechanism can be a microprocessor-controlled analog system (using a DAC and amplifier) or a PWM technique.

Figure 5.4 illustrates proportional control. The heater control is 100% on when the heater is cold, but as the heater temperature approaches the setpoint, the amount of control is reduced because the difference between the setpoint and the actual value is smaller. As you can see, the proportional control system has less overshoot and less oscillation around the setpoint. Figure 5.4 shows the oscillation to be about half that of the on-off control system. The actual difference between an on-off control and a proportional control will depend on the system.

Another advantage to proportional control is the ability to adjust the control signal based on the controlled object. If you are heating fluid flowing through a tube, you might use a larger proportion (larger gain) when the flow rate is higher. Denser fluids might require even more gain to ensure that the temperature is maintained.

In some systems, the output is the $G \times e$, as shown earlier. In many systems, including the heater example in Figure 5.4, the actual proportional control equation looks like this:

$$\text{Output} = (G \times e) + M$$

The M is an offset, and is needed in systems where some power is required to keep whatever you are controlling at the desired value. For the heater example, the basic proportional equation will reduce the power as the heater approaches setpoint ($G \times e$ gets closer to zero), and the end result is that the temperature will never get to the setpoint. However if the M offset is used, and if M is, say, 50% of the available heater power, then the system can reach the setpoint. The $G \times e$ term becomes an addition (if positive) or a subtraction (if negative) from the constant offset. As long as the system is cold, the $G \times e$ term will be very large, so the heater will operate at 100%. If the sum of $G \times e$ and the offset is greater than 100%, the output is limited to 100%, because that is all the power the system can provide. As the heater approaches the setpoint, the $G \times e$ term will become smaller and the heater power will be reduced toward the 50% offset value. If the temperature overshoots the setpoint, the $G \times e$ term will become negative and the sum of $G \times e$ and 50% will be less than 50%, reducing output power. If the sum is less than 0, then the output is turned off unless a negative output capability is available. An example of negative output capability would be a system that can provide both heating and cooling capability.

Note that M may have to change as the characteristics of the system change. If you are heating blocks of metal, a small block might be held at setpoint with only 20% of the available heater power, but a large block might need 80% of available heater power.

Designing a proportional control system is more complicated than designing an on-off control system. With an on-off control system, you have to live with

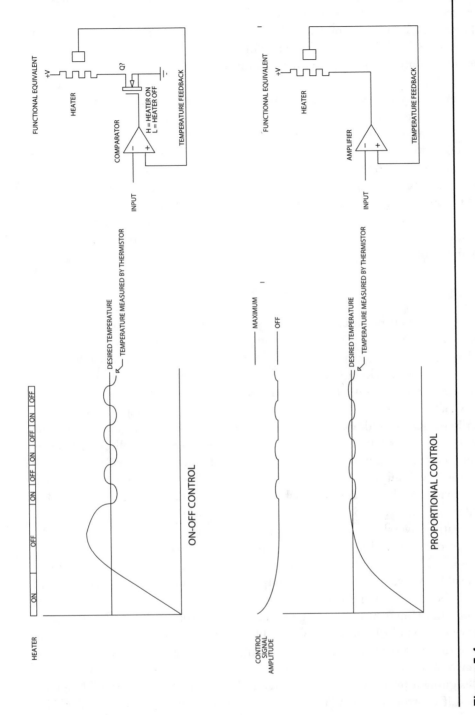

Figure 5.4
Proportional control.

Analog Interfacing to Embedded Microprocessor Systems

whatever overshoot and oscillation you get. As the load changes, the overshoot and oscillation will change, but as long as you can put enough energy into the system to make it reach the setpoint, it will eventually get there. With a proportional control system, you have to adjust the gain and the offset to the application. Too much gain, and you end up with an on-off control. Too little gain, and you never reach the setpoint. Worse, a proportional control system might work on the prototypes, but if someone in the field puts the product in an unheated outbuilding it might quit working in the winter. Proportional systems work best when the load is fixed or at least is known to the controlling processor. An example of a fixed load would be a heater that is always heating the same size and shape of plate. An example of a known load would be fluids, where the fluid flow rate and type vary, but the microprocessor always knows what they are.

Note that some proportional systems do not need the offset term. For example, a motor application that is driving the motor to a certain position and then stopping would not need the offset. Instead, the output value to the motor, which determines speed, would be the product of the gain times the error. In this case, the error is the difference between the actual motor position and the desired motor position, and when the error is zero the motor should stop. On the other hand, an application that requires the motor to hold a particular speed would require an offset because when the error is zero (actual speed equals desired speed), power must still be applied to the motor to maintain this condition.

In many cases, it is difficult to design a proportional control system that will reach the setpoint without oscillating. In most cases, the final value of the system (temperature, speed, whatever) is somewhat below the setpoint value. The actual value reached is dependent on the gain of the system, the offset, M (if used), and the size of the load.

The problem with a proportional control system is that it adjusts the control signal based on the difference between the measured point and the setpoint. There is no mechanism to adjust the amount of control based on conditions that the microprocessor doesn't know about. If you are heating plates of metal, what happens if someone puts on a plate that is twice the mass of the average one? Or one that is made out of aluminum instead of copper? You could add a weight sensor to the system, but what if the difference is in the shape instead of the weight? A tall, skinny piece of metal will have different heating characteristics than one that just matches the surface area of the heater.

There are similar problems with other control mechanisms. An automobile cruise control, for instance, has to handle things like headwinds, uphill and downhill grades, and the decrease in horsepower caused by turning on the air conditioner. A proportional control system would have problems with these conditions, because the right amount of throttle to apply going uphill in a strong headwind is different from the amount needed under the opposite set of conditions.

Proportional, Integral, Derivative Control

A control method that handles conditions like this is called proportional, integral, derivative (PID). The basic concept behind PID control is to add another input to the system, that input being the history of what actually happened when the control was applied. In the cruise control example, instead of just applying the throttle based on the amount of difference between the current speed and the desired speed (proportional control), the control system can look at how the car responded to the last throttle change. Did the car accelerate more slowly than it was expected to? Then it must be driving uphill or into a headwind, and more throttle is needed.

Figure 5.5 shows a block diagram of a PID control system. The difference between the actual value of whatever is being controlled and the setpoint is amplified. The derivative and integral of the amplified difference are summed with the amplified error to produce the output signal.

I don't want to write a book about calculus, nor do you want to read one. This book is about practical embedded control, so I want to focus on practical applications. However, we need to take a look at the general formula for calculating the output of a PID controller, which is:

$$\text{Output} = G\left(e + I\int e\,dt + D\frac{de}{dt}\right)$$

where G is the gain, e is the error (difference between setpoint and actual value), I is the amount of integral to apply, and D is the amount of derivative to apply.

If I and D are zero, then the output is:

$$G \times e$$

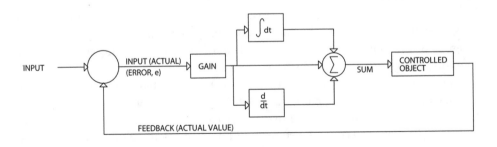

Figure 5.5
PID control system.

which is the formula for a proportional controller. If I and D are 0 and G is very large so that the output always saturates in one direction or the other, this describes an on-off controller. Like the proportional controller, the PID controller may need to use an offset to which the PID term is added or subtracted.

The things that set the PID controller apart from the proportional controller are the integral and derivative terms. These are time-based terms: the integral is an integral over some time period, and the derivative is the derivative between two time periods. Let's see what this means in practical terms.

Almost any system has some kind of inertia. When you turn on a heater, it gets hotter than whatever it is trying to heat (the load). It has to, or it will absorb heat from the load instead of transferring heat into it. When you turn the heater off, it doesn't cool off immediately. Instead, its temperature ramps down slowly. Until the heater cools down to the same temperature as the load, it will continue to raise the temperature of the load. Figure 5.6 illustrates this. The amount of difference between the heater temperature and the load temperature, and how fast each one heats up and cools off, is dependent on the mass, the amount of energy applied to the heater, the coupling between the heater and the mass, the shape of the mass, and so on.

Figure 5.6 also shows the effect of a light load versus a heavy load on the same heater. If the heater is heating metal blocks, the heavy load might be a bigger block of metal or one that is more massive (steel versus aluminum, for example). As you can see, the heavy load heats up and cools down more slowly because it has more mass—more inertia. If we were looking at the speed of a car instead of a heater, the heavy load might be an uphill acceleration and the light load might be a downhill acceleration.

Let's say that the heater is controlled by a proportional system. Because the amount of energy put into the heater is determined only by the difference between the desired temperature and the actual temperature, the control signal will be the same for the light load as for the heavy load. This means that the light load will overshoot the desired temperature by a greater amount. Once the right temperature is reached, there will be more oscillation (bigger temperature swings) around the setpoint. Accuracy of temperature is less precise than for a heavy load.

Derivatives

Adding a derivative term to the control equation allows better control. The derivative is a measure of how fast the error is changing. If the control system knows the size of the output applied to the heater, the rate of change in the error gives some indication of the size of the load. Mathematically, the derivative of a curve is the slope of a curve—in this case, the slope of the error. Practically, it is the rate of change in the error (volts per millisecond or pounds per second, or

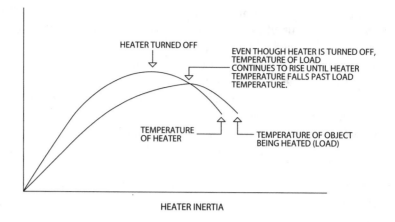

HEATER TURNED OFF

EVEN THOUGH HEATER IS TURNED OFF, TEMPERATURE OF LOAD CONTINUES TO RISE UNTIL HEATER TEMPERATURE FALLS PAST LOAD TEMPERATURE.

TEMPERATURE OF HEATER

TEMPERATURE OF OBJECT BEING HEATED (LOAD)

HEATER INERTIA

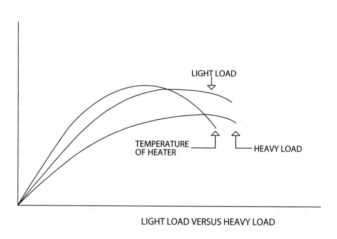

LIGHT LOAD

TEMPERATURE OF HEATER

HEAVY LOAD

LIGHT LOAD VERSUS HEAVY LOAD

Figure 5.6
Inertia in a control system.

whatever is being measured). If the error term is decreasing, the curve has a negative slope and the derivative will be negative. If the error term is increasing, the derivative will be positive. If the error term doesn't change at all, then the slope and derivative are both 0. Note that any error, even a very large one, will have a derivative of 0 if the error doesn't change. The original heater/load graph is shown in Figure 5.7, along with the resulting error term and the derivative term.

If we make the gain smaller and then add the derivative to the Gain × error term, our proportional control system will handle varying loads better. When the

Analog Interfacing to Embedded Microprocessor Systems

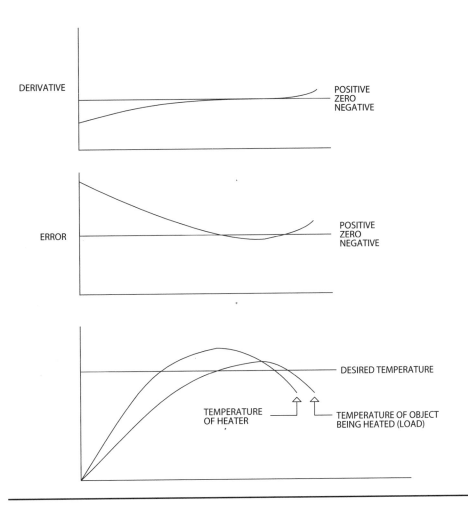

DERIVATIVE

POSITIVE
ZERO
NEGATIVE

ERROR

POSITIVE
ZERO
NEGATIVE

DESIRED TEMPERATURE

TEMPERATURE
OF HEATER

TEMPERATURE OF OBJECT
BEING HEATED (LOAD)

Figure 5.7
Derivative.

load is heating rapidly (light load), the derivative has a large negative value, so the output (G × e + D × derivative) is smaller. Smaller output equals less heat, so the load heats up more slowly. If the load is heavy, the derivative will be less negative, less is subtracted, the output is larger, the heater gets hotter, and the load heats up faster.

When the load temperature gets close to the setpoint, the gain term (G × e) becomes smaller. Lower heat also makes the derivative smaller, so there is less overshoot. When the load passes the setpoint temperature, the derivative becomes positive as the error term changes direction. This causes a larger positive value to be added to the gain term. The faster the load is cooling off, the larger the derivative is, and the less the output shrinks.

Output Control Methods

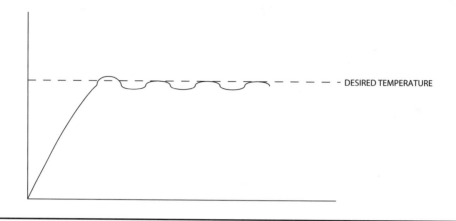

Figure 5.8
Proportional gain and derivative.

Figure 5.8 shows the result of a system using proportional gain and derivative. There is a small overshoot followed by an oscillation around the setpoint. Depending on system characteristics, the overshoot may be small or zero, and the oscillation may die out as the system settles on one value. As shown in the figure, the end result (temperature, in this case) is often a bit below the setpoint, just as with a proportional control system. This occurs because the gain isn't quite high enough to bring the temperature up to the desired value without the derivative term. When the temperature is near the setpoint, the slope of the error change is small, so the derivative term is nearly 0. Figure 5.9 shows a gain/derivative system where the final error is a small constant value.

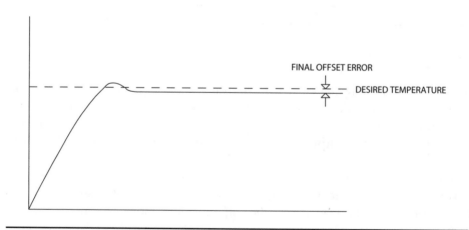

Figure 5.9
Offset error.

Analog Interfacing to Embedded Microprocessor Systems

Integrals

One way to solve the problem of settling a small distance from the setpoint is to add an integral term. Mathematically, the integral is the area under a curve. In practical terms, the integral is the sum (or accumulation) of the error term over a period of time. Figure 5.10 shows what the integral term looks like in graphic mode. Notice that, in this example, the integral never goes negative even though the error term does go negative. If the error stayed negative for a long enough period of time, the integral would eventually become negative.

Figure 5.11 shows the effect of the integral on the constant error in the proportional/derivative heater controller that we looked at earlier. When the system stabilizes with a small offset, the integral term begins to grow because it

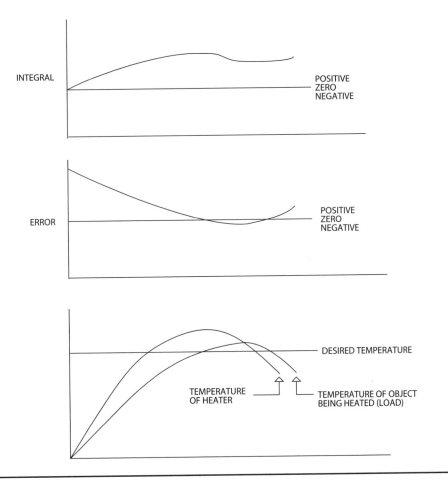

INTEGRAL — POSITIVE / ZERO / NEGATIVE

ERROR — POSITIVE / ZERO / NEGATIVE

DESIRED TEMPERATURE

TEMPERATURE OF HEATER — TEMPERATURE OF OBJECT BEING HEATED (LOAD)

Figure 5.10
Integral.

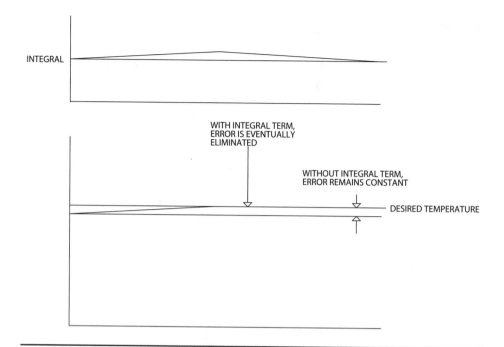

INTEGRAL

WITH INTEGRAL TERM,
ERROR IS EVENTUALLY
ELIMINATED

WITHOUT INTEGRAL TERM,
ERROR REMAINS CONSTANT

DESIRED TEMPERATURE

Figure 5.11
Effect of integral.

is the *accumulation* of errors (in this case, if the temperature is low, the error is positive and the integral grows to a positive value). Eventually the integral term becomes large enough to affect the output, pushing the temperature toward the setpoint.

Going back to the cruise control example, a proportional/derivative control mechanism might result in the car settling at 62 mph when the control was set on 65. If the car spent enough time driving at 62, the integral term would eventually produce a large enough error to push the speed up to the setpoint.

Summarized PID

The proportional part of a PID loop causes the output to follow the input (setpoint). The derivative allows the output to respond to rapidly changing inputs and to compensate for varying loads. The integral compensates for long-term errors.

All the examples so far have shown a system with overshoot and some oscillation around the setpoint. These waveforms are typical for a system with an underdamped response. Figure 5.12 shows a critically damped response. Here,

Analog Interfacing to Embedded Microprocessor Systems

Figure 5.12
Critically damped system.

the system rises rapidly to the setpoint but does not overshoot or oscillate when the setpoint is reached. In many systems, a small overshoot past the setpoint is an acceptable tradeoff for fast response. In other systems, no overshoot is acceptable, so a critically damped response is used. An example of this would be a cooling system that has to keep biological samples near freezing, but can't let the temperature dip below freezing or the samples will be permanently damaged.

In classical control theory, the integral and derivative gains are times, not scalar (unitless) multipliers like the proportional gain. In a microprocessor-based system, the system is sampled at a regular interval and it may not be possible to set the integration time or derivative period to a specific value. However, by using a gain factor on the integral and derivative values, the integral and derivative time factors can be multiples of the sample period while still obtaining the same control results.

Practical Considerations

Although a PID loop can compensate for varying loads, it still must be tuned. *Tuning* is the process of selecting the parameters (coefficients) of the three terms. That is, how much of the integral and derivative terms should be added to the $G \times e$ term, and how large should G be? There are a number of ways to adjust these values, such as the Ziegler/Nichols method. The primary difficulty in adjusting the parameters of the PID loop is that adjusting one parameter affects the other two—the adjustments are not independent. In addition, simulating the operational extremes of a real device is sometimes difficult.

In general, the tuning procedure for a PID loop is to make the gain term (G) large enough to provide sufficient response speed. Then the derivative term (D)

Output Control Methods   123 is made large enough to decrease overshoot to acceptable levels and to make the system stable (no oscillation). Finally, the integral term (I) is made large enough to eliminate steady-state error.

As an example, the Ziegler/Nichols method, mentioned above, uses the following steps:

- Turn off integral and derivative terms, making the controller a proportional-only controller.
- Increase the proportional gain until the output has a steady oscillation that does not increase or die out. Call this gain K.
- Measure the period, P, of the oscillation.
- Set the proportional gain (G) and the integral and derivative times (Ti, Td) according to the following:
- If controller is to be proportional only, gain = 05 K.
- If controller is to be proportional-integral, G = 045 K, Ti = 1.2/P
- If controller is to be PID, G = 06 K, Ti = 2/P, Td = P/8

The result of this process will probably require additional adjustments to optimize performance. As mentioned earlier, the result of this process may be integral and/or derivative values that are not possible with the sampling clock. The integral and derivative gain must be adjusted to compensate for this.

PID loop tuning sometimes runs into other problems, including the difficulty of making measurements. Measuring the ability of a motor controller to hold a specific speed may require hardware that is itself subject to error. In a refrigeration system, the cycle time may be several minutes or even hours. How long does the system have to run to detect a sustained oscillation for Ziegler/Nichols tuning? Problems like this can make control system design a challenge.

Practical systems often do not function as well as their ideal models. Potential problems for a PID system include the following.

Saturation

It is possible to calculate an output that the electromechanical system cannot possibly achieve. For instance, if someone places a huge block of very cold metal on our example heater, the system may calculate that an enormous amount of current is required to get to the right temperature. This current may be beyond the capability of the power supply and the heater. Or, the power supply may be large enough that the 100% ON condition will burn the heater out.

Another problem with saturation involves the integral term. If the heater is ON 100% because the microprocessor wants more output than the system can deliver, there will be an integral error that will grow larger with time. Because the system cannot respond as quickly as it would in a nonsaturated condition, the integral error may get very large. Once the setpoint is reached and the gain and derivative terms stop applying control to the load, the integral term will cause the output to continue to be driven in the same direction. This condition is called *windup*. Figure 5.13 shows how windup can affect the output.

Saturation can also occur in a sensor; an example would be the scaled thermistor we looked at in an earlier chapter. It is possible for the temperature in that case to be within the range of the thermistor, but for the opamp output to be saturated because the temperature is beyond the range we designed the circuit to handle.

Software Considerations

To avoid windup, the software should artificially limit the integral buildup when a saturated output (or saturated sensor) is detected. In addition, the software, unlike the theoretical mathematical model, has registers of limited size. Care must be taken to ensure that the registers do not roll over when performing mathematical calculations. In some cases, the integral is inhibited until the error is

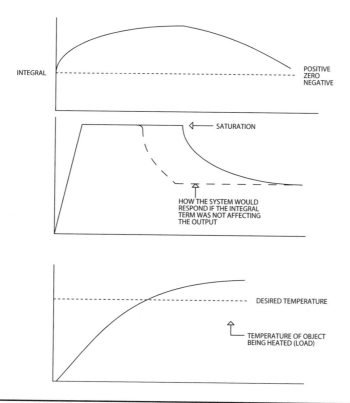

Figure 5.13
Windup.

Output Control Methods

within a certain percentage of the setpoint. This avoids building up a large integral term while the output is ramping toward the setpoint.

The derivative term in a PID design is the amount of change in the error over a specific unit of time. Because a microprocessor control system uses a regular sampling rate, the unit of time is usually the sample interval (or some multiple of the sample interval). The derivative is then calculated by subtracting two samples. Subtracting the error at time n from the error at time $n + 1$ gives the amount of change in one time interval. To prevent noise problems, the software may average two or more successive samples.

The integral is the sum of error over a period of time. In a practical microprocessor system, the integral is calculated as the sum or average of several successive samples. Again, precautions must be taken against rollover and saturation when performing calculations.

Time Delay

One subject that we have mentioned without taking a close look at it is time delay. Our example heater had some delays built in. These include:

- The time it takes for the heater to respond to a control change; the temperature of the heater does not change instantly just because the control signal to it did
- The time it takes the heat to be transferred to the load
- The time it takes the thermistor to respond to changes in the load temperature

All of these have the same effect on the control system—inaccuracy. The time from when a control change is applied until it registers in the sensor is called *deadtime*. If the microprocessor changes the control signal because the block is too cold, it takes a while for the heater to heat up, for the load to heat up, and for the thermistor to respond to the change. In the meantime, the microprocessor has sampled the thermistor many times, found that the temperature still isn't right, and pushed the output even higher. Or, in an on-off control, the heater stays on well past the optimum point for the right temperature, resulting in overshoot and oscillation. In either case, the controller overcompensates for the error. Using PID control instead of just proportional control can reduce some of these effects, as we have already seen. However, in some cases, PID control can make a deadtime situation worse, such as when windup occurs.

Compensating for deadtime usually involves predicting the effect of a control change and assuming that it will take place after the deadtime has elapsed. Once the real result of the change is available, a new change can be made that will correct for the difference between the theoretical result and the actual result. This process is called the *Smith Predictor*, and was originally modeled by Otto Smith in 1957. Implementing this involves modeling the system to determine what the response will be.

Analog Interfacing to Embedded Microprocessor Systems

Discontinuous Inputs

Many systems suffer from the application of sudden input changes that make a pure PID or even a proportional system impractical. A heater may be subject to having water splashed on it. This will rapidly cool down the heater and may be impossible to handle by tuning the PID loop. How do you predict how much water will be splashed on the heater? How do you predict that the user will suddenly remove the load?

Another example of sudden load changes is in automobile voltage regulators. If the driver suddenly switches off the car's headlights, the load on the electrical system is instantly reduced (called *load dumping*). The voltage produced by the alternator suddenly jumps up to a larger value because the alternator tries to produce the same power output but at a lower amperage. In a case like this, you don't want the system to respond along a PID curve—you want it to recognize the event and respond immediately. The typical way to handle an input change like this is to cut off the PWM output and let the system "coast" until things stabilize. The key thing here is to be sure the integral and/or derivative values don't result in an erroneous output when the control is reinitiated. You may have to reset or otherwise modify these values when a sudden input change occurs.

Special Requirements

Many systems that require PID control must handle specific inputs. A cruise control system may need to go to a quiescent state, resetting the integral and derivative values, when the driver hits the brake. The automobile voltage regulator may need to operate differently, with different PID parameters, at different motor speeds. A heater may have a differing ON time PWM power limitation for heating different materials. The software must ensure that all these special requirements are met, and that a change from one state to another (such as from one heated material to another) does not cause the PID loop to be confused. You don't want to use an integral value calculated using one set of PID parameters to generate an output when the PID parameters change. When PID parameters are changed for any reason, the software needs to reset or otherwise adjust the accumulated values.

Motor Control

So far we have used heaters as the primary example for control system operation, because they are easy to understand. The control methods described in this chapter apply to motors as well, but there are some additional complications when motors are involved. Figure 5.14 shows a PID loop controlling a motor.

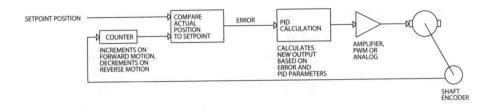

Figure 5.14
PID motor control.

The input to the system is a digital word that indicates the desired position. The motor position is an analog quantity (number of degrees of shaft rotation or something similar) but is measured as a digital quantity (number of encoder pulses). A counter counts up when the motor rotates one way and counts down when the motor rotates the other way. The output of this motor position counter is compared to the desired position. The difference is the error. This is exactly the same as the error in an analog control system, except that it is a digital word. The PID portion of the controller uses the error (and the history of the error) to calculate the new output value.

Figure 5.15 shows a round carousel with eight sample positions. This carousel might be used to rotate samples under a sampling arm for a chemical or medical

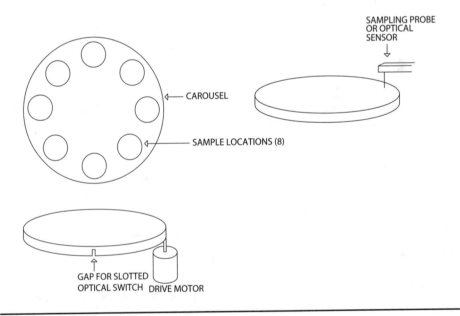

Figure 5.15
Rotating carousel.

sampling application, or it might be continuously rotated under a camera or other optical sensor in an automated image processing system. The carousel is driven with an internal gear (not shown), which matches a gear on the motor shaft with the motor underneath. One revolution of the carousel takes dozens of revolutions of the motor. A gap in the carousel and a corresponding slotted optical switch tells the controlling microprocessor when the carousel is at the home position. The motor shaft has an optical encoder for feedback to the microprocessor.

Constant Speed

The simplest case for this system is continuous rotation. The carousel is rotated at a constant speed, which may be required for synchronization with the optical pickup or camera. The control loop (proportional or PID) maintains the motor velocity. The slotted switch would typically be used to verify that the carousel is following the motor—in other words, that there isn't a stripped gear or some other mechanical malfunction.

The control system would ramp the motor up and hold it at a constant speed (Figure 5.16) until commanded to stop. Let's say that there are 100 motor revolutions per carousel revolution, and that the motor uses a 500-line encoder (500 encoder counts per revolution of the motor shaft). Figure 5.16 doesn't have enough resolution to show all the encoder counts, so the relative spacing between encoder pulses is shown—as if the picture were displaying every 100th count or something similar.

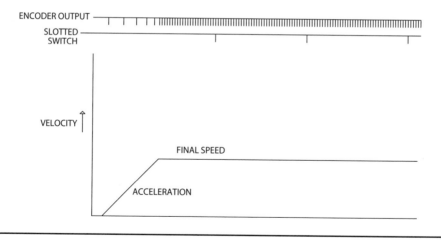

Figure 5.16
Motor ramps up and holds constant speed.

The motor control software (or the controller, if a packaged motor control IC is used) will typically check the velocity on a regular basis (a specific number of clocks from an internal reference clock). There is no point in designing the system so that the sample interval is shorter than the PWM frequency (if PWM is used). In fact, such a system would tend to be unstable, because a new PWM duty cycle would be assigned before the previous one had a chance to take effect.

Instead of sampling at a regular interval, you could check the count of an internal free-running counter on every encoder pulse, or every fourth pulse, or something similar. The time from the previous encoder pulse is measured, and if the velocity is low the control output is increased (more motor current). Figure 5.17 shows a simplified diagram of both measurement methods. In fixed-time sampling, all timing is synchronized to the sampling clock, which is usually a multiple of the PWM clock. The potential drawback is shown in the detail area; if the encoder pulse occurs just before the sample clock, the count will differ by 1 from the count that results if the encoder pulse occurs immediately after the sample clock. The actual amount of motor shaft rotation in both cases is almost identical, but the system will see a difference of 1 count.

The fixed-count sampling method, which samples after a fixed number of encoder pulses (3, in Figure 5.17), avoids this problem and can give better precision in the result. The catch is that the time measurement counter has to run at a fairly high clock rate and may have to be many bits wide to handle slow

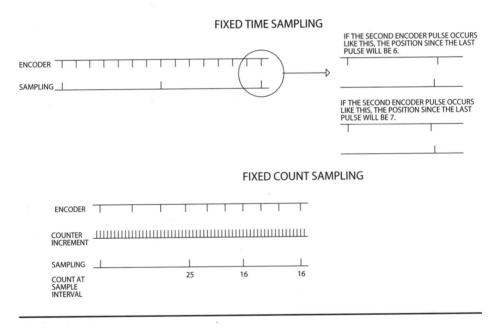

Figure 5.17
Motor sampling.

motor speeds. In addition, use of fixed-count sampling means that the sampling interval is no longer synchronized to the PWM frequency—the sample frequency varies with motor speed. For this reason, fixed-time sampling is more common.

If you use fixed-count sampling, you should include some kind of timeout to detect a stalled motor. If the motor stalls, no encoder counts will be generated and no sampling will occur. Whichever sampling method is used, the carousel in our example will run at a constant speed, with some fluctuation depending on the type of control and the control parameters. Because the home position occurs once every revolution of the carousel, and this is 100 motor rotations, then the home position indication will occur once every 50,000 motor revolutions (500 encoder counts revolution × 100 motor revolutions/carousel revolution). So if the first pulse occurs at count 10,000, the next pulse will occur at count 60,000 (usually plus or minus 1). So to check that the carousel is following the motor, the software could open a "window" and look for the pulse around count 60,000, 110,000, and so on.

Eventually, the counters that keep track of position will overflow, and the software (or controller IC) has to take this into account in controlling the speed.

Positioning

The case of our carousel in a sampling system is a bit more complex. The carousel does not rotate continuously, but moves to a fixed position and stops with one of the sample positions under the sampling arm. After the sampling probe has taken a sample of the contents, the carousel is rotated to the next position.

The typical waveform for this type of move is shown in Figure 5.18. The motor ramps up to some velocity, just like in the continuous rotation example, then runs at a constant speed, then ramps down and stops in the correct position (correct encoder count). The difficulty is in timing all this so that the final position is correct. A PID motion controller that is used in a positioning application usually has two loops operating together in parallel. The PID loop controls motor current to achieve the correct velocity. The input to the PID loop is the velocity setpoint. A second loop creates the trapezoidal waveform by passing velocity setpoint values to the velocity control PID loop.

Figure 5.19 shows a simple diagram of such a control system. This is typical of the position-control functionality in a motor control IC such as the LM628/9. In this figure, the velocity generator block is separate from the microprocessor, as it would be in a self-contained motion control IC. If you were writing software for a microprocessor or DSP to directly control a motor, the velocity generator and PID loops would be software functions. The position control loop generates position commands to the PID loop. This is the same position command that was an input to the PID loop in Figure 5.14. That figure shows a simplified table of position values for a move of 80,555 steps, which is a bit over 161 revolutions of

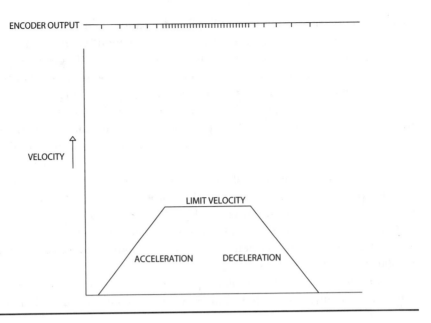

Figure 5.18
Trapezoidal motor move.

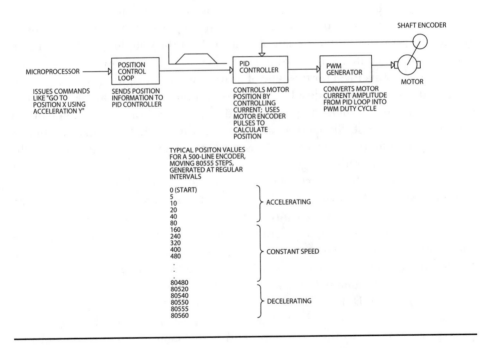

Figure 5.19
Motor position-control block diagram.

the motor shaft for a 500-count encoder. Notice that the position initially increases 5 steps per sample interval, then 10, then 20, and so on. This acceleration profile is reversed when the motor is stopping.

Software Considerations

The PID loop controls motor position. In many designs, having a critically damped waveform is crucial. Remember that this is a mechanical system—overshoot may result in broken parts.

The problem of offset in a PID loop, where the final position is just slightly different from the desired position, can cause a unique problem in a motor control application. There is usually a plus or minus 1 count ambiguity in any digital system. If the final motor position is different from the setpoint by 1 or 2 counts, and if the integral portion of the PID loop is too small, the system may draw excessive current and overheat the motor and/or controller. This is because the proportional part of the loop is trying to nudge the motor that final step or two to get the right position, but it can't generate quite enough current to do so. Instead of the motor current going off at the end of the move, it stays on. This can be a real problem in systems that have a lot of inertia or some kind of detent to overcome when starting, as the current can be relatively high. In addition, in a DC motor, this continuous current is not shared over all the motor windings, because the motor isn't rotating.

If the system is such that an integral term cannot be set to correct this problem (possibly because the load when stopped isn't known), then the software should detect this condition and shut off the motor output. If your application needs holding current (say, to keep a vertical arm from falling), then reprogram the setpoint position to the actual position. Notice that the position generator does not know what the motor position is. It is assumed that the PID loop will be able to meet the acceleration requested by the position generator. In a system with variable loads, the software may need to reduce the acceleration when the load is large.

Predictive Control

PID control is effective when controlling a single-input process that is fairly consistent. The drawbacks to PID are that it has to be tuned to a particular process; if the process changes appreciably, the PID parameters must be readjusted to provide good control. In addition, a PID loop is not usually effective in controlling systems with multiple input parameters, especially if the parameters interact. An example would be a control system for temperature and humidity, where the temperature affects relative humidity and vice versa.

To handle these conditions, some form of predictive control can be used. There are several variations on predictive control, such as model predictive control (MPC) and nonlinear model predictive control (NMPC). All model predictive control algorithms start with a model of the response of the system. This model is used to predict system behavior over some time period. The response prediction might span a single sample interval or the response delay of the system, if there is one. A control output is generated, the response is measured, and a new prediction is made for the next time interval. Some predictive systems adjust the parameters (typically gains) of the mathematical model as the system operates, so that the model more closely matches the actual system response.

Generally, the model for a predictive control system is a mathematical representation of the response, and so predictive control is often impractical for small microcontroller-based systems. The system model can be a table of values, but if there are multiple inputs, the number of tables can quickly grow beyond the available memory.

The model for a predictive control system can be generated by analyzing the electrical and mechanical components to determine their response, or by empirical testing. Either method has drawbacks; an analytical solution may be difficult to obtain and empirical testing may be difficult to perform, especially in a system where some control values may cause physical damage.

Measuring and Analyzing Control Loops

Development of a control system often requires that the control inputs and outputs be measured. This may be necessary to set the parameters for a PID loop or to debug a system that isn't functioning properly. Figure 5.20A shows a control system with monitoring hardware attached. The monitoring hardware measures the ADC output and the resulting control output.

The monitoring hardware in a system like this could be a logic analyzer that captures every read from the ADC and every write to the amplifier (the amplifier may be a linear or PWM output device). The idea is to capture the inputs and see what output the control system generates as a result. If a logic analyzer is used, the resulting data can be time-tagged and stored to disk, or sent over a network connection to a computer. There, it can be plotted or captured in a spreadsheet for analysis.

If you are debugging a problem in a control system, the logic analyzer may also accept other inputs that will allow you to trigger when the error occurs and see what the control system was doing just before that time. Instead of a logic analyzer, a relatively slow system might be analyzed using a PC and plug-in

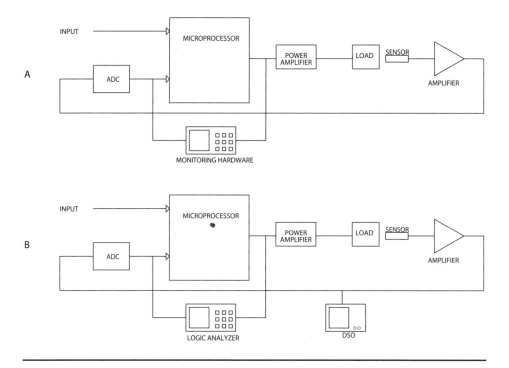

Figure 5.20
Monitoring a control system.

boards to make a data acquisition system. National Instruments makes several types of data acquisition boards and software that can be used for this purpose.

Another approach to monitoring is to add microprocessor code that outputs the sensor readings and resulting control values to a serial port or some other output mechanism. This approach requires less analysis of the resulting data, but it assumes that the software is working properly. For instance, this approach won't catch a problem that occurs if the software generates the correct control output value, but a software race condition prevents that value from actually being written to the PWM controller. The output will not reflect what the software thinks (and tells the world via the diagnostic output) is happening.

Combined Logic Analyzer/DSO

One problem with both the software and logic-analyzer approach to monitoring the system parameters is that the digital values may not represent the analog inputs. If a problem occurs because the ADC reference voltage varies too much with temperature, neither of these approaches will detect it because the ADC outputs look correct and the system responds to the ADC output correctly.

Figure 5.20B shows the addition of a digital storage oscilloscope (DSO) to the original setup. The DSO monitors the actual sensor signal while the logic analyzer monitors the ADC output and the resulting control output. The DSO trigger is coupled to the logic analyzer trigger output (or vice versa) so that the data on the two instruments can be correlated. Using a logic analyzer with an integrated DSO simplifies the data correlation process.

Whether you output monitoring data using software or use external equipment such as a logic analyzer, it is a good idea to provide the necessary components for monitoring early in the design. This may mean adding a header to the board for connection of a logic analyzer, or leaving one port bit on a microcontroller available to indicate interrupt entry and exit.

Measuring Motor Parameters

Measuring the effects of PID loop changes in a heater is fairly easy—you just monitor the thermistor and display the results on a DSO, or use an ADC to convert the results to digital values and capture them with a computer. A motor is more difficult to tune. There is no direct indication of speed; you have to measure the time between encoder pulses to determine how fast the motor is turning.

Figure 5.21 shows the block diagram of two simple circuits that can be used as an aid for tuning motor parameters. Figure 5.21A shows a circuit that measures the period between encoder pulses. A clock increments a counter. Each encoder pulse latches the count into a register and resets the counter. The counter can use synchronous or asynchronous reset, although the reset logic obviously has to match the counter characteristics.

The output of the register can be connected to a logic analyzer so the speed data can be captured, or it can connect to the input of a DAC to provide a voltage that corresponds to speed; the resulting waveform can be viewed on a DSO. Some logic analyzers provide a chart mode that allows state data to be viewed like a DSO. Or, the captured data can be saved to disk, input to a spreadsheet on a computer, and viewed/manipulated there.

The sample clock and counter width depend on the resolution needed and the motor/encoder characteristics. If your motor runs at 2000 rpm (33.3 rev/sec) and uses a 500-line encoder, then the time between encoder pulses is:

$$\frac{1}{500 \times 33.33} \text{ or } 60\,\mu s$$

If you want to use an 8-bit measurement and you want this speed to be 250 counts, then you need a clock of $250/60\,\mu s$, or $4.167\,MHz$.

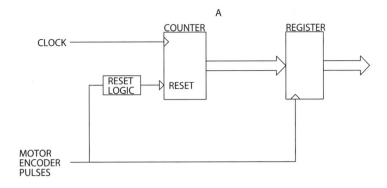

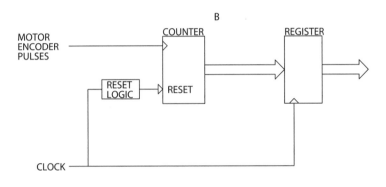

Figure 5.21
Motor-timing analysis aid.

If the slowest motor speed you want to measure is 100 rpm, then the encoder pulses will occur at a rate of 833 Hz, so the counter will accumulate 5000 counts between encoder pulses, and you will need a counter that is 13 bits wide. For this application, a 13-bit counter will prevent overflow at the slowest speed and still allow 8-bit resolution at the highest speed.

In this example, the counter resets to 0 and counts up, so a larger count corresponds to a slower motor speed. To make the count proportional to motor speed (larger count = higher speed), you can either invert the counter outputs or use a down-counter that resets to all 1s instead of to 0s.

Figure 5.21B shows an identical circuit, but with the encoder and reference clock inputs reversed. This circuit measures the frequency of the encoder pulses. Using the same 100-to-5000 rpm motor with the same 500-line encoder, a 10 ms sampling clock will give a count of 8 at 100 rpm and a count of 166 at 2000 rpm. The output of this circuit can also be connected to a logic analyzer or DAC/DSO combination. Of course, either circuit can be implemented with discrete logic or in a PLD.

Commercial Software

There are software packages that can aid in tuning PID loops. Examples are Wintune from BestSoft (www.bestsoft.com) and a PID analysis package from National Instruments (www.ni.com).

PID Software Examples

Following are some pseudocode examples for a simple PID controller, with various options implemented.

Basic PID Loop

Read input (actual position, speed, temp, whatever) from sensor, save as CurrentValue.

    Error = TargetValue − CurrentValue
    Derivative = Error − PreviousErrorValue
    Integral = Integral + Error

    ControlValue = K1*Integral + K2*Derivative + K3*Error
    PreviousErrorValue = Error (for use with next sample)
    Output ControlValue to control hardware

Definitions:
    K1 = Integral gain
    K2 = Derivative gain
    K3 = Error gain
    Integral = Integral term
    Derivative = Derivative term
    Error = Error term, setpoint minus actual value read from sensor
    TargetValue = Setpoint, the desired input
    CurrentValue = Current value read from sensor
    PreviousErrorValue = The value of Error from the previous sample

Note that Error, Derivative, and Integral must be stored in such a way that they can be negative values. This means floating point, 2's complement integers, or some other method. In this implementation, the derivative is simply the current error minus the previous error, which is a measure of how fast the error is changing. Technically, the derivative is the change that occurs over time; however, since the system samples at a regular interval, the derivative can be approximated as the difference between two successive samples. The integral is just the sum of previous error values so far.

Antiwindup

Adding antiwindup for the integral term looks like this:

Read input from sensor, save as CurrentValue.

$Error = TargetValue - CurrentValue$
$Derivative = error - PreviousErrorValue$
$Integral = Integral + Error$

If Integral > MaximumIntegralValue, then
   Integral = MaximumIntegralValue.
ControlValue =
$K1^*Integral + K2^*Derivative + K3^*Error$

PreviousErrorValue = Error(for use with next sample)
Output ControlValue to control hardware

Definition:
   MaximumIntegralValue = maximum value of integral term; represents 100 %

An alternative method, which inhibits the integral unless the output is within a specific range of the setpoint looks like this:

Read input from sensor, save as CurrentValue.

$Error = TargetValue - CurrentValue$
$Derivative = error - PreviousErrorValue$

If absolute value of Error < IntegralBand
   $Integral = Integral + Error$
Else Integral = 0.

ControlValue =
K1*Integral + K2*Derivative + K3*Error

PreviousErrorValue = Error(for use with next sample)
Output ControlValue to control hardware

Definition:

Integral Band = the range of error values for which the integral calculation is enabled. Note that IntegralBand can be a constant or a fraction of the setpoint.

Filtering Noisy Input

You might have a situation in which the sensor input is noisy. In this case, you may not want to use each sample as-is because an erroneous value for ControlValue might be calculated. In such a case, you may want to average multiple samples. The following code will average 8 samples together and then process that average as a new sample. Note that this only generates a new output once for every 8 samples. To generate a new output ten times per second, the code would actually have to sample 80 times per second.

```
Read input from sensor, add to CurrentValue.

Increment SampleCounter
If SampleCounter = 8,
[
SampleCounter = 0
CurrentValue = CurrentValue/8
  Error = TargetValue – CurrentValue
Derivative = error – PreviousErrorValue
  Integral = Integral + Error
  ControlValue = K1*Integral + K2*Derivative + K3*Error
  PreviousErrorValue = Error
  Output ControlValue to control hardware
  CurrentValue = 0 (reset to zero so next accumulation can start)
]
```

To simplify the code, you might not do the division of CurrentValue by 8. Instead, you can work with the sum, which avoids division. If the division value happens to be a nonbinary value, this can be a significant time savings on small microcontrollers without a divide instruction. Of course, this means all the terms derived from CurrentValue are also larger by a factor of 8. Be sure overflows don't occur.

Preventing Out-of-Bounds Control Output

The following code will prevent the control output from exceeding the maximum that the system can handle (say, to avoid burning out a heater element).

```
Read input from sensor, save as CurrentValue.

Error = TargetValue - CurrentValue
Derivative = error - PreviousErrorValue
Integral = Integral + Error
New control value = K1*Integral + K2*Derivative + K3*Error

If new ControlValue > MaximumControlValue,
   ControlValue = MaximumControlValue
   Set MaximumPowerExceeded flag.

PreviousErrorValue = Error
Output ControlValue to control hardware
```

In this code, if the maximum power is exceeded, the new ControlValue is limited to the maximum value, and a flag is set (MaximumPowerExceeded) to tell the code that the event has occurred. This flag might be processed by a separate piece of code that notifies the operator of an error or even shuts down the system.

Preventing Out-of-Bounds Average Output

In some cases, the maximum allowable control value is not a specific value, but an accumulation of value over time. For example, a heater may not burn out if too much current is applied for a few sampling intervals, but it might burn out if a total power rating is exceeded for more than a second. The following code adds an array, AvgPwrArray, which contains 10 elements. Each element in the array is the output value for one sample interval; added together and divided by 10, they represent the average power over the last 10 samples.

```
Read input from sensor, save as CurrentValue.

Error = TargetValue - CurrentValue
Derivative = error - PreviousErrorValue
Integral = Integral + Error
```

ControlValue $= $ K1*Integral $+ $ K2*Derivative $+ $ K3*Error

AveragePower $= $ sum of values in AvgPwrArray [0] through AvgPwrArray [9]

If AveragePower > MaximumAllowablePower*10,
Set MaximumPowerExceeded flag.
ControlValue $= $
MaximumAllowablePower $- $ AveragePower $+ $ AvgPwrArray [0]
If ControlValue < 0, ControlValue $= $ 0

(The following discards the oldest value in AvgPwrArray[0] and makes room for the newest)
For AvgPwrArray[0 through 8], AvgPwrArray [n] $= $
AvgPwrArray [n $+ $ 1]

AvgPwrArray [9] $= $ ControlValue
PreviousErrorValue $= $ Error
Output ControlValue to control hardware

The line

ControlValue $= $
MaximumAllowablePower $- $ AveragePower $+ $ AvgPwrArray[0]

calculates ControlValue as the maximum value that will bring the average below the maximum value after the next sample interval. The reason AvgPwrArray[0] is used is that it is the oldest sample and will be replaced in the array by the new ControlValue. If the result is negative, then ControlValue is set to zero. Note that, in your system, the value that produces zero output may not actually be zero.

This pseudocode fragment moves all the array values around to make room for a new value; a faster method (but not as easily understood) is to use a pointer that wraps from the end to the beginning of the array and allows the new value to overwrite the oldest value.

Implementing These Examples

Each of these examples has illustrated one basic principle. You can, of course, combine these methods as needed. Initialization is not shown in these examples. You will typically need to initialize the variables when the program starts or any time events cause the current values to be invalid. These examples are based on the assumption that the sensor input and control output are updated on a periodic, regular basis. You will typically implement this with an interrupt.

Implementing these examples in a microcontroller is often more difficult than on a larger microprocessor. Microcontrollers, especially 8-bit microcontrollers, often do not have good mechanisms to handle negative values, multiplication, or division. You can sometimes get around these problems by using binary values. For example, when averaging values to filter out noise, always filter 2, 4, 8, or some other binary number of samples. This allows the division to be simple shift operations. If you are using a microcontroller that does not handle 2's complement subtraction very well, you can make each variable a 2-byte (or 2-word) value. The first value is the unsigned value of the variable. The second variable is a flag to indicate whether the variable is positive or negative. The software looks at the flag before using the variable, and either adds or subtracts the variable based on the flag value.

Things to Remember in Control Design

- The accuracy of the system is only as good as the ability of the measurement sensor to measure the actual output. A thermistor that measures the temperature of the heater will not provide as precise control as one that measures the actual temperature of the heated object. This is especially true of a PID controller, which bases all the control parameters on the sensor input. If you are measuring the wrong thing, a higher-precision sensor will just give you wrong answers with more decimal places.
- Time delays can be introduced not only by the object you are controlling, but by the measurement sensor. A slowly responding thermistor can introduce as much delay as the rest of the system.
- Size the processor to the application. It is easy to design a mathematical model of a control system and simulate it with a 2 GHz, 64-bit desktop computer. Implementing the model, in real time, on an 8-bit processor with only a few kilobytes of code space can be much more difficult. For example, if your algorithm requires complex math, be sure the target CPU can perform it. If it can't, you may have to resort to lookup tables.
- If you do have to resort to lookup tables or something similar in a real application, be sure there is sufficient memory for it. It doesn't take very many 256-byte tables to fill the memory of most small microcontrollers.
- Have some plan for analyzing and debugging the finished design, and include whatever hardware and software are necessary.

Solenoids, Relays, and Other Analog Outputs

Solenoids

A solenoid is an electromagnet that activates a mechanical function, such as a plunger. Solenoids are used to latch safety covers closed so they can't be opened while a machine is in operation, or to unlock the doors in your car when you push the keyless entry button on the remote. Solenoids can open and close valves in industrial processes or push the record head against the tape in a tape player.

Solenoids come in many shapes and sizes, and are capable of exerting a force from less than an ounce to several pounds. There are two basic varieties: continuous duty and pulse duty. Continuous-duty solenoids are designed to be energized all the time. An application such as holding a safety cover closed would use a continuous-duty solenoid. A pulse-duty solenoid might be used for the doors in your car. Pulse-duty solenoids will overheat if left energized all the time—they are designed for intermittent operation. A pulse-duty solenoid allows a high-force solenoid to be smaller and cheaper because continuous operation is not a concern.

Relays

A relay is a solenoid that operates electrical contacts. When the relay is energized, the contacts are shorted or opened, just like a mechanical switch.

Interfacing to Solenoids and Relays

For the sake of simplicity, this section will address relays, but the same considerations apply to solenoids. Figure 6.1A shows a relay as it might be connected to a microprocessor. A single bit is used to turn the relay on and off. The figure shows an NPN

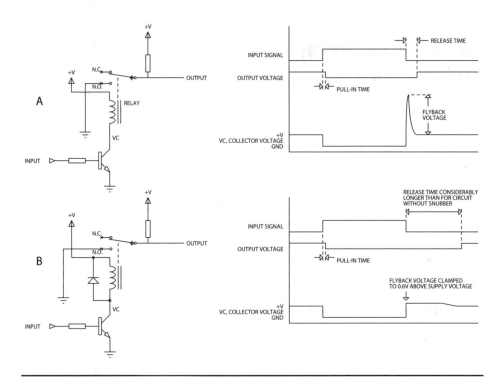

Figure 6.1
Relay control and clamping.

transistor connected to a port bit on the processor; you could also use a MOSFET. Some microprocessors have outputs that are capable of sinking sufficient current to activate a relay, as long as the relay is operating from the same voltage as the processor.

Because the relay or solenoid is activated by a coil, there is a flyback voltage that occurs when the drive transistor is turned off and the magnetic field collapses in the coil. This voltage can reach high enough levels to damage the drive transistor. Figure 6.1B shows how a diode can be used to clamp the voltage across the coil to safe levels. When the transistor turns on, activating the relay, the diode is reverse biased. When the transistor turns off, the top end of the coil is tied to the drive voltage, so a voltage spike appears at the lower end (transistor collector). As soon as this voltage reaches the supply voltage plus one diode drop (about 0.6 V for a silicon diode), the diode conducts.

There are two considerations when using a diode clamp on a relay. The first is that the energy in the coil doesn't just disappear. It has to go somewhere, and it gets dumped into the positive supply through the diode. This results in a current surge into the supply. For this reason, the supply needs to be well bypassed. If the relay is on a board that is some distance from the power supply, there may be a noise spike on the ground as well. The second problem with this technique is that it slows the release time down.

Figure 6.2 shows a method that can be used to speed up the relay release by using a zener diode. When the transistor is turned on and the relay pulls in, the normal diode keeps current from flowing through the zener. When the transistor turns off and the flyback pulse occurs, the normal diode is forward biased and the zener is reverse biased. The result is that the transistor collector voltage is clamped at the zener voltage plus one diode drop above the positive supply. Of course, the resulting voltage has to be lower than the transistor breakdown voltage or damage will result. Typical numbers for a generic 6 V relay with no clamp, a diode clamp, and two zener clamps are as follows:

Clamp	Open time
none	1 ms
12 V zener	1.5 ms
6 V zener	2.2 ms
diode	5.5 ms

These numbers were obtained by switching off the relay coil and measuring the time until the contacts open. You can see that the higher the flyback voltage is allowed to rise, the faster the field dissipates and the faster the contacts open.

Tranzorbs can also be used to clamp a relay or solenoid. A Tranzorb is a zener-like device that is used for clamping high-energy transients. A Tranzorb clamps at the same voltage in both directions, so no blocking diode is needed.

Pick/Hold

The DC current drawn by a relay has to be high enough to pull the relay contact from one end of its travel to the other. However, the current needed to hold that

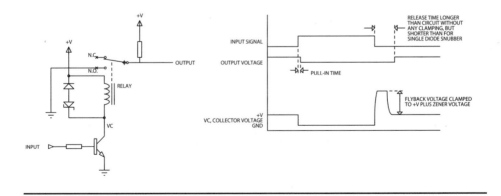

Figure 6.2
Using a zener clamp to speed up relay release time.

position is much lower—typically 50% of the pull-in (or pick) voltage. In many cases, a smaller power supply can be used if the current is reduced once the relay contacts are pulled in, especially if several relays are to be activated at once. In addition, using a lower hold current decreases the release time, because there is less energy stored in the coil when the relay is turned off.

Figure 6.3A shows a simple method for reducing the hold current once a relay is picked. An electrolytic capacitor in parallel with a resistor is in series with the collector of the drive transistor. When the transistor turns on, the capacitor looks like a low impedance and the full current is drawn through the relay coil. As the capacitor charges up, the current through the coil is reduced until eventually the current through the coil is limited by the resistor.

The drawbacks to this circuit are two. First, the capacitor tends to be large because it has to supply current to the coil until the contacts pull in. Second, the resistor dissipates power and, depending on the size of the relay, may have to be a large power resistor. It may get hot in operation.

Figure 6.3B shows an alternative means of implementing a pick/hold circuit. This circuit requires two outputs from the controlling microprocessor. Input 2 is driven high to pick the relay. After a short delay (implemented in software), Input 1 is driven high and Input 2 is driven low. This holds the relay closed. This circuit eliminates the capacitor, but still requires a resistor and takes two outputs from the microprocessor, as well as some additional software.

Figure 6.3C shows how the relay can be controlled by *chopping* the current with PWM—turning it on and off. The ON input goes high to pull the relay in. After a delay (again, implemented in software), the HOLD input goes high. The relay current is now the time-average of the chopping waveform; if the waveform is 50% high and 50% low, the average current through the coil will be half the pick current.

An alternative version of this method can be implemented if you are using a microcontroller with PWM outputs (Figure 6.3D). You drive the relay with a single transistor from the PWM output. To pull the relay in, you program the output to be 90% or 100% on. After the relay pulls in, you switch to 50% or some other PWM ratio to reduce the current.

Figure 6.3E shows how two PNP transistors can be used to implement pick/hold if two power supply voltages are available. To pull the relay in, Input 1 is driven high and transistor Q2 turns on, applying voltage V2 to the coil. After the relay pulls in, Input 2 is driven high and Input 1 is driven low. V2 is higher than V1. V2 might be 12 V (for a 12 V relay) and V1 might be 8 V or 6 V. Note that the transistors in this circuit must be driven from a source that can withstand the supply voltages.

Finally, you can avoid timing the pick/hold function if there is an extra set of contacts on the relay. You can use one set of contacts for whatever you are controlling, and the second set of contacts to switch between pick and hold. This has the advantage of always having the correct timing, because the circuit doesn't change from pick to hold until the contacts have actually pulled in.

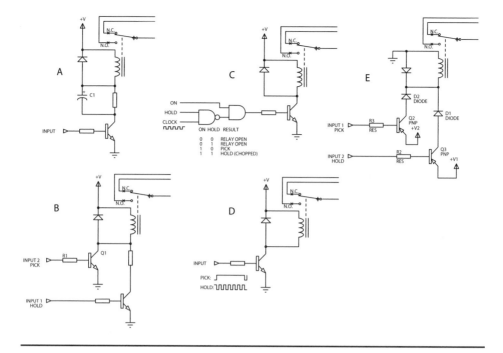

Figure 6.3
Pick/hold.

Heaters

A heater is driven much the same as a solenoid, usually using a transistor. Most heaters have negligible inductance, so the clamping diodes are not necessary. In most cases, heaters are controlled by a feedback loop, with a temperature sensor mounted somewhere to measure the temperature. Figure 6.4 shows a typical temperature control loop using a microprocessor. The heater is mounted on whatever is to be heated, along with some kind of temperature sensor. The microprocessor turns the heater on and off to control the temperature.

Open Heater

What happens if the heater opens up? You get no heat. How do you detect it? Figure 6.5 shows a means to detect an open heater condition. A resistor (R1) is connected across the control MOSFET to ground. R1 is much larger than the heater resistance—at least ten times larger. When the heater is off, the junction of the heater, MOSFET, and R1 will go almost to +V because the resistance of the

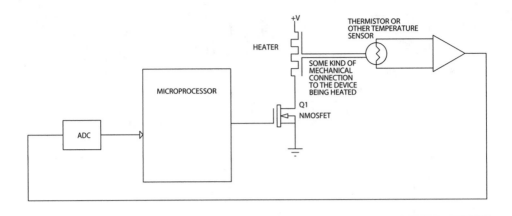

Figure 6.4
Microprocessor-controlled heater.

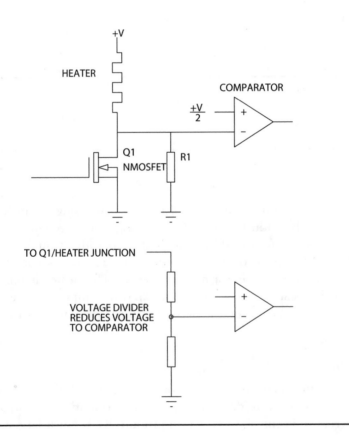

Figure 6.5
Detecting an open heater.

heater is much less than the R1 divider. The output of the comparator is low. However, if the heater is open, there is no resistance to +V, so R1 pulls the noninverting comparator input to ground and the output of the comparator is high.

If the comparator used cannot handle an input that goes all the way to the supply rail, you can either run the comparator from a higher voltage than the heater, or make R1 a voltage divider and monitor the voltage at the tap to reduce the voltage at the comparator input. If you use the voltage divider, the reference voltage has to be proportionally lower as well. Of course, you can only check for an open heater when the heater is turned off, so the software has to synchronize the test with heater operation. In addition, if the heater is ever 100% on, the microprocessor must occasionally turn it off to check for heater failure.

Open Sensor

What happens if the temperature sensor in a heater system opens up? For most sensors (NTC thermistor, solid-state sensor, thermocouple) this condition looks like a very cold temperature. This can be a disaster because the microprocessor will leave the heater on 100%, attempting to reach the target temperature. There are several ways to handle this condition. In software, you can monitor the amount of time the heater is on and declare an error if it stays on for an unreasonable amount of time. This only works if your system can ensure that no damage will result before the error is detected. If the normal operating temperature range is limited, you can detect an out-of-bounds cold condition as an open.

Figure 6.6 shows a circuit that I used in a design. This is the scaling circuit that we looked at in an earlier chapter, to amplify and scale an NTC thermistor to the 0–5 V range needed by an ADC. In this case, the operating range was between about 30 °C and 50 °C. I couldn't just declare a low temperature as an error, because room temperature (about 25 °C) is outside the measurement range, but it is a valid temperature until the system heats up.

What I did was add a second opamp, wired as a buffer (no gain, no scaling) and connect the input to the thermistor. The output went to a second ADC channel. If the thermistor opens, voltage V1 will go to the reference voltage, 2.5 V. In this system, 2.5 V corresponds to a temperature below 0 °C, outside the allowable range of operation for the instrument. So the microprocessor used the scaled/amplified signal to measure temperature, and monitored the unscaled signal for a voltage greater than about 2 V to detect an open thermistor.

If you don't have a second ADC channel, the same thing can be implemented with a comparator. In this case, one side of the comparator would connect to the

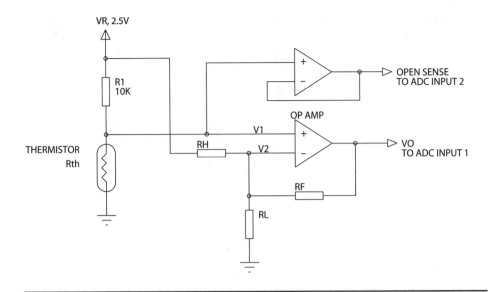

VR, 2.5V

R1
10K

THERMISTOR
Rth

RH

V1

V2

OP AMP

OPEN SENSE
TO ADC INPUT 2

VO
TO ADC INPUT 1

RF

RL

Figure 6.6
Detecting an open thermistor.

thermistor and the other side would connect to a 2 V reference. The output of the comparator then goes to a digital input that can be monitored by the microprocessor.

RTD Heater

The RTD heater is a special type of heater that is composed of an RTD material, usually iron-nickel. The heater element doubles as the thermistor. These heaters are often printed onto a high-temperature, flexible backing. Because a thermistor is not required, overall system cost can be lower.

Figure 6.7A shows a method of driving an RTD heater. A MOSFET transistor controls the heater, and the transistor is driven by the microprocessor. The resistance of the heater element is related to its temperature. When the heater is on, the current through it is given by:

$$\frac{V+}{Rs + Rh}$$

where Rh is the heater resistance and Rs is the value of the sense resistor. By measuring the voltage across the sense resistor with a differential amplifier, the

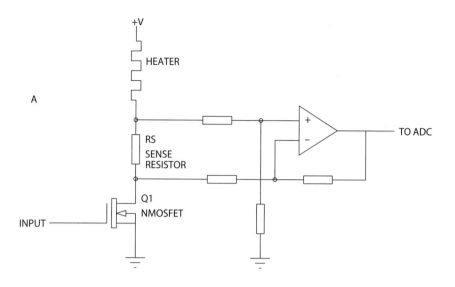

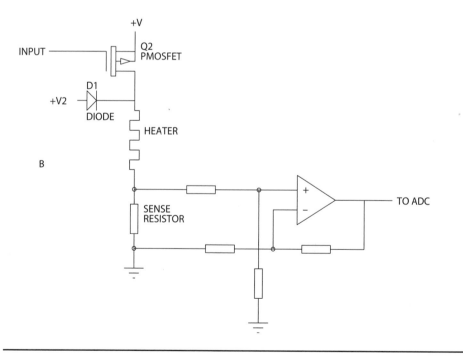

Figure 6.7
RTD heater.

value of the heater resistance can be determined. The catch is that the heater has to be on for the temperature to be measured.

Figure 6.7B shows a means to use an RTD heater and measure temperature with the heater off. A P-channel MOSFET switches the high side of the heater to V+ to turn the heater on. When the heater is off, diode D1 supplies a lower, well-regulated measurement voltage to the heater. For a 24 V heater, a typical measurement voltage might be 2.5 V. The measurement voltage must be small enough to prevent any significant heating.

An alternative to this approach is to eliminate the sense resistor, use the N-channel, low-side switching MOSFET, and use a large-value resistor in parallel with the MOSFET. The voltage across this resistor is then measured to determine the heater resistance. The problem with this approach is that the measurement resistor must be significantly larger than the RTD resistance, so there is little change in voltage with temperature.

Finally, some MOSFET transistors have a fourth lead that provides a fraction of the current passed through the MOSFET itself. By connecting a resistor from this lead to ground, a voltage is developed that is proportional to the current in the device. This can be used to measure the heater resistance when the heater is on. International Rectifier makes a line of MOSFETS, called SENSEFETS, with this feature.

RTD heaters have some drawbacks. The first drawback is the tolerance of the heater element itself. Unlike RTD sensors, RTD heaters are usually sprayed or sputtered onto some kind of flexible substrate. Consequently, they have a typical tolerance of about 10%, although some vendors will allow you to specify 5% tolerance at additional cost.

Another problem with RTD heaters is that the temperature measurement is dependent on the supply voltage. A 24 V supply with 5% tolerance results in a 5% variation in temperature measurement (compared to actual temperature). You can get around this problem by using a separate ADC channel to measure the actual supply voltage and correct the RTD measurement value. This typically means using a voltage divider to bring the heater supply voltage down to a range the ADC can handle.

When using an RTD circuit, you can measure only when the heater is on or off (depending on which type of circuit you use), but not both. If using a measure-when-on circuit, you have to turn the heater on momentarily to get a measurement, so you can't get a 0% duty cycle. If you are using the measure-when-off circuit, you have to turn it off occasionally, so you can't get a 100% duty cycle. In either case, the software has to synchronize temperature measurement with the correct heater state (ON or OFF).

Finally, when you use an RTD heater, you are measuring the temperature of the heating element, not the object you are trying to heat. If you have good thermal contact between the two, this may not be an issue. However, if the thermal contact is poor or, worse, varies during operation, the results you get may be a poor representation of the actual conditions.

Coolers

A solid-state (Peltier) cooler consists of a series of PN junctions, usually fabricated from bismuth telluride, that can draw heat from one side and exhaust heat on the other side. A Peltier cooler can be controlled much like a heater, using a thermistor to measure the temperature. PWM can be used, although to avoid thermal stress on the semiconductor elements, a minimum PWM frequency is usually recommended. The minimum is typically around 2 kHz.

One concern with a Peltier cooler is, what happens if the thermistor opens? Unlike with a heater, you won't overcool anything, but the cooler will never turn on. If you are trying to keep medical samples cold, this can ruin them. If your application calls for a cooling temperature above the lower limit of the thermistor, you can use the same technique as for a heater thermistor—looking for an out-of-bounds condition on the temperature. If you will be operating the cooler near the ends of the thermistor range, you may need a second thermistor in the system so you can verify that everything is working. In some cases, you might be able to use a PTC thermistor, which has a positive temperature/resistance curve.

Fans

Cooling fans may seem like mundane things. You turn them on and off when the power goes on and off, right? Actually, you do occasionally find a need to control or monitor fan operation. For instance, you might want to control fan speed to limit noise in a system.

If your system has multiple cooling fans, you might not need all the fans all the time, so you can make the system quieter by turning off the ones that aren't needed. As the temperature goes up, you can turn fans on, increasing the cooling (and the noise level). DC fans can be controlled by a MOSFET transistor. Some fans can be speed modulated by using PWM techniques, but be sure your fan will operate this way. Some fans use electronic controllers that don't like PWM inputs.

In many systems you need to monitor the fan to be sure it is operating because fans tend to have a high failure rate relative to other parts of the electronics. In fact, you can make a case for the concept that if you don't need to monitor the fan, then you don't need a fan. Or, the corollary is that if you need a fan to keep things from overheating, then you must monitor it to be sure it is working.

There are several ways to monitor fan operation. One is simply to put a semiconductor temperature sensor somewhere in the electronics and see if things overheat. Another way is to use an airflow sensor near the fan to sense if air is really moving. Some fans include an internal sensor that generates a pulse at least once per revolution.

Figure 6.8 shows a typical circuit for a fan with an internal sensor. An optical (or Hall effect) sensor output is pulled up to the fan's supply voltage with a resistor. The voltage out is limited with a zener diode to 4.7 V. The intent is that this will connect to the timer input of a microprocessor so that the speed can be measured.

Another way to use this is to connect it to one side of a set/reset flip-flop. The other input to the flip-flop is connected to a port bit or decoded address strobe so the microprocessor can reset it. Finally, the output of the flip-flop is connected to a digital input on the processor.

In operation, the microprocessor will periodically check the input and clear the output. If the fan is running, it will eventually (in a few milliseconds) set the flip-flop again. This does not measure fan speed, but it does give an indication that the fan is running.

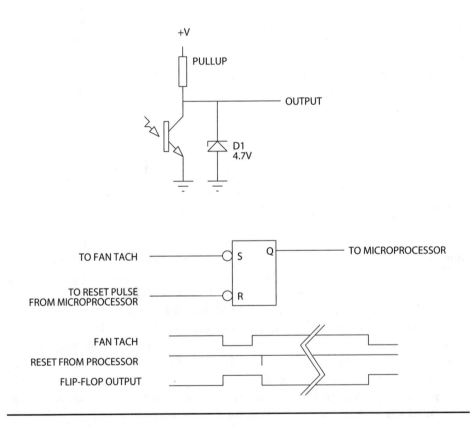

Figure 6.8
Fan tach.

Analog Interfacing to Embedded Microprocessor Systems

One problem with built-in fan tachs is that they have to run from the fan supply voltage (+V in Figure 6.8). The output is clamped with a zener. But what happens if the fan is plugged in while power is on and the +V and output connections are made before the ground connection is made (Figure 6.9)? Because the zener ground is floating, you instantly get the fan power supply (typically 24 V) applied to the digital input that is monitoring the fan tach. This can damage the device. (I've seen it happen.)

If you use a fan with this type of tach, it is a good idea to add a zener on the board where the fan plugs in to prevent such damage. The added zener will be in parallel with the zener in the fan circuit, so it will not affect normal operation, but it will prevent overvoltage if the fan is connected or disconnected with the power on.

LEDs

LEDs are simple, right? You put a current-limiting resistor in series with the LED and connect it between the positive supply and ground. In many cases, that is adequate. But this can cause problems in other situations. Figure 6.10 illustrates such a case. Here, the LED operates from an unregulated supply. You might do this in a battery-operated system in which you want the LEDs to remain off so they don't drain the battery when the AC power is removed. In this example, the DC supply has AC ripple from the full-wave rectifier in the supply. The LED

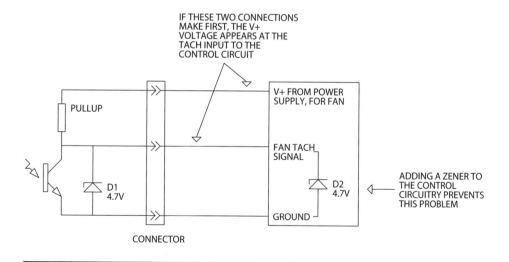

Figure 6.9
Protecting against fan-tach overvoltage.

Solenoids, Relays, and Other Analog Outputs   157

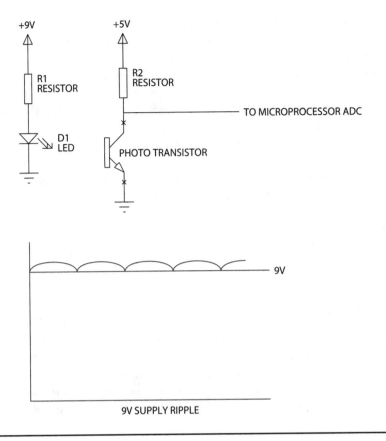

Figure 6.10
LED ripple.

current will follow this ripple, and the result will show up on the phototransistor output and in the ADC results.

One way to prevent this problem is to drive the LED with a constant current. Figure 6.11 shows a simple circuit that will provide a constant current to the LED. The opamp will keep the voltage across the sense resistor equal to the input voltage. The current through the LED is given by:

$$I_{LED} = \frac{\text{INPUT VOLTAGE}}{\text{SENSE RESISTOR}}$$

So if the input voltage is 2.5 V and the sense resistor is 250 ohms, then the LED current will be 10 ma. The precision of this current control is dependent on the transistor gain, the input voltage tolerance, and the tolerance of the sense resistor.

Analog Interfacing to Embedded Microprocessor Systems

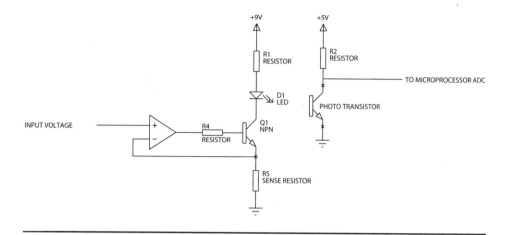

Figure 6.11
LED constant-current drive.

This circuit requires that the opamp operate from positive and negative supplies, or from a single-supply opamp that can drive its output to within 0.6 V of ground.

The input voltage that sets the LED current can be connected to a fixed voltage, such as a reference diode. Figure 6.12 shows how a microprocessor can turn the LED on and off. When ON, the LED operates at a constant current, determined by the diode voltage. The microprocessor port output must be able to source current to the reference diode, so a low-current reference should be used here. The reference diode voltage must be less than the voltage on the microprocessor port bit when in the high state.

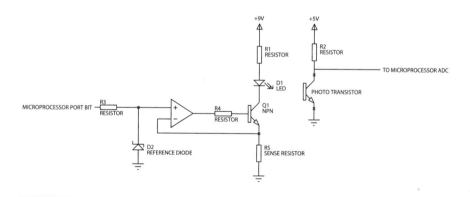

Figure 6.12
LED constant-current drive with microprocessor control.

Optoisolator Outputs

Optoisolators were shown in Chapter 3. Optoisolators can be used to isolate an external input from your microprocessor circuit. They can also be used to generate an output that is isolated from an external circuit. The LED of an optoisolator is driven the same way as any other LED. You need to ensure that there is sufficient current through the LED to turn on the output transistor. The output current is determined by multiplying the LED current by the CTR of the optoisolator. To ensure that the circuit will always work, use the minimum CTR specified by the manufacturer.

In cases where the output is driving another logic input, you typically do not need a small-value pull-up resistor on the output transistor, so you can select something reasonable (4.7 K or 1 K) and provide enough LED current to ensure that the output transistor saturates. Or, use an optoisolator with a logic-level output and ensure that sufficient LED current is provided to switch the output.

In addition to transistor and logic outputs, optoisolators are also available with triac outputs. These are typically used to turn on large power triacs or SCRs for switching AC power. They provide a simple means to turn on an AC semiconductor while isolating the microprocessor from the AC voltage.

Driving Multiple LEDs

Sometimes you need to drive multiple LEDs from a single input; for example, you may need to turn on multiple optocouplers or optical switches at the same time. Figure 6.13 shows a method that is sometimes tried: hooking the LEDs in parallel with a single limiting resistor. This doesn't work reliably. The LEDs have a forward voltage drop, usually 1–2 V. However, this is dependent on temperature

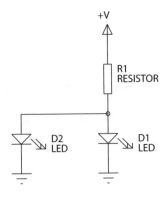

Figure 6.13
Multiple LEDs in parallel.

Analog Interfacing to Embedded Microprocessor Systems

and the specific LED, so one LED tends to hog most of the current. The circuit in Figure 6.14, with one limiting resistor per LED, is more reliable. Also shown is a constant current driver for multiple LEDs, with the LEDs wired in series. The supply voltage for the series connection has to be higher than the forward drop of all the LEDs plus the sense resistor voltage. Of course, with this arrangement, if one LED opens, they all quit working. However, using a series connection and

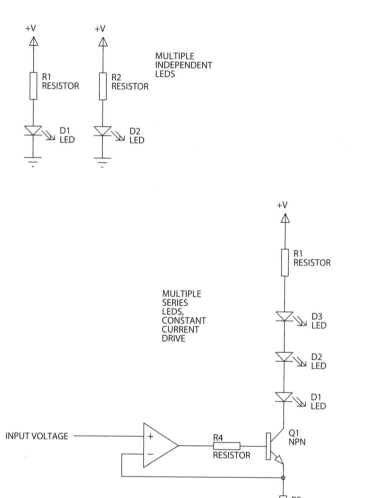

Figure 6.14
Multiple series LEDs.

driving with a constant current provides more uniform illumination in cases where that is important.

Figure 6.15 illustrates a method that can be used to drive multiple LEDs with a single pull-up resistor. In this circuit, each LED is turned on one at a time (by driving the corresponding port bit low), so the differing forward drops do not cause a problem.

DACs

As discussed in Chapter 2, DACs convert a digital word to a corresponding analog voltage (or current). A DAC is at the heart of most ADCs. Other applications for a DAC range from controlling the reference to a voltage comparator to simulating a sine wave. I used a DAC in an unusual application years ago in a piece of military gear that was replacing older equipment. The original equipment had an analog signal that controlled a horizontal situation indicator (a meter) in an aircraft. We were performing these functions in software, so the DAC, under software control, generated the voltage to drive the analog meter.

The Analog Devices AD7801 is a typical 8-bit, voltage-output DAC. The microprocessor interface consists of 8 data bits, a –WR signal and a –CS signal. Data is written to the device by toggling –WR while –CS is low. The AD7801 can operate at voltages from 2.7 to 5.5 volts. The part also has a –CLR pin that, when low, loads the DAC with all 0s.

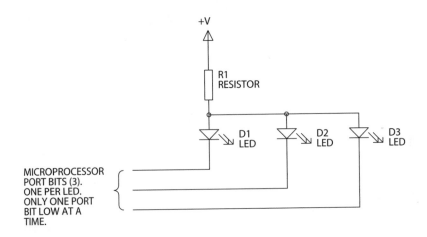

Figure 6.15
Multiple multiplexed LEDs.

Analog Interfacing to Embedded Microprocessor Systems

The output of the AD7801 can swing from ground to the positive rail. The reference for the device can be either the positive supply or an external reference voltage. The output can source or sink several milliamps.

Like ADCs, DACs are available with both parallel and serial interfaces. The Analog Devices AD5300 is an 8-bit DAC with a rail-to-rail output and an SPI-compatible interface. Like the AD7801, the AD5300 can operate with supply voltages from 2.7 to 5.5 volts.

Specialized DACs

DACs designed for special applications are also available. The Analog Devices ADV7120 is a triple 8-bit video DAC designed for video use. The part contains three DACs for the RGB (red green blue) video signals. The ADV7120 also has SYNC and BLANK inputs that force all three outputs to the sync and blanking levels, respectively (Figure 6.16). Other specialized DACs include audio parts with built-in volume control and mute functions, and DACs that are optimized for use in voice transmission systems such as telephones.

Digital Potentiometers

Although a DAC can provide a voltage or current output for control, sometimes a design calls for a variable resistance. Typical examples would be a volume or tone control in a stereo or gain control in an opamp circuit. In these cases, a digital potentiometer is often the ideal solution. Like a DAC, a digital potentiometer takes a digital word from a microprocessor, but it converts the word to a resistance instead of to a voltage.

The Analog Devices AD5220 is a typical digital potentiometer (Figure 6.17). It comes in an 8-pin package, either DIP or surface mount, and in resistance ranges

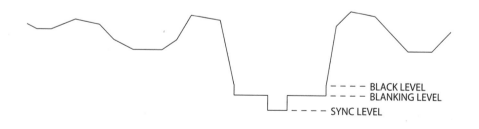

Figure 6.16
Video levels.

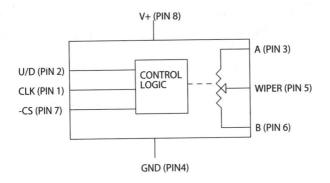

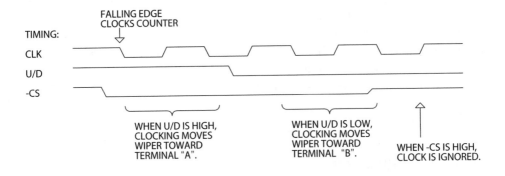

Figure 6.17
Analog Devices AD5220.

of 10 K, 50 K, and 100 K. It can operate at voltages from 3.3 V to 5 V. The AD5220 simulates a three-terminal potentiometer with two terminals (A and B) and a wiper (W). An internal 7-bit counter is decoded to determine one of 128 positions for the wiper.

The AD5220 inputs consist of a clock (CLK), a chip select signal (–CS), and an up/down control pin (U/D). When –CS is low, the device is selected, and falling edges on the CLK signal will move the wiper. Clocking with the U/D pin high moves the wiper toward terminal A (away from terminal B), and clocking with the U/D pin low moves the wiper toward terminal B (away from A). To use the AD5220 with a microprocessor, the clock input could be connected to a decoded write strobe and the U/D connected to a microprocessor data line. Assuming data line D0 is used, to move the wiper toward terminal A, the processor would write to the AD5220 address with a "1," and to move the wiper the other way the processor would write a "0."

A mechanical potentiometer can be connected without concern about the absolute voltages on the pins, as long as the dissipation of the device is not

Analog Interfacing to Embedded Microprocessor Systems

exceeded. A digital potentiometer has some limitations because it uses analog switches to connect to taps on a solid-state resistor. The AD5220 resistor terminals (A, B, and W) cannot be driven above the positive supply or below ground. The AD5220 would not work as a volume control in the circuit shown in Figure 6.18A because the coupling capacitor causes the A terminal to swing below ground. In Figure 6.18B, a resistor, the same value as the AD5220 resistance, biases the A terminal at 2.5 V, half the supply voltage. In this circuit, the AD5220 potentiometer connections will remain within the 0–5 V operating range of the part, as long as the audio input signal amplitude doesn't exceed 5 V peak to peak (p-p).

An alternative connection is also shown in Figure 6.18, with two biasing resistors at the B terminal of the AD5220. A bypass capacitor places the B terminal at AC ground without affecting the DC level. This configuration has the advantage that the biasing resistors don't load the signal input, but the bypass capacitor must be large enough that it looks like a low impedance at all frequencies of interest. For audio applications, this typically means an electrolytic capacitor.

If the amplifier were a single-supply opamp, the AD5220 could be placed in the feedback network to control the gain. Because an opamp will not drive the resistor terminals beyond the supply rails, no biasing resistors are needed. Of course, biasing resistors may still be needed to keep the opamp inputs between the rails.

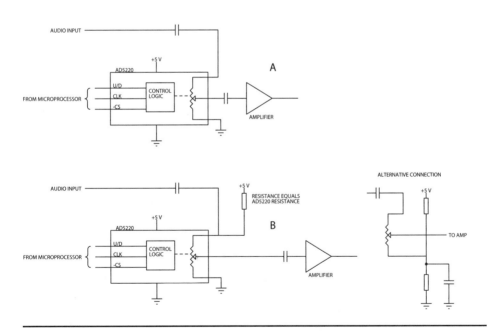

Figure 6.18
Digital potentiometer biasing to keep inputs between the supply rails.

The Analog Devices AD5203 is a quad digital potentiometer with an SPI-like serial interface. The AD5203 potentiometers each have 64 positions and have the same voltage range limitations as the AD5220 (0 V to the positive supply). The AD5203 comes in 24-pin DIP and surface-mount packages. The AD5203 has a shutdown feature; by bringing the SHDN pin low, all four potentiometer wipers are taken to the B terminal. When SHDN goes high again, the wipers resume their previous position. A typical application for this would be a mute function in a stereo.

One issue with digital potentiometers that does not occur with mechanical potentiometers is power-up operation. A mechanical potentiometer will stay in its last position when power is turned off, unless someone changes it. On power-up, the AD5203 wipers go to their center position. This may not be the position you want, and it probably isn't the position it was last in. The only way to ensure that the digital pot remembers its position is to use nonvolatile storage. On power-up, the software looks up the last position of each pot and sets the pot accordingly. The software also needs to ensure that the power-up state of the potentiometer doesn't damage whatever it is controlling.

Potentiometers that retain their setting when power is turned off are available. Xicor makes a series of EEPOT devices with SPI, I^{2}C, and increment/decrement interfaces. The EEPOT series of parts contain an EEPROM and remember their settings when power is removed.

Analog Switches

An analog switch can be thought of as a solid-state relay allowing a microprocessor to open or close a switch between two points. An analog switch is faster and smaller than a relay, does not have contact bounce, and consumes considerably less current.

Figure 6.19A shows the symbol for an analog switch and the internal construction. Inside the switch, an N-channel MOSFET is connected in parallel with a P-channel MOSFET. Control circuitry turns both MOSFETs on or turns both of them off. When both MOSFETs are on, current can flow in either direction, from IN to OUT or from OUT to IN. The OUT and IN pin labeling is arbitrary; the analog switch will work the same if the two pins are swapped.

Figure 6.19 shows the analog switch as having V+ and V− inputs; in practice, some switches can operate from a single positive supply voltage and ground (V− connected to ground, in other words). Some switches require a third voltage input equal to the logic supply voltage.

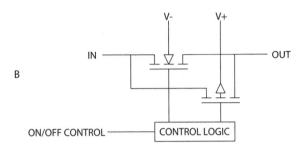

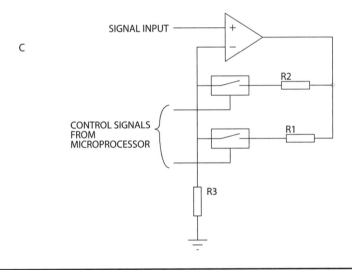

Figure 6.19
Analog switch.

Practical Parts

Although an analog switch can be thought of as a solid-state relay, there are some differences. For instance, the contacts of a relay are completely isolated from the coil. You can switch hundreds of volts with no danger of the voltage reaching the microprocessor circuits. An analog switch requires power supplies for the switching transistors, so the voltage on the input and output pins cannot exceed the V+ and V− voltages. If the input or output pin is connected to a voltage outside this range, the switch can be destroyed due to excessive current flow between the out-of-range voltage and one of the supply voltages.

Some analog switches are fault protected, permitting the input and output pins to exceed the supply voltage. Note that they won't switch voltages outside the supply range, but they won't be damaged if that condition occurs. This feature is intended for applications in which the supply voltage may be turned off while the signals that the switch is controlling (such as audio signals from external equipment) are still present. Typical parts include the Maxim MAX4511 and MAX4512.

Because the analog switch is constructed using MOSFETs, there is some finite ON resistance for the switch, equal to the drain-to-source resistance of the transistors. Early analog switches had ON resistance values of a few hundred ohms; modern parts can be less than an ohm.

The turn-on and turn-off time of an analog switch is specified as Ton and Toff and usually ranges from a few tens of nanoseconds to a few microseconds.

Applications

Analog switches can be used to control the gain of an opamp circuit, as shown in Figure 6.19C. In Figure 6.19C two feedback resistors (R1 and R2) are selected by an external microcontroller to adjust the gain. Three gain values can be selected: R1, R2, and R1 in parallel with R2. Note that the analog switches must be supplied from a voltage that exceeds the maximum input and output voltages that will be applied to them. This typically means the supply voltages of the opamp, because the opamp output can go to the supply rails on power-up or if both switches are open. In actual operation, once power has been applied and the circuit is stable, the switch supply voltages would only need to be a little bit more than the maximum input signal voltage on the noninverting opamp input.

Multiplexers

Figure 6.20 shows a 4:1 analog multiplexer. An analog multiplexer consists of two or more analog switches with one common contact (labeled Y on the diagram). The control inputs select which switch is closed, and therefore which of the inputs (X1–X4) are connected to signal Y.

Analog multiplexers have the same operating characteristics as analog switches with respect to input voltage range, ON resistance, and switching time. A typical application for an analog multiplexer would be to select the audio input source for a sound system.

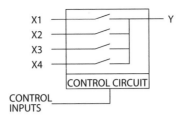

Figure 6.20
Analog multiplexer.

The Maxim MAX349 is a single 8-to-1 analog multiplexer with an SPI interface. The MAX350 is a dual 4-to-1 analog multiplexer, also with an SPI interface.

Motors 7

Motors are key components of many embedded systems because they provide a means to control the real world. Motors are used for everything from the vibrator in a vibrating pager to moving the arm of a large industrial robot. All motors work on the same principles of electromagnetism, and all function by applying power to an electromagnet in some form or another. We won't spend our time on magnetic theory here. Instead, we will look at the basic motor types and their applications in embedded systems.

Stepper Motors

Stepper motors come in three flavors: permanent-magnet, variable-reluctance, and hybrid. Figure 7.1 shows a cross-sectional view of a variable-reluctance (VR) stepper motor. The VR stepper has a soft iron rotor with teeth and a wound stator. As current is applied to two opposing stator coils (the two "B" coils in the figure), the rotor is pulled into alignment with these two coils. As the next pair of coils is energized, the rotor advances to the next position.

The permanent magnet (PM) stepper has a rotor with alternating north and south poles (Figure 7.2). As the coils are energized, the rotor is pulled around. This figure shows a single coil to illustrate the concept, but a real stepper would have stator windings surrounding the rotor. The PM stepper has more torque than an equivalent VR stepper.

The hybrid stepper essentially adds teeth to a permanent magnet motor, resulting in better coupling of the magnetic field into the rotor and more precise movement. In a hybrid stepper, the rotor is split into two parts, an upper and lower (Figure 7.3). One half is the north side of the magnet and one is the south. The teeth are offset so that when the teeth of one magnet are lining up with the mating teeth on the stator, the teeth on the other magnet are lining up with the

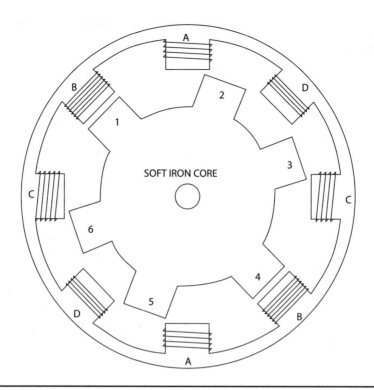

Figure 7.1
Variable-reluctance stepper.

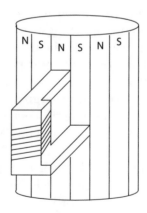

Figure 7.2
Permanent magnet stepper.

Analog Interfacing to Embedded Microprocessor Systems

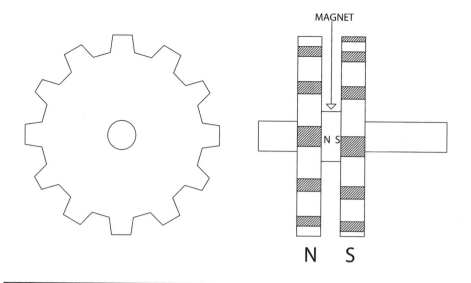

Figure 7.3
Hybrid stepper.

grooves in the stator (in the side view in Figure 7.3, the tops of the teeth are crosshatched for clarity). Some hybrid steppers have more than one stack of magnets for more torque.

Bipolar versus Unipolar

All steppers work by creating a rotating magnetic field in the stator, to which the rotor aligns itself. There are two types of stator winding methods for stepper motors: bipolar and unipolar. Bipolar windings use field coils with no common connections. The coils must be driven independently to reverse the direction of motor flow and rotate the motor. Unipolar motors use coils with centertaps. The centertap is usually connected to the positive supply, and the individual coils are grounded (through transistors) to drive the motor. Figure 7.4 shows the difference between bipolar and unipolar motors. Each time the field is changed in a bipolar motor or a different coil is turned on in a unipolar motor, the motor shaft steps to the next rotation position. Typical step sizes for a stepper are 7.5° or 15°. A 7.5° stepper will have 360/7.5 or 48 steps per revolution. The step size depends on the number of rotor and stator teeth.

Resonance

When a stepper motor rotates, it aligns the rotor with the magnetic field of the stator. In a real motor, the rotor has some inertia and is moving when it reaches

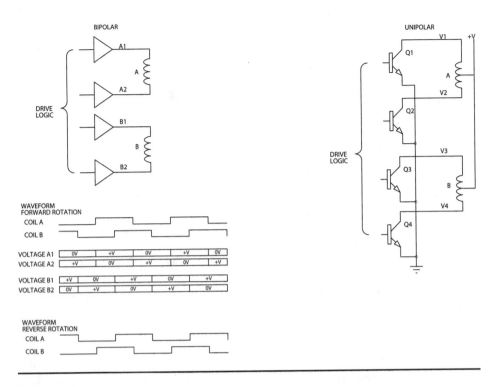

Figure 7.4
Bipolar versus unipolar operation.

the ideal alignment, so it overshoots the final position. Because it is now out of alignment with the magnetic field, it "bounces" back and overshoots in the other direction. This continues, with smaller oscillations, until the rotor finally stops. Figure 7.5 illustrates this. The frequency at which the rotor oscillates depends on the motor characteristics (rotor mass and construction, for instance) and the load. If the motor is connected to a load that looks like a flywheel (a mechanical shutter in an optical system, for example), resonance may be more of a problem than it is with an unloaded motor. A load with a lot of friction, such as a belt-driven pulley, has a damping effect that will reduce resonance (unless the belt is connected to a flywheel).

Many stepper motors exhibit a sudden loss of torque when operating at certain step rates. This occurs when the step rate coincides with the oscillation frequency of the rotor. The torque can change enough to cause missed steps and loss of synchronization. There may be more than one band of step rates that cause this effect (because the motor has more than one resonant frequency). In a design that uses only one step rate, these frequency bands (usually fairly narrow) can be avoided by simply picking a step rate that is not a problem.

174   *Analog Interfacing to Embedded Microprocessor Systems*

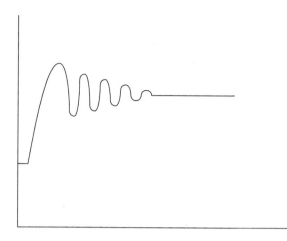

Figure 7.5
Step motor ringing.

In a design in which the step rate has to vary, the system may need to be characterized to identify the problem frequencies. The software may then need to avoid operating the motor at these step rates. When accelerating a stepper up to a particular speed, the software may have to accelerate rapidly through these problem areas (Figure 7.6). This is particularly true if the acceleration ramp is fairly slow, which would otherwise cause the step rate to spend some time in the resonance area.

Half-Stepping

As was already mentioned, the rotor in a stepper motor aligns itself to the magnetic field generated by applying voltage to the stator coils. Figure 7.7 shows a simple stepper with a single pair of rotor poles and two stator coils. Say that coil A is energized, and the rotor aligns itself to magnet A with the north pole up (position 1), as shown in the figure. If coil A is turned off and B is energized, the rotor will rotate until the north pole is at position 3. Now if coil B is turned off and coil A is energized but in the reverse direction of what it was before, the rotor will go to position 5. Finally, if coil A is turned off and coil B is energized with the reverse of its original polarity, the rotor will move to position 7. This sequence is called *one-phase-on drive*.

Say that instead of energizing one magnet at a time, we energize coils A and B at the same time. The rotor will move to position 2, halfway between magnets A and B. If we then reverse the current through coil A, the rotor will move to position 4. If we reverse B, the rotor moves to position 6, and, finally, if we reverse A again the rotor moves to position 8. Each of these methods generates a

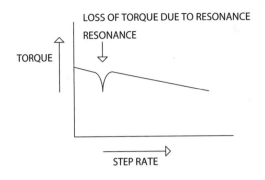

LOSS OF TORQUE DUE TO RESONANCE

RESONANCE

TORQUE

STEP RATE

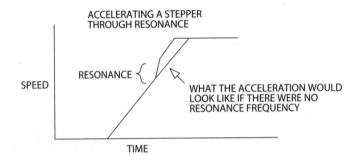

ACCELERATING A STEPPER
THROUGH RESONANCE

SPEED

RESONANCE {

WHAT THE ACCELERATION WOULD
LOOK LIKE IF THERE WERE NO
RESONANCE FREQUENCY

TIME

Figure 7.6
Step motor resonance.

full step of the rotor (in this case, 45° per step), but the actual position is different for the two drive methods. If we combine the two, we can half-step the rotor:

A+, B off: position 1

A+, B+: position 2

A off, B+: position 3

A−, B+: position 4

In this simple example, half-stepping permits a step angle of 22.5°, as opposed to 45° for a full step. The same principle applies to a real motor with several rotor teeth. A motor with a 15° full step can be half-stepped in 7.5° increments.

Figure 7.8 shows all three drive methods. Half-stepping provides smoother rotation and more precise control. It is important to note, though, that for the positions where only one phase is energized (positions 1, 3, 5, 7), the coils need more current to get the same torque. This is because there is only one coil (electromagnet) pulling the rotor. Switching from two coils to one coil reduces the torque by approximately 30%, so two coils have about 140% of the torque of a

Analog Interfacing to Embedded Microprocessor Systems

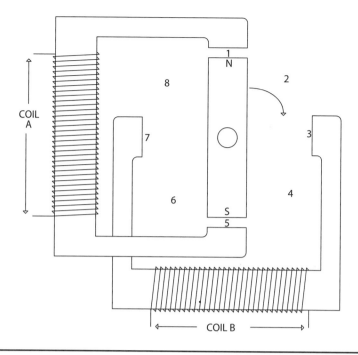

Figure 7.7
Half-stepping.

single coil. You can compensate for this loss of torque by increasing the coil current by 140% when driving a single coil.

Microstepping

If you examine the drive waveform for half-stepping a motor, you can see that it looks like a pair of digitized sine signals, offset by 90°. When the rotor is at position 1, coil A is at the maximum voltage and coil B is at minimum voltage. At position 3, coil A is off and coil B is at maximum voltage. For half-stepping, each coil has three possible drive values: positive drive, off, and negative drive.

If the rotor is at position 1 and coil B is energized slightly, the rotor will rotate toward position 3. If the current through coil A is gradually decreased as the current through coil B is increased, the rotor will slowly move toward position 3, where it ends up when the current in coil A is zero and the current in coil B is maximum. If coil A and B are driven with sine signals that are offset by 90°, the motor will rotate smoothly. Figure 7.9 shows the discrete drive waveform with the equivalent sine/cosine drive and the corresponding rotor positions. A stepper can actually be driven this way.

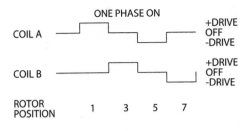

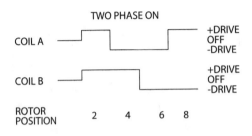

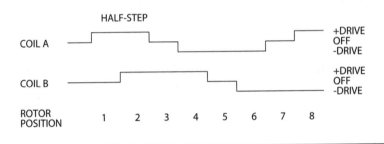

Figure 7.8
Half-step drive waveforms.

If the drive signals are generated from a DAC, the motor can be moved to discrete points between the normal step or half-step positions. This is called *microstepping*. It provides finer control of shaft position, but at the expense of more expensive analog drive circuitry. The actual resolution obtainable by microstepping depends on the resolution of the DAC, the torque of the motor, and the load. For instance, say the motor is very close to position 2 and you want to microstep it to position 2. If the load is too large, you may find that you have to apply more torque than you wanted to to move it, and then it may overshoot the position and stop in the wrong place.

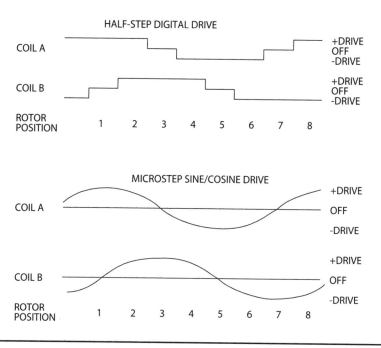

Figure 7.9
Microstepping.

If you do need to perform small steps, you can use a bigger motor that can overcome the load. In some cases, this may be a lower-cost solution than other possibilities, such as a geared DC motor. Microstepping also reduces resonance problems because the motor does not receive discrete steps, so the mechanical ringing is less likely to occur. In a real application, a high-precision DAC is not usually needed because the stepper will not respond to very small changes in the drive waveform. Typical microstep increments are 1/3 to 1/16 of a full step. In other words, using a 10-bit DAC to microstep a stepper motor will not provide any practical advantage over using an 8-bit DAC.

Driving Steppers

The coils of a bipolar stepper are typically driven with an H-bridge circuit. Figure 7.10 shows a circuit that will drive both coils in a two-coil bipolar stepper. This circuit consists of a pair of N-channel MOSFETs and a pair of P-channel MOS-FETs for each coil. When input "A" is high, transistors Q1 and Q3 are turned on and current flows from the positive supply, through Q1, through the motor winding, through Q3, and to ground. When "A" is low and "B" is high, Q2 and

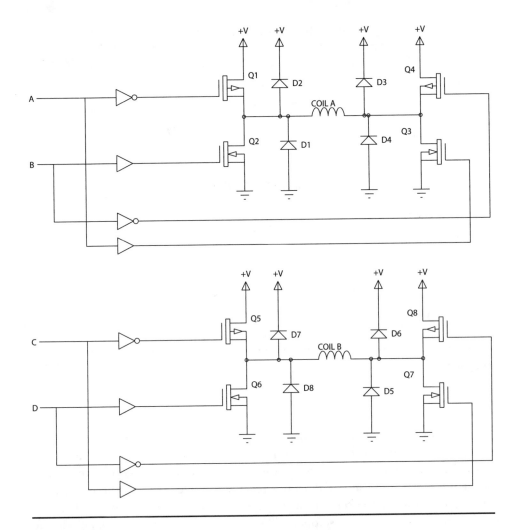

Figure 7.10
H-bridge circuit.

Q4 are on and current through the motor winding is reversed. The circuit for the other coil works the same way.

The diodes, D1-D8, protect the transistors against the coil flyback voltage when the transistors are turned off. The motor shaft is rotated by applying drive voltage to each input in the proper sequence.

Cross-Conduction

One common problem for designers who want to build their own H-bridge circuits from discrete transistors is cross-conduction, also known as shoot-through. This is the condition that occurs when the upper and lower transistors on the same side of the coil turn on at the same time. In the example in the previous section, this would be transistors Q1 and Q2 or Q3 and Q4. If Q1 and Q2 turn on at the same time, there will be a very low impedance between the supply voltage and ground— effectively a short. This usually destroys one or both transistors. In a high-power circuit, the results can be quite dramatic, with blue sparks and pieces of transistor flying across the room.

Shoot-through can be caused (again going back to the same example) by bringing inputs "A" and "B" high at the same time. As shown in Figure 7.11, it can also be caused by bringing one input high while simultaneously taking the other input low. If one of the transistors in the bridge turns off a little more slowly than the others turn on, the result will be momentary shoot-through. It may not be enough to destroy the part, but over time it can cause premature failure. Or,

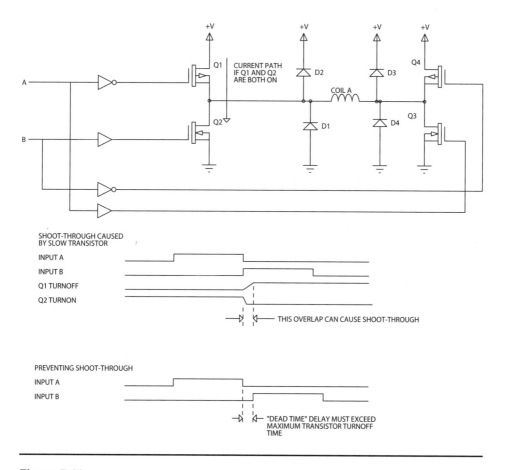

Figure 7.11
Shoot-through.

worse, the problem may show up only at high or low temperatures, making failures that only happen in the field.

The usual method to avoid shoot-through is to introduce a short delay between turning off one side of the H-bridge and turning on the other. The delay must be long enough to allow both transistors to turn off before the other pair turns on.

I saw a design once (Figure 7.12) that used optocouplers to provide isolation between the motor-control circuitry and the driving circuitry. The problem was that optocouplers have a wide variation in turn-on/turn-off times. In production, the only way to make the circuit work reliably was to hand-select optocouplers that had similar characteristics. If the operating temperature varies widely, it is possible that a circuit like this can fail in the field.

If you drive an H-bridge directly from the port outputs of a microcontroller, be sure to take power-up conditions into account. Until they are initialized, the port bits of most microcontrollers are floating. Depending on whether the H-bridge logic sees this condition as logical "1" or "0," it can turn on both sides of the bridge and cause shoot-through. Be sure everything comes up in a safe condition and add pull-ups to the port pins if necessary. If the H-bridge drive inputs cannot be guaranteed during power-up, use a power supply for the stepper motor that has the ability to be disabled with a shutdown input.

Keep the motor power off until everything on the control side is stable. It may be tempting to depend on the microprocessor getting out of reset and getting its port bits set to the right state before the motor power supply comes up to a high enough voltage to do any damage. This is a risky approach, as a faulty processor may never get the ports set up right. If you use an emulator for debugging, there may be a considerable delay between applying power and getting the ports set up correctly. And what happens if you turn the power on but you forget to plug the

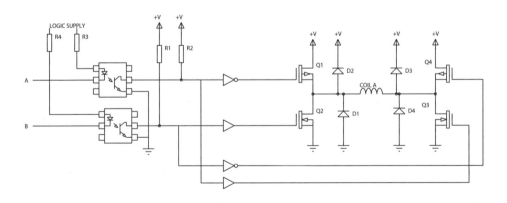

Figure 7.12
Shoot-through caused by optoisolator delay.

emulator in? You could destroy the entire prototype setup. This can be a real problem if there is only one of them. The safest route is to ensure that the power-up state of the processor can't do any damage.

Shoot-through can also be caused by the driver transistors themselves. Figure 7.13 shows one half of an H-bridge driver constructed with MOSFET transistors. MOSFETs have a fairly high capacitance between the gate terminal and both of the other terminals (source and drain). In the figure, the capacitance is represented by the capacitance C, between the gate and drain of Q2. This capacitance is usually on the order of a few tens of picofarads for a typical MOSFET used in a motor application.

If transistor Q1 turns on to apply voltage to one side of the motor (the transistor opposite Q2, not shown, on the other side of the bridge would turn on as well), there will be a voltage spike at the junction of the drains of Q1 and Q2. This voltage spike will be coupled to the gate of Q2 by the capacitance C. If the impedance of the device driving the gate of Q2 is high enough, the voltage spike may be enough to turn on Q2 and cause shoot-through. Remember that the voltage on the motor may be 24 V, 36 V, or more, and the gate of Q2 may need only a few volts to turn on. So even if the signal is significantly attenuated, it still

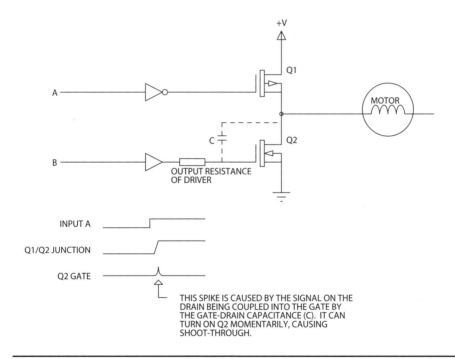

Figure 7.13
Shoot-through caused by MOSFET capacitance.

may be able to turn on the MOSFET. This problem can be minimized by ensuring that the impedance of the driver is low; if a series resistor is used to limit current flow into the gate in case of transistor failure, make the value as small as possible. Minimize trace lengths between the MOSFET and the driver device.

Current Sensing

Many designs need to sense the current through the stepper motor coils. The usual method for doing this is to place a small-value precision resistor in series with the ground lead of the driver circuit (Figure 7.14). When the motor is turned on, the current through the winding must pass through the sense resistor to reach ground. This develops a voltage across the resistor that can be amplified and sensed with an opamp amplifier. The amplifier output can be connected to an ADC so it can be read by a microprocessor, or it can connect to one side of a comparator for digital detection of an overcurrent condition.

To avoid stealing excessive power from the motor winding, the sense resistor is usually small, on the order of 1Ω or less. Even a 1Ω resistor will take a watt in a motor drive circuit that uses one amp. This is a watt of power that is wasted as heat. Generally, you want to make the sense resistor as small as possible without making sensing difficult. As already mentioned, International Rectifier makes a series of MOSFETs known as SENSEFETs with an extra pin that mirrors a fraction of the transistor current. This can be used for current sensing.

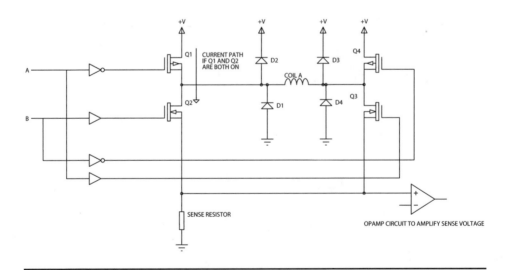

Figure 7.14
H-bridge current sensing.

Analog Interfacing to Embedded Microprocessor Systems

Motor Drive ICs

There are a number of ICs that can control and drive stepper motors. The L6201 from SGS-Thompson is a typical part. The L6201 can drive motors up to 5 A with supply voltages up to 48 V. The L6201 includes internal flyback protection diodes and includes a thermal shutdown that turns the motors off if the part overheats. The L6201 is available in DIP, SMT, and multiwatt packages.

The LM18200 from National is another motor driver IC. This part includes a pin that provides a thermal warning when the device is about to overheat. Unlike the L6201, the LMD18200 does not require a sense resistor in the ground connection of the driver transistors. Instead, the LMD18200 has a separate pin that mirrors the current in the H-bridge. This pin (CURRENT SENSE OUTPUT in Figure 7.15) typically carries $377\,\mu A$ per amp of current in the bridge. If a motor winding draws 2 amps, and a 4.99 K resistor is connected from the current sense pin to ground, then the voltage developed across the resistor will be:

$$377 \times 10^{-6} \times 2 \times 4990 = 3.76\,\text{V}$$

The current sense output pin can be connected directly to an ADC or comparator input.

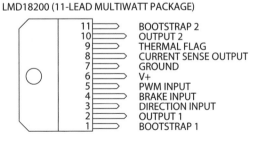

Figure 7.15
L6201 and LMD18200 multiwatt packages.

Chopper Control

Torque in a stepper motor is controlled by adjusting the current through the windings. Because the winding is an inductor, applying voltage to the coil doesn't cause the current to change instantly (Figure 7.16). As the current in the coil increases, torque increases. So, if we want to have a particular torque, it takes a while to get there once voltage is applied. However, as shown in Figure 7.16, if we operate at a higher voltage (V2 in the figure), we get to the original torque value much more quickly because the current increases along an exponential curve. The problem is that we end up with too much current in the winding because the current keeps climbing past the torque we wanted.

One way of generating torque faster is to use a higher drive voltage to get fast current buildup, but turn off the voltage to the coil when the current reaches the desired value. The chopper circuit in Figure 7.17 illustrates a way to do this. The voltage from the sense resistor (amplified if necessary) is applied to one input of a comparator. The other side of the comparator connects to a reference voltage that sets the drive current.

A chopper oscillator, typically operating from 20 kHz to 200 kHz (depending on the motor and driver characteristics) sets a flip-flop. The output of the flip-flop enables the H-bridge outputs. When the flip-flop output is low, the H-bridge is disabled, even if one of the control inputs is high.

When voltage is applied to the coil and the current builds to the desired level, the voltage across the sense resistor becomes greater than the comparator reference, and the comparator output goes low. This turns off the flip-flop and disables the H-bridge until the next oscillator pulse occurs. As long as the current is less than the desired level, the H-bridge will remain enabled.

The circuit shown in Figure 7.17 illustrates the concept. In practice, the comparator reference voltage could be fixed, or it could come from a micropro-

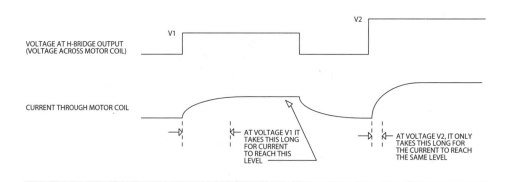

Figure 7.16
Coil current as a function of supply voltage.

Analog Interfacing to Embedded Microprocessor Systems

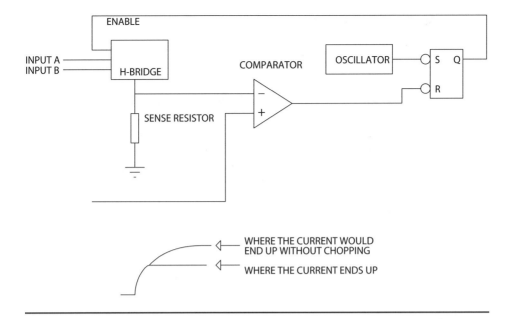

Figure 7.17
Chopper control of coil current.

cessor-controlled DAC. This would permit software control of the current and therefore the torque. This would allow a stepper motor to be used in an application with varying loads, as long as the microprocessor knows approximately what the load is. It could also be used to compensate for the torque variation between a single-coil and two-coil drive when half-stepping, or to generate the varying signals needed for microstepping.

The chopping frequency has to be high enough to be significantly greater than the maximum step rate of the motor, but low enough that the transistors can respond. If the chopping frequency is too high, the drive transistors will spend too much time in the linear region (during the turn-on and turn-off times) and will dissipate significant power (see appendix B).

The chopper oscillator and comparator could be eliminated and this entire function could be performed in software. A regular interrupt at the chopping frequency would be used as a time base. Each time the interrupt occurred, the microprocessor would examine the sense resistor voltage (via an ADC) and either enable or disable the H-bridge. Of course, the processor must be able to service interrupts at the chopping frequency, which would limit that frequency in a practical design. Using a microprocessor just to chop a single motor would probably be overkill, but it might be cost-effective to use a single microprocessor to control several motors if all motors were chopped with the same clock.

Control Method and Resonance

Stepper motors driven with constant current drive (chopped or analog) are more likely to have resonance problems at low step rates. Using half-stepping or microstepping can usually overcome these problems. Of course, going from a simple on-off H-bridge to a DAC-controlled microstepping scheme is a large step in system complexity.

Steppers that are driven with constant voltage are more likely to have resonance problems at higher step rates. Half-stepping and microstepping will not solve these problems. However, a load with a significant damping effect (such as a high-friction load) reduces resonance effects overall. If your application calls for high step rates and a load that doesn't provide much damping, use constant current drive and half-stepping or microstepping to avoid low-frequency resonance problems. What is a high step rate? It depends on the motor, but will generally be in the range above 200 to 500 steps/sec.

Linear Drive

If you don't want to use chopping to get a constant current drive, you can use a circuit like that shown in Figure 7.18. In this circuit, a power opamp, capable of controlling the current required by the motor coils, drives the top of the coil. The voltage across the sense resistor (amplified if necessary) drives the inverting input of the opamp. The opamp will attempt to keep the motor current equal to the reference voltage.

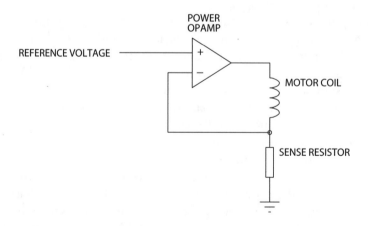

Figure 7.18
Linear constant-current drive.

A circuit like this is electrically quieter than the chopper, but it is much less efficient. The power opamp will dissipate considerable power because it will carry the same current as the motor coil and will usually have a significant voltage drop. The power dissipated by the opamp at any time is given by where V is the supply voltage, Vm is the motor coil voltage, and I is the coil current.

A linear drive like this requires a negative supply voltage. It is possible to build a bridge driver using two opamps that operates from a positive supply and works like the H-bridge, driving one side of the coil positive or negative with respect to the other.

The L297 (Figure 7.19) from SGS-Thompson is a stepper-controller IC. It provides the on-off drive signals to an H-bridge driver such as the L6201 or to a discrete transistor driver design. The L297 controls current in the motor windings using chopping. It has an internal oscillator, comparators, and chopping logic. The oscillator frequency can be set by using an external resistor/capacitor or an external clock. The chopping clock is also used to time turn-on and turn-off of the phases to prevent shoot-through.

The L297 provides four phase outputs (ABCD) and two inhibit outputs for chopping (INH1, INH2). An open-collector HOME signal goes low when the L297 phase outputs are at the home position (ABCD = 0101). The L297 can control a stepper in half or full steps.

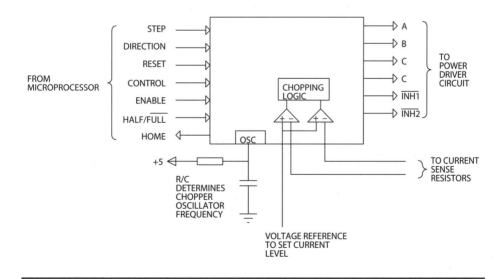

Figure 7.19
SGS-Thompson L297.

DC Motors

Figure 7.20 shows a cross-section of a DC motor, sometimes referred to as a permanent magnet DC (PMDC) motor. A DC motor consists of a permanent magnet stator and a wound rotor. Connection to the rotor windings is made with brushes, which make contact with a commutator that is affixed to but insulated from the shaft. When power is applied, the rotor rotates to align its magnetic field with the stator. Just as the field is aligned, the commutator sections that had been in contact with the brushes break contact and the adjacent commutator sections make contact. This causes the polarity of the windings to reverse. The rotor then tries to align its new magnetic field with the stator. The rotor rotates because the brushes keep changing the winding polarity. The example shown in Figure 7.20 has four rotor arms, four brushes, and four commutator contacts. Some high-performance DC motors do not use wound rotors, but instead print the rotor winding as traces on a printed circuit. This provides a very low-inertia motor, capable of high acceleration.

DC motors do not lose synchronization as stepper motors do. If the load increases, the motor speed decreases until the motor eventually stalls and stops turning. DC motors are typically used in embedded systems with position encoders that tell the microprocessor what the motor position is. Encoders will be covered in detail later in this chapter.

A DC motor is typically driven with an H-bridge, like a bipolar stepper. However, a DC motor requires only one bridge circuit, because there are only two connections to the motor windings. DC motors will typically operate at higher speeds than equivalent stepper motors.

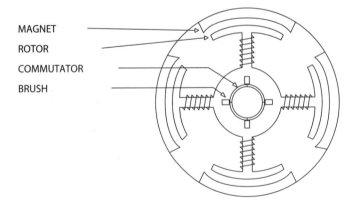

Figure 7.20
Cross-section of PMDC motor.

Analog Interfacing to Embedded Microprocessor Systems

Driving DC Motors

Like steppers, DC motors can be driven with an on-off chopped H-bridge or by an analog driver such as a power opamp. However, where a stepper motor typically uses an analog drive or chopped PWM signal to control motor current, the DC motor driver design does not usually depend on current control. Instead, the DC motor controller provides sufficient current to meet a particular acceleration curve (as measured by the encoder feedback). If the motor has a larger-than-normal load, then the driver circuit will increase the current to force the motor to the correct speed. In other words, the DC motor controller increases or decreases the current to maintain a particular speed. Speed is monitored, not motor current. DC motor control circuits do sometimes sense current in the H-bridge, but it is usually to detect an overcurrent condition, such as occurs when the motor stalls.

Figure 7.21 shows a typical DC motor operation with two different loads. The motor accelerates to a constant speed, runs for a certain time, then decelerates back to a stop. With light loading, the motor current profile is lower than with higher loading. However, the controller applies sufficient current to the motor to produce the required speed/time curve regardless of motor load. For this reason, DC motors are usually better for applications with large load variations.

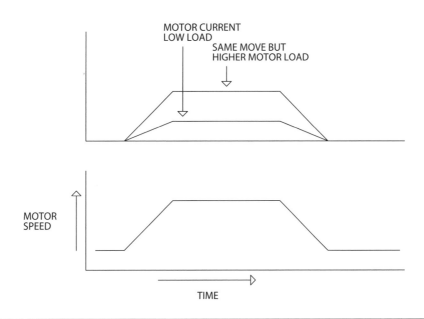

Figure 7.21
DC motor operation with different loads.

One feature of DC motors is the ability to brake them. If you manually turn the shaft of a DC motor, you get a small generator. If you short the terminals of a DC motor, it becomes difficult to turn the shaft because of the electromotive force (EMF) the motor generates when it turns. If you short the motor terminals while the motor is running, it quickly comes to a halt. This is called *dynamic braking*.

Figure 7.22 shows the H-bridge we've looked at before, but with a modification. Here, we have separated the motor control inputs so we can turn each transistor on and off separately. If we take inputs "A" and "D" high at the same time, transistors Q1 and Q3 both turn on and the motor turns in one direction. If "B" and "C" are both high, the other pair turns on and the motor turns in the opposite direction.

Now, suppose the motor is turning and inputs "B" and "D" go low, then inputs "A" and "C" are both driven high. This turns on transistors Q1 and Q4. One side of the motor will be more positive than the other; let's say it is the left side for this example. Current will flow from the positive supply, through Q4, through the motor winding, through D2, and back to the positive supply. The motor is effectively shorted out by Q4 and D2. This will stop the motor quickly. If the right side of the motor is the positive one, the current will flow through Q1 and D3. If we drive inputs "B" and "D" high instead of "A" and "C," we get the same effect, with the current flowing through Q3/D1 or Q2/D4.

Many motor H-bridge ICs include braking capability. These include the L6201 and LMD18200. The L6201 has two inputs to control the two halves of the bridge circuit. If both inputs are brought to the same level (high or low), the driver will brake the motor. The LMD18200 has a separate input signal for braking.

Braking can be used to stop a motor quickly, or to hold it in position. One limitation on dynamic braking as a holding force is that there will be no braking

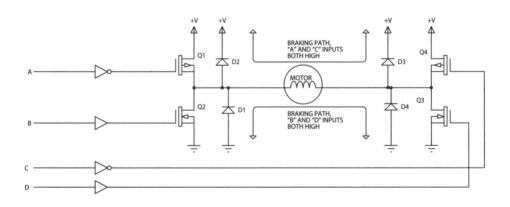

Figure 7.22
DC motor braking.

Analog Interfacing to Embedded Microprocessor Systems

until the EMF generated by the motor exceeds the forward drop of the diode in the braking circuit.

There are ICs that provide a motor drive subsystem for DC motors; we will examine this subject after covering brushless DC motors and encoders.

Brushless DC Motors

Figure 7.23 shows a cross-section of a brushless DC motor. This looks very much like a stepper motor, and in fact a brushless DC motor works much the same way. The stator in this motor consists of three coils (A1/A2, B1/B2, and C1/C2). The coils are connected in a three-phase arrangement, with a common center point. A brushless DC motor is more efficient than a brushed DC motor of the same size. This is because the coils in a brushless DC motor are attached to the case (instead of to the rotor), so it is easier to get the heat generated in the windings out of the motor.

A brushless DC motor functions essentially as a DC motor, but without the brushes. Instead of mechanical commutation, the brushless DC motor requires that the drive electronics provide commutation. A brushless DC motor can be driven with a sine signal, but is more typically driven with a switched DC signal. Figure 7.24 illustrates both drive waveforms. For sinusoidal drive, the current can be controlled with a chopper circuit, or a linear drive can be used. Because the

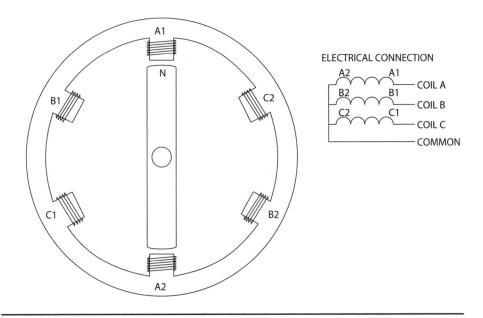

Figure 7.23
Brushless DC motor.

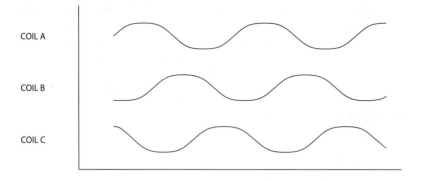

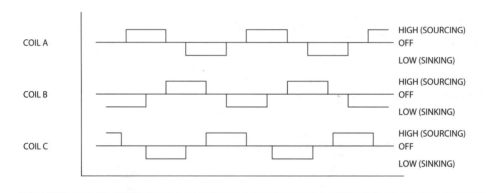

Figure 7.24
Brushless DC motor waveform.

coil positions are 120° apart, the sinusoidal drive waveforms for the coils are 120° apart. The sum of the currents in the three coils is 0. For the switched DC waveform, there are always two phases on (one high, one low), and the third phase is floating (off).

Note that if you use a sinusoidal drive, the driver does not need a negative supply; the sinusoid can swing between ground and a positive voltage (or for that matter, between two different positive voltages). If the drive goes from 0 V to 5 V, when all three coils are at the same voltage there is no current flowing. So the midpoint between the two drive voltages (in this case, 2.5 V) can be picked as a "virtual ground."

For digital drive, the driver circuitry for a brushless DC motor is simpler than for a stepper or brushed DC motor. Because each phase is either high, low, or off (high

Analog Interfacing to Embedded Microprocessor Systems

impedance), an H-bridge is not needed. Instead, the driver circuitry can just be a totem pole output. Figure 7.25 illustrates how two MOSFETs can be used to drive a brushless DC motor. The inputs to this circuit could come from a controller IC or a microprocessor. Note that flyback protection diodes are needed in this circuit.

A brushless DC motor usually has at least one Hall-effect sensor (and more-typically three) to indicate position. However, it is possible to drive a brushless DC motor without any sensors. If you look at the digital drive waveforms in Figure 7.24, you will see that there are always two phases that are on (either positive or negative drive) and one that is off. The moving rotor will generate a voltage in the coil that is not driven. This voltage will cross zero once during the OFF period, and can be sensed to indicate the rotor position. Note that the voltage being measured is the voltage across the unused coil—in other words, the difference between the coil connection and the common connection point for all the coils.

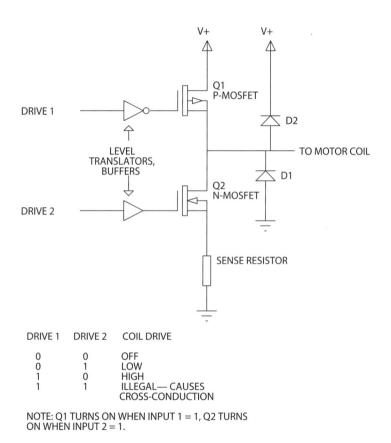

Figure 7.25
Brushless DC motor drive.

Figure 7.26 shows a sensorless drive configuration for a brushless DC motor. This circuit brings the common connection point of the three motor coils back to the ADC circuitry as a reference. This is not always necessary; however, this technique can reduce the noise in the measurement. If the common point cannot be used as a reference, it could be connected to a fourth ADC channel and the value subtracted from the sensed coil in software. If the common point isn't brought out of the motor, you can calculate its value in software if the microprocessor is powerful enough. If the processor isn't powerful enough to perform the calculation in real time, you can calculate the values and put them in a lookup table.

When using the sensorless technique with a microprocessor, you will find that there are noise spikes on the sensed coil when the transistors switch on and off. You can filter this out with capacitors on the sense line, as shown in Figure 7.26, or you can just ignore the samples from the sensed winding during this interval.

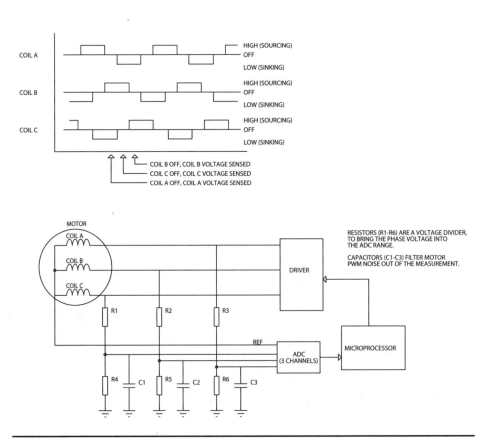

Figure 7.26
Sensorless brushless DC motor drive.

Analog Interfacing to Embedded Microprocessor Systems

There are a number of brushless DC motor drivers that can take advantage of sensorless, EMF-based position sensing. The Philips TDA5140 will drive motors up to about 8A and can use either a sensor or sensorless driving.

Encoders

PMDC and brushless DC motors are usually used in embedded systems with an encoder attached to the shaft. This provides feedback to the microprocessor as to motor position. A typical encoder is shown in Figure 7.27. In this scheme, four magnets are placed around the shaft of the motor and a Hall-effect sensor is placed on the case. The Hall-effect sensor will produce four pulses per revolution of the motor shaft.

Four pulses per rotation of the motor shaft is sufficient to regulate motor speed for a low-resolution application such as a cooling fan. If the motor is geared, so that it takes many revolutions of the motor shaft to produce one revolution of the (geared) output shaft, then this type of encoder is also suitable for more precise applications. However, for cases where you need accurate information about the position of the motor shaft within a single rotation, an optical encoder is normally used.

Figure 7.28 shows a simple optical encoder. A glass disk is printed with opaque marks, 16 in this example. The glass disk is attached to the motor shaft and a slotted optical switch straddles the edges of the disk. Every time an opaque spot passes through the slotted switch, the phototransistor turns off and a pulse is generated. This encoder will produce 16 pulses for every rotation of the motor shaft. The controller can count pulses to determine the angle of the motor shaft and the number of revolutions.

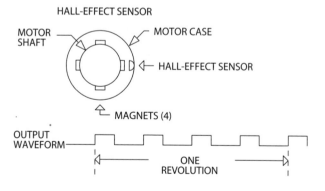

Figure 7.27
Hall-effect motor shaft encoder.

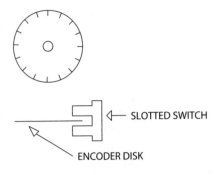

Figure 7.28
Simple motor encoder glass disk.

This simple encoder has one major drawback, common to the simple Hall-effect encoder—how do you tell which way the motor is turning? Figure 7.29 shows a practical encoder arrangement that provides direction information. This encoder still uses a glass disk with opaque stripes, but now there are two slotted switches, located next to each other. The opaque stripe is wider than the distance between the switches. As the opaque stripe moves under switch A, the output (channel A) goes high. As the opaque stripe moves under switch B, that output (channel B) goes high. As the motor shaft continues to rotate, the stripe clears switch A and its output goes low, followed by switch B.

If the motor reverses direction, switch B is covered first, followed by switch A. So this two-channel encoder (called a *quadrature* encoder) provides information on position, speed, and direction. Typical encoders of this type produce between 50 and 1000 pulses per revolution of the motor shaft.

Encoders are also available with an index output, which uses a third encoder and a single opaque stripe closer to the center of the disk. As shown in Figure 7.29, there is a single index stripe, so only one pulse is produced per revolution of the shaft. This allows the system to know the absolute starting position of the motor shaft, for cases in which this is important.

Figure 7.30 shows the pattern for a section of an absolute encoder. The absolute encoder encodes the opaque stripes in a binary fashion so that the absolute position is always known. Of course, this requires as many slotted switches and stripe rings as there are bits of resolution. The figure shows the outer four rings; an encoder with 6 rings would require 6 switches and would divide one revolution into 64 unique codes. An encoder that provides 1024 unique positions would require 10 switches and 10 concentric rings on the encoder disk. Absolute position encoders are extremely expensive. Their primary use is in systems where the position of the motor shaft needs to be known at power-up.

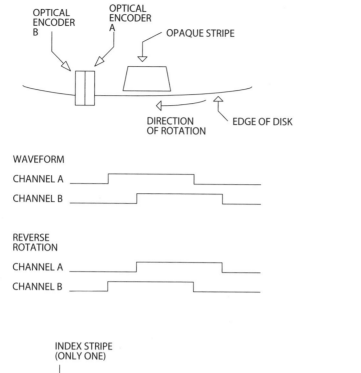

Figure 7.29
Practical quadrature encoder.

DC Motor Controller ICs

There are ICs that are designed for the control of DC motors. The LM628/ LM629 from National Semiconductor are typical devices. Figure 7.31 shows how these two devices would work in a system. The LM628 has an 8-bit or 12-bit output word (selectable) for driving the motor through an analog interface using a DAC. The LM629 has PWM outputs for driving a motor, using PWM,

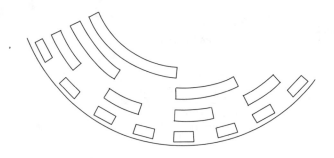

Figure 7.30
Absolute position shaft encoder.

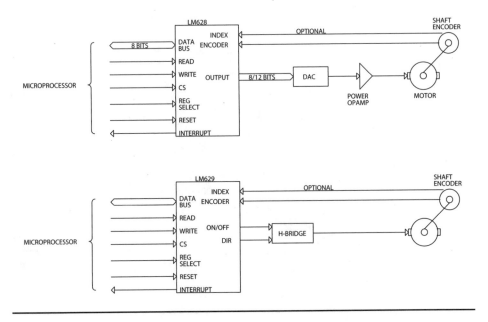

Figure 7.31
National Semiconductor LM628/LM629.

through an H-bridge. Both parts use a similar microprocessor interface. There is an 8-bit data bus, READ and WRITE signals, a chip select, a reset, and a register select signal. The LM628/9 also provides an interrupt output to the microprocessor. The motor interface includes the output (PWM or DAC) and an input for a two-channel quadrature encoder. There is also an input for an index pulse from the encoder if the encoder provides one; this input is optional and need not be used.

Analog Interfacing to Embedded Microprocessor Systems

When connected to a DAC and power opamp (LM628) or an H-bridge driver (LM629), the LM628/9 provides a complete motor control subsystem. The microprocessor issues a series of commands such as "move to position x with acceleration y," and the LM628/9 will execute a trapezoidal move, accelerating the motor to a particular speed, holding that speed, then decelerating the motor to a stop at the right position. (The "position" is a count of encoder pulses, maintained in a 32-bit register.)

The LM628/9 uses two addresses. One address is a command address and the other is for data. A command sequence starts with an 8-bit command opcode, written to the command register by the microprocessor. This is followed by anywhere from 0 to 14 bytes of data, either read from or written to the data register. The commands for the LM628/9 are as follows:

Command	Opcode	Data following
Reset	00	None
Select 8-bit DAC output	05	None
Select 12-bit DAC output	06	None
Define home	02	None
Set index position	03	None
Interrupt on error	1B	2 bytes, written
Stop on error	1A	2 bytes, written
Set breakpoint, absolute	20	4 bytes, written
Set breakpoint, relative	21	4 bytes, written
Mask interrupts	1C	2 bytes, written
Reset interrupts	1D	2 bytes, written
Load filter parameters	1E	2 to 10 bytes, written
Update filter	04	None
Load trajectory	1F	2 to 14 bytes, written
Start motion	01	None
Read signals register	0C	2 bytes, read
Read index position	09	4 bytes, read
Read desired position	08	4 bytes, read
Read real position	0A	4 bytes, read
Read desired velocity	07	4 bytes, read
Read real velocity	0B	2 bytes, read
Read integration sum	0D	2 bytes, read

The LM628/9 index input is intended for use with an encoder that provides an index output. The LM628/9 can capture the encoder position count and store it in a separate register when the index pulse occurs. However, the index input does not have to be connected to an encoder output. I have used the LM628/9 index input to indicate other conditions. For instance, in one system we had a rotating carousel that was connected to the motor shaft via a gearbox. It took many revolutions of the motor to produce one revolution of the carousel. We did not need to know when the motor shaft reached a specific position, but we did need to know when the carousel reached its home position. So the sensor (slotted switch) that indicated when the carousel was at home was connected to the index input.

One caution if you use this technique: the LM628/9 responds to the index input when both the encoder channels are low, so the sensor output has to be low while both encoder channels are low. To avoid multiple index capture events from a single sensor input signal, be sure the index input to the LM628/9 occurs for only one encoder cycle, regardless of how long the actual sensor input lasts. In the actual application, a small CPLD handled the index inputs for multiple LM629s. Figure 7.32 shows how the timing worked.

The interrupt output can be asserted for any combination of various conditions, including a breakpoint, index pulse, wraparound, position error, or command error. The software determines which conditions generate an interrupt, by setting a mask byte in the LM628/9. The interrupt output is level sensitive and true when high. When using the LM628/9 motor controller, there are some software considerations:

- The position registers in the device have a limited size: 32 bits for the LM628/9. This means that if enough forward movements are made, or if the motor continuously rotates, the registers will eventually overflow. The software must

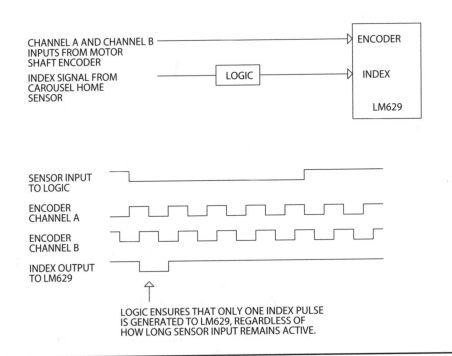

Figure 7.32
LM628/LM629 index timing.

take this condition into account. This is especially true if the software uses, say, 64-bit math. It would be possible, in software, to add an offset to a current position and get an answer that is greater than 32 bits: for example, C017B390 (hex) plus 40000000 (hex) results in a result larger than 32 bits and cannot be stored in the LM628/9 registers.

- When using the index input, the LM629 will capture the count. This becomes, in effect, the "zero" or "home" position of the motor, and all moves are relative to that position. However, the 32-bit position counter is not reset by the index. So the software must offset moves from the index position.
- The fact that the LM628/9 uses two addresses (command and data) means that there is the potential for a race condition. If an interrupt occurs in the middle of a command sequence and the ISR also communicates with the LM628/629, the original command will be corrupted. An example would be an interrupt that notifies the processor that the index pulse has occurred. If the ISR reads the index position, and the interrupt happens in the middle of another command, the non-ISR code will get garbage data. Figure 7.33 illustrates this. To avoid this condition, the software should disable interrupts around non-ISR code (or interruptible ISR code) that accesses the LM628/9.

These restrictions are typical and are not unique to the LM628/9. There are other motor controller ICs available, and all have their quirks. The MC2300 series from Precision Motion Devices (PMD) is a two-chip set that can control up to four brushless DC motors. These parts can control two-phase or three-phase brushless motors and can provide several motion profiles. The MC2300 can provide a digital word for a DAC/amplifier driver, or PWM outputs for an H-bridge.

The MC2100 series, also from PMD, is a two-chip set for brushed DC motors. Like the MC2300, the MC2100 parts support one to four motors, have 32-bit position registers, and support multiple types of motion profiles. Both of the PMD devices are based on a fast DSP that performs the actual motor manipulation.

The Agilent HCTL-1100 is a single-motor controller with a 24-bit encoder counter and PWM or 8-bit digital outputs. The HCTL-1100 does not use an

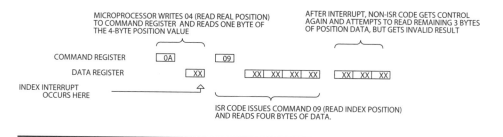

Figure 7.33
LM628/LM629 interrupt timing.

address- and data-register scheme, but instead multiplexes the address signals with 6 of the 8 data lines.

Software Controllers

In some cases, a DC motor might be directly controlled by a microcontroller, using software, instead of using an off-the-shelf controller such as the LM628. Reasons for this include the following:

- **Cost**: An off-the-shelf controller must be coupled with a microprocessor anyway, so why not do away with the controller and just use the processor?
- **Simplicity**: In an off-the-shelf controller, you pay for all the generalized functionality that the part provides. If you need only slow speeds, simple controls, and limited features, you may be able to implement them in software.
- **Flexibility**: You can design the control algorithms to your requirements, instead of just modifying PID parameters. You can also make very deep position registers, 64 or 128 bits for specialized applications.
- **Custom design**: If your system has special requirements, such as special sensors or a move-to-stop-and-apply-pressure for x milliseconds, you can implement this because you will develop and control the algorithms.

If you decide to roll your own controller, there are a few things to consider. The processor has to be fast enough to keep up with whatever processing demands are required. This means also servicing encoder interrupts in a timely fashion. In a software-based controller, the encoder on a DC motor typically connects to one or more interrupt inputs. Figure 7.34 illustrates this. One method of handling interrupts is to let one channel ("A" in the figure) generate an edge-sensitive interrupt to the microcontroller. When the interrupt occurs, the microcontroller reads the state of the other encoder channel ("B" in the figure). If channel B is low, motor motion is forward, and if "B" is high, motion is reversed. For forward motion, the software-maintained position register would be incremented, and for backward motion the register would be decremented.

As shown in Figure 7.34, if there is enough latency between the rising edge of channel "A" and the state of the ISR, channel B may have changed states and the wrong result will be calculated by the firmware. If you implement a motor controller with a system like this, be sure that your interrupt latency never allows this condition to occur, even at maximum motor speed.

It is a good idea to make the interrupt a timer input if one is available. As described in Chapter 4, the timer can be set one count before rollover, and the encoder input will cause the timer to roll over and generate an interrupt. If an interrupt is missed, the timer count will be 0001 instead of 0000 (for a timer that increments starting from FFFF) and the missed interrupt can be detected. The

Analog Interfacing to Embedded Microprocessor Systems

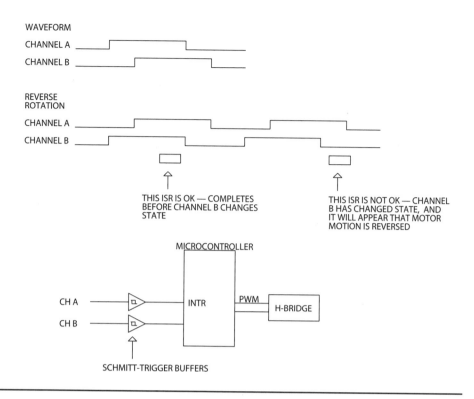

WAVEFORM

CHANNEL A

CHANNEL B

REVERSE
ROTATION

CHANNEL A

CHANNEL B

THIS ISR IS OK — COMPLETES
BEFORE CHANNEL B CHANGES
STATE

THIS ISR IS NOT OK — CHANNEL
B HAS CHANGED STATE, AND
IT WILL APPEAR THAT MOTOR
MOTION IS REVERSED

MICROCONTROLLER

CH A

CH B

INTR

PWM

H-BRIDGE

SCHMITT-TRIGGER BUFFERS

Figure 7.34
Encoder interrupt to microcontroller.

system as shown in Figure 7.34 will have only 1/4 the resolution of a typical system using a motor controller IC, because it captures new position information on only one encoder edge (rising edge of "A") instead of on all four edges. You could compensate for this by using an encoder with more lines, but that could cost as much as a motor controller IC. You can double the resolution of this circuit by connecting both encoder channels to interrupts on the microcontroller. Most microcontrollers permit you to read the state of an interrupt input as if it were a port pin. When an interrupt occurs, the software reads the state of the other input to determine motor direction.

Finally, to get the same resolution as a motor controller IC, you could add an external PLD that generates interrupts on any input transition. This would also let you filter the signals to eliminate spurious edges if necessary.

Another way to get higher resolution in a microprocessor-based controller is to use a microcontroller that can generate interrupts on either clock edge. The Microchip PIC16C series has an interrupt-on-change feature that can generate an interrupt when selected pins change state.

Tradeoffs between Motors

The tradeoffs between DC motors, brushless DC motors, and steppers are as follows:

- Stepper motors require no encoder and no feedback system to determine motor position. The position of the shaft is determined by the controller, which produces step pulses to the motor. However, this can also be a disadvantage. If the load is too high, the stepper may stall and there is no feedback to report that condition to the controller. A system using a DC motor with an encoder can tell when this condition occurs.
- Steppers have no brushes, so they produce less EMI.
- A stepper can produce full torque at standstill, if the windings are energized. This can provide the ability to hold the rotor in a specific position.
- A stepper can produce very low rotation speed with no loss of torque. A DC motor loses torque at very low speeds because of lower current.
- DC motors deliver more torque at higher speeds than equivalent steppers.
- Because there is no feedback, a stepper-based system has no means to compensate for mechanical backlash.
- Brushless DC motors require electronic commutation, which is more complex than the drive required for brushed DC motors. However, the availability of driver ICs for brushless DC motors makes this less of a concern.

Without feedback, there is no way to know if a stepper is really doing what it is told to do. Consequently, stepper motors are typically used where the load is constant or at least is always known. An example would be stepping the read/write head mechanism in a floppy disk drive. The load in this application is fairly constant. If the load varies greatly during operation, a stepper may stall out or it may overshoot the desired position when trying to stop.

If the load varies but is known, a stepper may be useable by reducing the drive current when the load is low and increasing the current when the drive is high. An example of a known load would be a system that has to move something, but sometimes just has to position the motor into the correct position when there is no load. On the other hand, if the "something" that is being moved varies greatly in mass, friction, and so on, then the load isn't really known and a stepper may not be the best choice. When the load varies a lot, and especially if the load isn't known to the controller, a DC motor with an encoder is usually a better choice than a stepper. The encoder allows the controller to increase the current if the speed and/or position are not correct.

One way to achieve the benefits of the stepper and the encoder/feedback DC motor is to add an encoder to a stepper. This provides most of the advantages of both systems, but at higher cost. The maximum speed of such a system will still be slower than an equivalent DC motor, however.

Power-Up Issues

One problem with DC motors is what happens when power is applied. We've already looked at the issues surrounding the power-up state of microcontroller outputs. There are similar issues surrounding any DC motor design, including designs that use packaged controllers.

Typically, the logic that controls the motor H-bridge or analog amplifier operates from 5 V or 3.3 V. The motor power supply may be 12 V, 24 V, or even 50 V. If the motor power supply comes up first, the inputs to the H-bridge or amplifier may be in an invalid state and the motor may jerk momentarily. In a system with a limited range of motion, such as a robotic arm, the motor may slam up against whatever limits the travel. This can be hard on the mechanical components and gears connected to the motor shaft. A DC motor can apply considerable torque in this condition—it is equivalent to a 100% PWM duty cycle.

The best way to eliminate this problem is to ensure that the motor power supply comes on after the logic supply is on and everything is stable. Some multiple-output power supplies have an inhibit input for the high-voltage output that can be used for this purpose. But how do you control the inhibit signal if the power supplies come up together? The logic supply is not available to power the logic that inhibits the motor supply. Some supplies have a low voltage (5 V or 12 V) output that comes up before all the other supplies and is intended for precisely this purpose. This auxiliary output is usually designed to supply minimal current (<100 ma). In some cases, you can just connect the inhibit input on the motor supply to a pull-up resistor from the auxiliary supply (to inhibit the motor supply) and then pull the inhibit input to ground when the logic electronics is stable. Figure 7.35 illustrates a one-transistor approach to this.

If the motor power supply cannot be controlled in this way, it may be necessary to inhibit the H-bridge in some manner, possibly by using a gate between the PWM output of the controller and the PWM input to the H-bridge. Of course, the gate logic has to operate from the motor supply or another supply that is stable when the motor voltage is.

Figure 7.36 shows a method I used in such a situation. The system used a National LMD18200 H-bridge. The LMD18200 has a brake input that is normally used for braking the motor. In this application we weren't using braking, so the brake input pin was available. When the 24 V motor supply is turned on and the 5 V supply is not yet on, the MOSFET is turned off (because the gate is low). A resistor pulls the MOSFET drain up to +24 V, but the voltage is clamped to 4.7 V by a zener diode. This voltage is recognized as a logic HIGH by the LMD18200, which brakes the motor and prevents motion. Some time after +5 V comes up (delay determined by R/C values at gate of MOSFET), the MOSFET gate goes high, the MOSFET turns off, and the motors can operate normally.

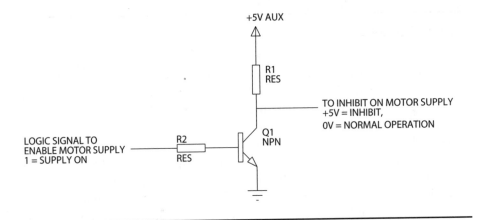

Figure 7.35
Motor inhibit using auxiliary power supply and power supply inhibit.

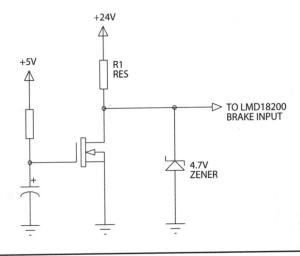

Figure 7.36
Motor inhibit circuit for LMD18200.

Motor Torque

How do you know if the motor you have chosen is powerful enough for the application? How do you know if you've picked a motor that is too big, adding unnecessary cost to the system? Motors are specified with a particular torque, the amount of force they can exert. The Pacific Scientific 4 N series of brushed DC

Analog Interfacing to Embedded Microprocessor Systems

motors is specified with torque ranging from 55 to 163 oz-in (0.39–1.15 N-m), depending on the model. These values are at some specific rated current—6.8 to 14.1 amps in this case. There is also a maximum current that the motor can withstand momentarily. The torque determines how much force the motor can exert and therefore how fast it can accelerate a load to a given speed.

Stall Torque

The stall torque is the torque that the motor will generate if the rotor is locked so that it can't turn.

Back EMF

When you spin a coil of wire in a magnetic field, you generate electricity—this is how the generator in a car works. A DC motor is a coil of wire spinning in a magnetic field. When operating the motor generates a DC voltage, a back EMF, that voltage opposes the voltage applied to make it move. The faster the motor spins, the more back EMF is generated.

Torque versus Speed

The torque of a DC motor falls off with speed. This is due to several factors, including the back EMF. This limits the maximum speed of a DC motor in a practical application and the maximum torque it can generate at a given speed.

A Real-World Stepper Application

A final example will serve to illustrate certain real-time concepts and bringing together some of the concepts described in this chapter. Figure 7.37 shows a microcontroller controlling a five-phase stepper motor. This circuit is a simplified diagram of an actual application that I designed. In this circuit, the microcontroller directly controls the high- and low-side driver transistors for the five stepper phases. This motor controlled an agitator that mixes the contents of bottles for a medical application. The gate drive logic allowed the microcontroller to turn either transistor in the pair on or off, allowing the phase to be driven high, driven low, or allowed to float.

The PWM output is wrapped back around to another timer, which generates an interrupt. This causes an interrupt every T states, where T is the value in the second timer. This interrupt rate is the step rate of the motor; larger values of T result in a slower step rate and higher values of T result in a faster step rate. By

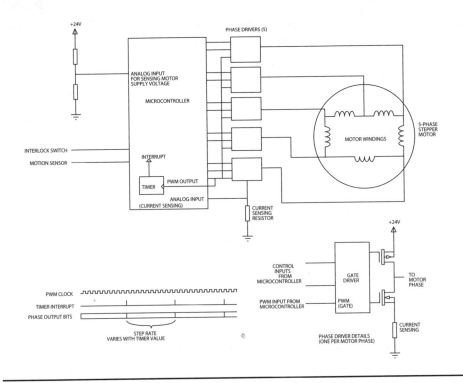

Figure 7.37
Five-phase stepper motor system.

clocking the step rate timer from the PWM timer, the circuit ensures that changes to the output state occur while the drive transistors are turned off.

This circuit has several requirements.

- When the door is closed, the microcontroller will ramp the stepper up to a predetermined speed. If the user opens the door, the interlock switch opens and the stepper ramps down.
- Motor current is controlled by the duty cycle of the PWM output, which chops the current in the low-side MOSFETs. Motor current is increased as speed increases to ensure that sufficient torque is maintained.
- When the motor stops, it must stop in a specific position to allow the operator to add and remove bottles.
- The microcontroller has to monitor motor current, shutting down the motor and generating a fault output if excessive current is drawn. An internal ADC is used for this purpose.
- The position sensor generates a pulse once per revolution; the microcontroller has to count steps from the position sensor pulse to the stopping position. A fault output is generated if a full revolution is made without a pulse from the

Analog Interfacing to Embedded Microprocessor Systems

position sensor. The motor continues to operate in that case, but the stopping position will be undefined and the external system displays a message for the operator.

- The motor has to be ramped up when starting because the stepper motor will stall if the full step rate is applied while the motor is standing still.
- The motor must not start until the motor supply voltage is present. If the motor supply voltage fails, the motor must stop until the voltage is restored. This is handled by providing the motor supply voltage to one of the microcontroller analog inputs via a voltage divider. The microcontroller will not start motor operation until the motor voltage is present.
- Finally, another timer generates a timeout every five milliseconds for debouncing the interlock. This timer does not generate an interrupt, but is polled by the main loop. This is to ensure that the step rate interrupt is serviced immediately, while the PWM output still has the transistors off. If the debounce timer were to generate an interrupt, the code would sometimes be executing the debounce interrupt routine when the step rate interrupt occurred, and this would delay servicing the step rate interrupt.

The system state is based on what the motor is doing:

- Stopped
- Ramping up to speed
- Ramping down to stop
- Running constant speed
- Seeking stop position
- Overcurrent (fault condition, requires power cycle to clear)
- Bad voltage (motor drive voltage not present)

Firmware

The firmware executes a continuous loop, servicing various functions as needed. A simplified description of the various routines follows.
The logic for the main loop looks like this:

If interrupt flag is set, update speed and current.

If 5-millisecond timer times out, debounce interlocks.

If position sensor pulse occurs, reset position count.

Update motor state.

If PWM active, start ADC conversion.

If ADC conversion complete, process motor current.

If position count passes one revolution, set position fault.

Speed and current update logic is as follows:

If motor Ramping Up,

Decrease speed timer value (increases speed).

Increase PWM duty cycle (increases motor current).

If speed timer value = terminal value, change motor mode to Running Constant Speed.

If motor Ramping Down,

Increase speed timer value (decreases speed).

Decrease PWM duty cycle (decreases motor current).

If speed timer value = minimum, change motor mode to Stopped and turn off PWM output.

Motor state update logic is:

If motor drive voltage not present and motor mode not Overcurrent, set motor mode to Bad Voltage.

If motor drive voltage present and motor state = Bad Voltage, set motor mode to Stopped.

If door open and motor Running Constant Speed and no position sensor fault, change motor state to Seeking Stop Position.

If door open and motor Running Constant Speed and position sensor fault, change motor state to Ramping Down.

If door open and motor Seeking Stop Position and position count is at rampdown point, change motor state to Ramping Down.

If door closed and motor stopped, start PWM and change motor state to Ramping Up.

Switch debounce logic is:

If interlock indicates door closed and if door state indicates door open, increment debounce counter 1 and clear debounce counter 2.

If debounce counter 1 = debounce value, change door state to closed.

If interlock indicates door open and if door state indicates door closed, increment debounce counter 2 and clear debounce counter 1.

If debounce counter 2 = debounce value, change door state to open.

Motor current uses the following logic:

If motor current exceeds overcurrent threshold, stop PWM, set motor to Overcurrent, set fault output.

Analog Interfacing to Embedded Microprocessor Systems

Interrupt routine (step rate interrupt) logic is as follows:

Generate the next step in the sequence to the drive transistors (uses a lookup table).

Set a flag to indicate that the interrupt occurred.

Increment the position count.

As mentioned in the pseudocode, the interrupt routine uses a lookup table. The table contains bits for each high-side and low-side transistor; a 1 turns the transistor on and a 0 turns the transistor off. Each entry in the table is the value needed to advance the motor to the next step in rotation. The key real-time requirement for this design is fast, repeatable update of the motor phases. To accomplish this, some tradeoffs were made, such as making the switch debounce timer polled instead of letting it generate an interrupt.

Debugging outputs from the microcontroller included a port bit that was set at the start of the main routine and cleared at the end. Another port bit was set at the entry to the ISR and cleared just before exiting the ISR. Because most port bits were used in the design, these two bits were shared with bits used for in-circuit programming.

Electromagnetic Interference   *8*

Electromagnetic interference (EMI) can be a problem in many designs. EMI is broadly divided into two types: what your equipment does to the world around you, and what the world around you does to your equipment. The first type is called *interference*, and the second type is called *susceptibility*. Of course, susceptibility effects are caused by interference from somewhere else and vice-versa. If you've ever placed a television too close to an operating computer, you've probably seen both: the clocks in the computer create interference that results in snow on the screen of the television.

This chapter will not focus on interference generated by your equipment, except where that interference is self-generated. We will concentrate on susceptibility—what causes it and what you can do about it.

Ground Loops

The term EMI usually conjures images of high-frequency signals interfering with normal circuit operation. However, errors also can be caused by simple AC and DC circuits. The classical case of a ground loop occurs when you have two return paths for ground current and one carries more current than the other. Figure 8.1 illustrates a microprocessor system connected to an external sensor system. The microprocessor ground is connected through its power supply back to the building ground. The sensor system is also connected to the building ground, on a different circuit. Let's say that the sensor ground is shared with some large AC load, such as an air conditioner.

In theory, there is no current flowing in an AC safety ground, but in some cases this current is not really zero. When the AC load is operating, the voltage at the sensor circuit ground is different from the voltage at the microprocessor circuit ground. The result is a ground-loop current flowing through the ground in the

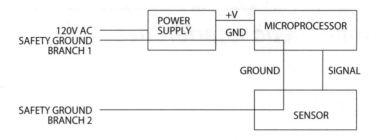

Figure 8.1
Ground loop.

cable connecting the sensor circuit to the microprocessor circuit. Ground loops like this can cause measurement errors or even damage to the electronics. If the potential difference between the grounds gets large enough, it can even burn open the ground connections between the systems. I have seen driver electronics destroyed when a large load (an air conditioner) switched on in a case like this. The resulting ground surge pulled one end of an interconnected system several volts away from the other and blew out the driver ICs.

In the circuit shown, the ground current would probably be an AC current, causing an AC error. A similar situation can occur with DC currents if the DC grounds vary. This situation can also occur with two computers that are connected together with a cable (such as RS-232) but are plugged into different AC branches. The ground connection that causes a ground loop between two systems does not have to be a ground wire in a signal cable. A shielded cable can cause ground loops if the shield is connected to the chassis of both systems.

If you are designing a system that involves components that operate from differing line voltages (such as a 208 V, three-phase machine controlled by a 110 V computer), you might consider using Ethernet between the two systems. Although you may not need the speed of Ethernet, the transformer-coupled cabling eliminates common grounds and most AC ground-induced failures. Another option is to use a fiber-optic interface, which has no electrical connection. If one end of the system is too simple to make a high-speed interface feasible (such as a design that uses a microcontroller), you could use an optically isolated serial interface. You can either buy off-the-shelf RS-232 isolators or define your own optical isolation scheme.

Finally, in some cases, you might be able to specify that one of your system components must have its own safety ground. In large systems that typically require an electrician to come out and wire power, this may be feasible. In the 208 V/110 V example, you would specify that the 208 V equipment have its own safety ground (not shared with anything else in the building). This doesn't protect your equipment from ground spikes on the 110 V line, but it will provide some

Analog Interfacing to Embedded Microprocessor Systems

protection from voltage surges caused by large industrial equipment such as air conditioners. Of course this solution is only as good as the building grounds themselves; in an older building, you may have to improve the grounding where the power enters the building to avoid problems.

Figure 8.2 shows a simple system that is similar to one I worked on. Here, a microprocessor-based system was connected via a cable to a sensor board that had several things on it, among them a thermistor. In this case, the thermistor amplification circuitry was on the microprocessor board, but the thermistor was located remotely, where the temperature needed to be measured.

Say that the thermistor signal to the microprocessor is on the order of 10 mv per °C. The thermistor is at room temperature (25 °C), so the thermistor signal is 250 mv. The problem with this circuit is that the thermistor connects to ground on the sensor circuit board. The sensor signal back to the microprocessor board is a single wire, and there is a single ground wire between the sensor circuit board and the microprocessor circuit. If the sensor circuit draws any significant current, there will be a DC offset between the microprocessor board and the sensor circuit. This introduces an offset to the thermistor signal, affecting the temperature measurement.

Figure 8.3 shows the same circuit, but with resistances in all the lines. These resistors represent the sum of the wire resistance and contact resistance in the

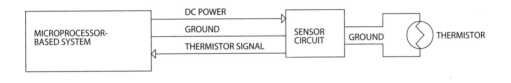

Figure 8.2
Thermistor system.

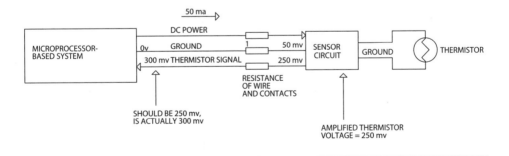

Figure 8.3
Thermistor circuit with wiring resistance shown.

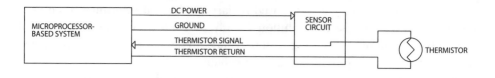

Figure 8.4
Thermistor circuit with separate ground.

connectors. Say that the total resistance in the ground wire is 1 ohm. If the sensor circuit draws 50 ma, then the drop across the ground wire is 50 ma × 1 ohm, or 50 mv.

The result of this is that the thermistor signal, which is 250 mv at the sensor board, becomes 300 mv at the microprocessor board—an error of 5 °C. If the sensor circuit also controls an output, such as a heater that shares the same ground, then the thermistor signal will jump every time the heater is on. This is due to the increased voltage drop across the wiring when the heater turns on and draws current. The microprocessor will respond as if the temperature had actually changed. In addition, the error will vary with the current drawn by the sensor circuit, which in turn varies with components from different manufacturing lots, and so forth.

The solution to this problem is shown in Figure 8.4. Another wire is added to the cable, providing a separate return for the thermistor signal. The thermistor is no longer connected to ground on the sensor circuit board. The added wire can be connected to ground on the microprocessor board, or it can be connected to one side of a differential amplifier. Either way, there is no significant current flowing in that wire, so the voltage offset (and the corresponding error) is minimal. Of course, this solution requires another wire in the cable and another pin on the connector.

In general, it is a good idea to avoid sharing grounds when using any remote, low-level voltage source. Thermistors and millivolt-level signals should have separate grounds to avoid problems with IR drop in the wiring.

Motor Current

Figure 8.5 shows a motor control circuit in which a motor controller drives a PWM driver. The connection to the PWM driver includes the control signals and the ground return. The problem with this approach is that there will be a current spike every time the PWM driver turns on. Because some of the PWM ground current flows back through the controller ground circuit, the current spike will result in a small voltage spike on the controller ground. If this voltage is large enough, the controller logic may interpret it as a level change on the control

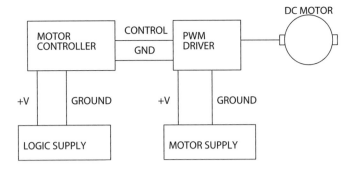

Figure 8.5
PWM motor controller.

signals coming in. In addition, any ADCs on the controller board will see a variation in the ground level, which may affect their accuracy.

This approach can be made to work if the return path has sufficiently low impedance so that the voltage excursions on the ground are minimal. However, if the motor draws significant current and you are also trying to measure anything with millivolt accuracy, it may be impossible to get the grounds quiet enough with this arrangement.

Another approach to this design is shown in Figure 8.6, where the logic supply and motor supply have separate returns connected together at the power supplies.

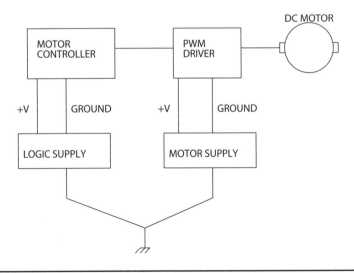

Figure 8.6
Motor controller with separate grounds.

This point is usually the chassis connection point. This arrangement fixes the original problem because all the PWM current is now forced to flow through the motor return, but it introduces a potential new problem. If the wiring resistance is too high, the PWM current spike may cause the PWM controller to see invalid logic inputs as its ground varies with respect to the controller ground. The solution to this is to ensure that both grounds are low-impedance connections. For the motor side, this may mean very large wire gauges or even wire braid. In other words, the wire size may need to be selected to minimize EMI, not just to ensure that it can handle the motor current.

Motor grounding and noise issues often arise because the system aspects of grounding were ignored. In a large piece of equipment with subsystems designed by different teams of people, the grounding is often not consistent. One subsystem may have a connection between its logic return and chassis ground, introducing a ground loop because the chassis ground is repeated elsewhere. In a system such as this, it is a good idea to consider the grounding as a separate system, designed and managed to minimize EMI issues.

Self-Induced Current Errors

If you have a system controlling multiple motors, you can induce ground-offset problems in software. If the software turns on all the motors at once, the resulting current surge can yank the ground far enough to cause problems, even if the ground impedance is fairly low. The solution to this is to sequence motor startup so that the motors don't all start at once, and limit the number of motors that are on at one time (where possible) to reduce the total current drawn. In cases where motor current causes noise in the system that affects ADC measurements, take the ADC readings when motors are off. This will minimize ground-noise-induced errors.

Electrostatic Discharge

Electrostatic discharge (ESD) is the electric spark you sometimes get when you walk across a carpet on a cold, dry day and touch a metal doorknob. This type of high-voltage discharge can destroy electronic circuits. ESD typically has a large amount of high-frequency energy because of the short, pulselike nature of the discharge. Circuits can often be protected against ESD by adding ferrite beads or EMI filters in series with the affected inputs.

Just like ordinary ground loops, ESD can get into your circuits via the grounds. ESD can affect circuits with grounds that are otherwise excellent for carrying their intended current because the ESD energy is high frequency. A good ground at DC is not necessarily a good (low-impedance) ground at RF frequencies. In fact, one way to find grounding problems is to use an artificial ESD generator and zap the chassis of your equipment. The circuits most affected (or most often affected) are often those with grounding problems.

Self-Induced ESD

Any time you have a motor-driven system with belts, pulleys, plastic gears, or other insulating, moving components, you have the potential for self-induced ESD. Depending on the materials used, a belt running over a pulley can be an excellent Van DeGraff generator. Figure 8.7 illustrates a practical system that I worked on that had serious self-induced ESD problems. A plastic band heater was wrapped partway around a rotating drum. Objects to be heated were guided under the heater, and the pressure between the heater and the drum performed a sealing action. The problem was that, somewhere between the prototype and production, someone discovered that they could get better heat transfer by changing the drum material from a conductive to a nonconductive plastic. The result was that, under the right conditions, you could draw a spark a quarter-inch long from the back of the heater band. This caused serious problems with the electronics, including random resets of the microprocessor. If you have rotating drums, pulleys, belts, or other elements, be careful of the materials you choose.

ESD Protection

Figure 8.8 shows how diodes can be used for ESD protection. In Figure 8.8A, two diodes are used to protect an input line against ESD. Diode D1 prevents the signal from rising more than one diode drop above the supply voltage. Diode D2 prevents the signal from falling more than one diode drop below ground. The problem with this approach is that the connections to power and ground have some impedance, and the diodes may be slow to turn on, relative to the rise-time

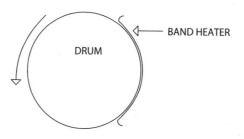

Figure 8.7
Self-induced ESD from insulating, rotating drum.

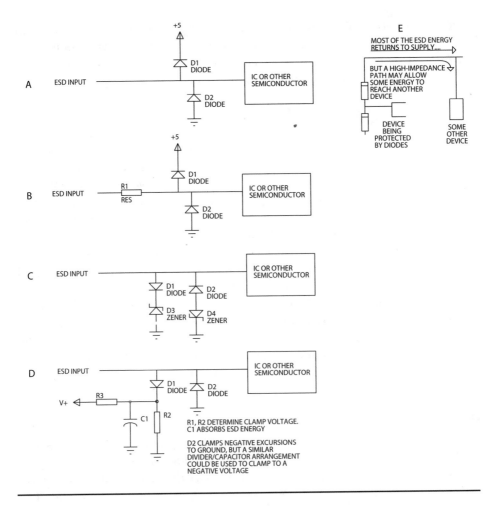

Figure 8.8
ESD protection.

of the ESD pulse. Figure 8.8B shows how the addition of a resistor in series with the signal provides some protection against these effects; because of the capacitance in the circuit, the resistor limits the risetime of the ESD pulse at the junction of the two diodes. In circuits where a resistor cannot be used, a ferrite bead will often work just as well.

The protection diodes themselves must also be able to handle the ESD energy. Where does the ESD energy go? To the place that is often overlooked—the power supplies. The ESD energy will travel through the diodes to either ground or power. If there is insufficient bypassing of the supply or if the PCB traces have too much impedance, the device connected to the input may survive the ESD, but

Analog Interfacing to Embedded Microprocessor Systems

something else may be affected (Figure 8.6E). Most designs use power and ground planes on the PCB, which minimizes this problem, but if you have power or ground traces, be careful about ESD effects. Similarly, if the board with the diodes is at the end of a cable, it is possible for the ESD to yank the board ground around, damaging whatever the board is connected to.

Many of these effects can be minimized with the addition of ferrite beads on the power and signal cables. Of course, you have to consider what the beads will do to the intended signals as well—adding beads to a high-speed video cable may fix the ESD problem, but it will also probably attenuate the desired video signal.

In some cases you cannot clamp to the power supply because even that is too much voltage. A typical example would be an opamp circuit, operating from ±12 V, that is driving a logic-level output. Although the opamp will normally not drive the output beyond the limits of the logic circuitry, an ESD pulse that is clamped to the 12 rails might. An excursion beyond the logic supply voltage could cause latch-up in the logic.

Figure 8.8C shows how zener diodes can be used to clamp the signal to some voltage less than the supply rails. Finally, Figure 8.8D shows how a resistor divider and filter capacitor can clamp the voltage; the capacitor must be large enough to absorb the ESD energy without an appreciable voltage change. This may require a low-value capacitor, around .01 μf, in parallel with a larger electrolytic. The smaller capacitor responds quickly to the ESD pulse, compensating for the limited high-frequency performance of the electrolytic. This technique has the added advantage that the incoming ESD is clamped to ground if the power supply is turned off.

When adding ESD protection, take system considerations into account. Adding protection diodes to the inputs may prevent damage when ESD occurs, but the system may still see an erroneous input. What will the system do in this case? It may be necessary to perform some filtering in software to ignore transient conditions on the inputs. In some cases, you might actually want to reset the system under certain interference conditions. This may require the addition of a watchdog timer to the microprocessor.

High-Precision Applications 9

In this chapter we will look at high-precision applications. *High precision* is not an easy term to define, but for our purposes, we will say that it is any application that requires more than 10 bits of accuracy.

A requirement for high precision usually stems from one of two places: a need to measure very small values, or a need to measure a wide dynamic range. High precision typically translates into more resolution: a 12- or 16-bit ADC instead of an 8- or 10-bit part. However, added resolution brings new problems. A 10-bit ADC with a 5 V range has a resolution of 4.88 mv per ADC step. A 12-bit ADC has a resolution of 1.2 mv per step. Just to pick one example, a signal fluctuation of 3 mv will cause at most a plus or minus 1 count variation in a 10-bit system— which amounts to 2 or 3 counts at 12 bits and 10 counts at 16 bits.

Some of the errors in high-precision applications can be caused by the opamps in the circuit. Figure 9.1 shows a simple noninverting opamp configuration. We can write the basic opamp equation like this:

$$Vo = Av(V_+ - V_-)$$

where Vo is the output voltage, Av is the opamp open loop gain, V_+ is the voltage at the noninverting opamp input, and V_- is the voltage at the inverting opamp input.

Because V_+ pin is connected to the input, V1, and V_- is a voltage divider with Vo and ground:

$$V = \frac{Vo \times R1}{R2 + R1}$$

substituting these values into the basic opamp equation makes the following equation:

$$Vo = Av\left(V1 - \frac{Vo \times R1}{R1 + R2}\right)$$

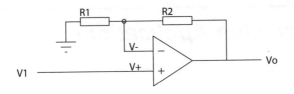

Figure 9.1
Noninverting opamp circuit.

Expanding leads to

$$Vo(R1 + R2) = (Av \times V1 \times R1) + (Av \times V1 \times R2) - (Av \times Vo \times R1)$$

Solving for Vo is performed in the following equation:

$$Vo = \frac{Av \times V1 \times R1}{R1 + R2 + (Av \times R1)} + \frac{Av \times V1 \times R2}{R1 + R2 + (Av \times R1)}$$

Dividing both terms on the right by Av/Av is performed in the following equation:

$$Vo = \frac{V1 \times R1}{\dfrac{R1}{Av} + \dfrac{R2}{Av} + R1} + \frac{V1 \times R2}{\dfrac{R1}{Av} + \dfrac{R2}{Av} + R1}$$

If Av is very large, we are left with

$$Vo = V1 + \frac{V1 \times R2}{R1} \quad \text{or} \quad Vo = V1\left(1 + \frac{R2}{R1}\right)$$

This is the equation normally used for the transfer function of a noninverting amplifier. However, it was derived by assuming that Av is large enough to make anything divided by Av in the previous equation effectively zero. What happens in a practical opamp? The LM318, a low-power opamp, has a gain that ranges from 50,000 to over 200,000. Suppose we have a noninverting amplifier with R1 = 10 K and R2 = 50 K, and V1 is 1.2 V. Using the ideal equations we get an output voltage of

$$Vo = V1\left(1 + \frac{R2}{R1}\right) = 1.2\,V\left(1 + \frac{50K}{10K}\right) = 7.2V$$

Now, if the opamp is an LM318 with a gain of 100,000, and using the nonideal equation, we get this:

$$Vo = \frac{Av \times V1 \times R1}{R1 + R2 + (Av \times R1)} + \frac{Av \times V1 \times R2}{R1 + R2 + (Av \times R1)}$$

$$= \frac{100,000 \times 1.2\,V \times 10k}{10K + 50K + (100,000 \times 10k)} + \frac{100,000 \times 1.2\,V \times 50k}{10K + 50k + (100,000 \times 10K)}$$

$$= 7.199568V$$

This is close to the ideal 7.2 V result, but it is off by $432\,\mu v$. This error would not be a problem in an 8-bit, 0–5 V system, but it is 5 steps in a 16-bit ADC system. The problem gets worse with higher closed-loop gain. Suppose that R2 is 110 K (gain = 12) and the input is 0.6v. The ideal output is still 7.2 V. The actual output with a gain of 100,000 is 7.199136, which is $864\,\mu v$ from the ideal value.

Input Offset Voltage

In an ideal opamp, the output will be 0 any time both inputs are at the same voltage. In a real opamp, the internal transistors are not precisely matched and may not be at exactly the same temperature. This produces an input offset voltage. The input offset voltage of an opamp is defined as the voltage that must be applied across the inputs to produce 0 volts at the output. To see the effect of input offset voltage on an opamp, we will look at the noninverting amplifier again. The equation for the output, when taking offset voltage into account is

$$Vo = Av(V_+ - V_- + V_x),$$

where V_x is the input offset voltage. Adding this new term into the original opamp equations gives

$$Vo = Av\left(V1 - \frac{Vo \times R1}{R1 + R2} + Vx\right)$$

Solving the equations for Vo, and assuming that Av is very large, we get

$$Vo = V1 + \frac{V1 \times R2}{R1} + Vx + \frac{Vx \times R2}{R1} \quad \text{or} \quad Vo = (V1 + Vx)\left(1 + \frac{R2}{R1}\right)$$

As you can see, the offset voltage is multiplied by the same gain factor as the input voltage is (including the effects of real, versus ideal, values of Av). The effect is to introduce an error term into the output. If we use the LM318 opamp again, we find that the data sheet shows an input offset voltage of 4 mv (typical) to 10 mv (maximum). Using the maximum offset and a gain of 6, we get an output offset of 6×10 mv, or 60 mv. This is three ADC steps, or 2 bits of imprecision, in an 8-bit, 0–5 V system. In a 16-bit system, it is 786 steps or 9 bits of imprecision! Clearly, the LM318 is not suitable for a high-precision application.

To be fair, the LM318 is an excellent example to illustrate the offset voltage problem, but it is an older part, originally designed for high speed and low power, not high precision. A better part for precision designs is the Maxim MAX400, with a maximum offset voltage of 10 μv. In our circuit with a gain of 10, the MAX400 input offset voltage would produce an output error of only 60μv. This is less than 1 bit of error even in a 16-bit, 0–5 V system.

Input Resistance

Opamp designs usually assume that the current flowing into the opamp inputs is zero because the input impedance is infinite. A real opamp has some current flowing into the inputs because the impedance is finite. The LM318 data sheet specifies an input resistance from 0.5 MΩ (minimum) to 3 MΩ (typical). Just for simplicity, we will assume that the source driving the noninverting input has a low enough impedance that the current is negligible. This will allow us to examine the inverting input only.

Figure 9.2 shows the effect of input resistance, Ri, from the inverting to noninverting inputs. If we assume that the input resistance is equal to the typical value, 3 MΩ, then the opamp output equation looks like this:

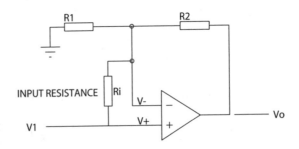

Figure 9.2
Opamp input resistance.

Analog Interfacing to Embedded Microprocessor Systems

$$Vo = \frac{R1Ri + R2Ri}{\dfrac{R1Ri + R2R1 + R2Ri}{Av} + R1Ri}$$

If Av is very large, then the /AV term goes to zero, the Ri term cancels out, and the result is equal to the ideal equation. So the effect of input resistance is dependent on the open-loop gain of the opamp.

The input impedance range of the LM318 is fairly low as opamps go; the MAX400 has an input resistance at least 30 MΩ. Clearly, choosing a better opamp will alleviate errors caused by input resistance. Another approach is to change the impedances; changing to smaller resistors for Rf and R1 will reduce the error caused by input resistance. Of course, this increases the output current of the opamp and may affect other parts of the circuit.

We ignored the input resistance of the noninverting input in this example. If the application calls for connecting the opamp input to a high-impedance source, then the input resistance of the noninverting input must be taken into account; it has the effect of making a voltage divider with the resistance of the source.

Frequency Characteristics

Figure 9.3 shows an approximate, typical, gain-versus-frequency plot for the LM318. The open-loop gain falls off with increasing frequency, approaching 0 dB (gain of 1) at around 10 MHz. As shown before, using actual gain versus ideal gain for the LM318 resulted in a noninverting amplifier with an ideal gain of 6 having an actual gain of 5.99964 (7.199568/1.2). Using the chart in Figure 9.3 to estimate the open-loop gain, we find that it falls from 100,000 at 0 Hz to 3000 at 1 kHz, and to 500 at 10 kHz. If we plug this into the output equation for a 1.2 V input signal, we get the following results:

- Output voltage at 0 Hz = 7.199568 V (gain = 5.99)
- Output voltage at 1 kHz = 7.185 V (gain = 5.98)
- Output voltage at 10 kHz = 7.115 V (gain = 5.93)

Even with an 8-bit system, there are 2 bits of error at 10 kHz. The frequency characteristics of an opamp affect the accuracy in high-precision applications. The effects get worse with higher gain; if the same opamp has an ideal gain of 60 instead of 6 (R1/R2 = 10 K/599 K), then the gain falls to 59.688 at 1 kHz and 54.28 at 10 kHz.

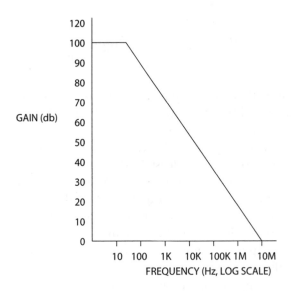

Figure 9.3
LM318 gain versus frequency.

Temperature Effects in Resistors

The value of a resistor changes with temperature. The relationship between resistance and temperature is defined as the temperature coefficient (TC) and is specified in parts per million per degree centigrade (ppm/°C). Typical temperature coefficients for film resistors range from 25 ppm/°C to 100 ppm/°C. The formula for calculating the temperature coefficient is as follows:

$$TC = \frac{R2 - R1}{(T2 - T1)R1} \times 10^6$$

where TC = temperature coefficient, T2 = temperature 2, T1 = temperature 1, R2 = resistance at temperature 2, and R1 = resistance at temperature 1. To find the new resistance at a new temperature, we can rearrange the equation to look like this:

$$R2 = \frac{TC \times R1 \times (T2 - T1)}{10^6} + R1$$

Analog Interfacing to Embedded Microprocessor Systems

Using the noninverting opamp circuit we've been looking at, suppose that the resistors have a 100 ppm temperature coefficient, and the resistors have nominal value at 25 °C. If the 10 K resistor is next to a power IC that raises the temperature of the resistor by 10 °C, what happens? Using the preceding equation, we get a new resistance of 10,010 ohms. This changes the (ideal) opamp gain from 6 to 5.995. The output voltage goes from 7.2 to 7.194 volts—no appreciable effect on the 8-bit system we've been looking at, but a 1-bit error in a 10-bit system, and a 2-bit error in a 12-bit system.

This example is a bit contrived to illustrate the point, because one resistor is considerably hotter than the other. This example does point out that things such as circuit-board layout (how close the 10 K resistor is to a power IC) can also affect accuracy. Moving the 10 K resistor farther from the hot component could reduce this specific error. You could also see this kind of error if the two resistors had different temperature coefficients. Using resistors with lower temperature coefficients will reduce temperature-induced errors overall.

Voltage References

All ADC systems require some kind of voltage reference. All voltage references have some nominal value, but they also have a tolerance that specifies how much they can vary from this value. Because references are semiconductor devices, they are susceptible to temperature effects as well.

The LM336A-2.5 is a 2.5 V reference diode that is used much like a zener is used (Figure 9.4). When operated within its specified current range and at 25 °C, it has a voltage range between 2.44 and 2.54 volts (the B version has a wider range). If an LM336 is used as a reference to measure voltage with an 8-bit ADC, an input of 1 V will result in an output value between 100 (at 2.54 V) and 104 (at 2.44 V). In a 10-bit system, the same 1 V input will result in an output value between 403 and 419.

Figure 9.4 shows what happens in an ADC system using an LM336 with nominal, maximum, and minimum values. At an input voltage of 0, the output code will be 0. As the measured voltage rises, the code read from the ADC diverges from the nominal value by a constant percentage.

Unlike a zener, which has two leads, the LM336 has three leads. Figure 9.4 shows how the third lead can be used to adjust the voltage of the device. In the circuit shown, the adjustment range will be about 120 mv. Of course, this requires a manual adjustment in the system.

Compensation for the voltage variation could also be accomplished in software. If a known, precise voltage is applied to the system, the software can calculate what the offset is. In the example we just looked at, if 1.000 V is applied to a 10-bit

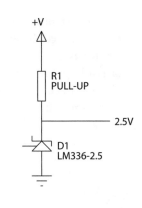

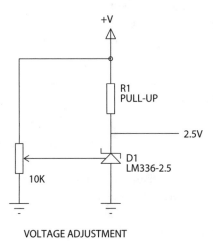

VOLTAGE ADJUSTMENT

Figure 9.4
LM336 voltage reference.

ADC using an LM336 reference, the output value will be 409 if the LM336 is at exactly 2.5 V. If the output is 419, then the software knows that the LM336 voltage is low and that all results should be multiplied by 409/419 or 0.976. If the result is 403, then the results should be multiplied by 1.014.

Of course, many systems cannot implement floating-point calculations, but the same thing can be accomplished with a 1024-entry table. Each value read from the ADC is used as an index into the table to get the corrected value. This has the advantage of requiring the calculation to be made only once, when the table is created, but at the expense of memory usage. Such a scheme requires a calibration step after the product is built, and nonvolatile storage to hold the results. As

Analog Interfacing to Embedded Microprocessor Systems

with any such calibration scheme, field replacement of parts means that the field engineer either must be able to calibrate the system, or the calibration values (microprocessor and/or memory) must be changed if the part of the system containing the reference is changed.

Microcontroller-based designs often do not have any leftover pins to tell the CPU when to operate normally and when to capture a calibration value. If your design uses a pin as an output, you can pull it up with a resistor and use a switch or shunt jumper to ground it. On power-up, the software checks the pin. If the pin is high, it is programmed as an output and the normal code is executed. If the pin is low, it has been externally grounded and the code executes the calibration function.

The LM336 voltage also varies with temperature, typically 30 mv over the range from $-55\,°C$ to $+125\,°C$. This drift has the same effect on the result as the voltage tolerance, but it is temperature dependent.

More precise voltage references are available. The Maxim MAX6225 is a 2.5 V reference with a voltage range between 2.499 V and 2.501 V at 25 °C. The part is available in different versions with temperature coefficients as low as 2 ppm/°C. The MAX6225 also has the capability to add a potentiometer that allows adjustment of the voltage range by about 30 to 50 mv.

Temperature Effects in General

As was already mentioned, the opamp offset voltage varies with temperature, resistor values vary with temperature, and other components vary with temperature, including voltage references for ADCs and opamp biasing. All of these errors accumulate in one direction or another, affecting the overall result.

If the components for a particular high-precision subsystem can be collected in one place, such as one corner of a circuit board, it may be possible to compensate for them in software. You can do this by placing a temperature sensor near the high-precision part of the circuit. The system can then be calibrated at various temperatures, with the software maintaining a table of actual ADC results for a known input at each temperature.

Say you are measuring some input voltage generated by a sensor. You could apply a precise voltage to the input of your high-precision measurement system and then put the system in an environmental chamber where you can control the temperature. The microprocessor measures the input voltage, then measures the temperature. The result is placed into a table. At each temperature point and each input voltage point, a new table entry is made. The results are stored in some kind of nonvolatile memory, such as EEPROM. In operation, every time the system makes a measurement, it also reads the temperature and looks up the actual input value that corresponds to that measurement value at that temperature. If there are a lot of data points, the table will get very large, so you may want to calculate the compensation value instead of using a table. To make use of this technique, you must be able to do the following:

- Ensure that all the high-precision parts of the circuit and the temperature sensor can be collected into one area and are at the same temperature. This may require potting the parts or using a fan. The non-high-precision parts, such as the microprocessor, do not need to be controlled in this way.
- The software must have sufficient storage or throughput to build a table or calculate compensation values.
- Provide precise inputs and hold the temperature during calibration. The results are only as good as the input value and the temperature control. The example just mentioned used a simple voltage monitor to illustrate the concept. In some systems, such as something that measures light or sound, providing precise inputs may be problematical.
- If any components in the high-precision part of the circuit produce significant self-heating, such as power dissipated in a resistor, the results will be less precise.

This technique does not lend itself to large production volumes, due to the need to calibrate every system. And if the sensor is remote, temperature effects at the sensor cannot be compensated this way (but a second temperature sensor mounted with the remote input sensor would permit such compensation).

Noise and Grounding

Figure 9.5A shows a high-resolution ADC and a crystal-controlled oscillator. When the oscillator output switches, current flows through the oscillator ground connection back to the power supply. Because the ground connection will never have zero impedance, the ground connection for the ADC will have a voltage "spike." The size of this voltage pulse will depend on the impedance of the ground connection and the amount of current produced in the ground by the oscillator. The higher the resolution of the ADC, the lower this voltage can be and still cause problems. Even if the ADC is too slow to respond to the individual voltage spikes, the average variation can result in noise in the ADC output. Figure 9.5B shows how the grounding arrangement can be changed to

Analog Interfacing to Embedded Microprocessor Systems

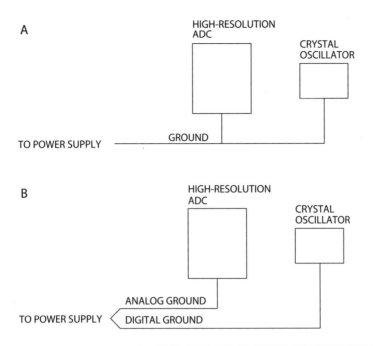

Figure 9.5
Ground noise.

minimize this error. The oscillator has a separate connection back to the power supply. This is typically implemented with a separate ground plane for the analog circuitry, connected to the digital ground plane either at the ADC ground pin or at the point where the power supply connects to the board. A single-point connection minimizes the amount of digital current that can flow in the analog ground plane.

This example used an ADC, but the same principles apply to DACs, sample-and-hold circuits, and opamps. Most high-precision circuits will need a separate ground plane for analog signals. Sometimes multiple analog ground planes, for different analog sections, are required.

Finally, some ground noise immunity can often be gained simply by amplifying the signal you are trying to measure. If you are measuring with a 12-bit ADC, going from 0-to-100 mv to 0-to-2.5 V changes the ADC step size from 24.4 μv to 610 μv. With a 100 mv range, a ground offset or noise signal of 24.4 μv will result in a 1-bit error in the result. With a 2.5 V range, the noise/offset has to reach 610 μv to produce a 1-bit error. Of course, any noise or offsets that appear on the inputs will be scaled by the same amount, but any noise added to the signal after the scaling (such as ground noise on the ADC) will not.

High-Precision Applications

Printed Circuit Board Layout

The layout of the printed circuit board (PCB) is important in any analog system. Poor board layout can result in ground loops and noise. As resolution goes up, these add more to the error.

PCB Grounding

This has been mentioned already, but you generally want to avoid having any current flowing in the analog ground except what is associated with the analog signals. If digital signals flow through the analog ground, they will induce noise on the grounds of the analog parts such as the opamps and ADCs. In some cases, you have to supply power to a PCB at the end of a cable. The cable resistance can cause significant offset in low-level analog signals if the current is high. For high-resolution applications, use a separate analog ground plane and add a separate analog ground to the cable. This means at least one extra pin on the connector, but it minimizes the offset caused by DC currents.

Some noise coupling into analog systems comes from capacitive coupling between traces. Run analog traces at right angles or at 45° to digital traces. Use two analog ground planes and sandwich the analog traces between them. If an analog trace must run next to a digital trace, move it as far away as possible and run a ground trace between them.

An ADC must have both analog and digital sections, and many ADCs have both an analog and a digital ground pin. Keeping digital noise out of the analog part of the circuit is a key factor in high-precision designs. Many ADC data sheets say to connect the analog ground to the digital ground at the digital ground pin. But what do you do if your design requires two ADCs? You can't have two single-point connections to a single ground plane.

Figure 9.6 shows two ways of handling this. In Figure 9.6A, a board has a digital ground plane and two analog ground planes. Each analog ground plane has a single-point connection to the digital ground plane. This approach will work if the two analog sections have no common connections.

Figure 9.6B shows a method you can use if the two analog sections have some common signals such as a common ground. A single analog ground plane is tied to the digital plane at one point. In this arrangement you will typically connect the ADC digital grounds to the digital ground plane, not to the analog ground plane.

Power Supplies

An analog circuit sometimes has to be designed into a circuit board for a standard bus, such as PC/104 or VME. The power supplies on these buses are often not

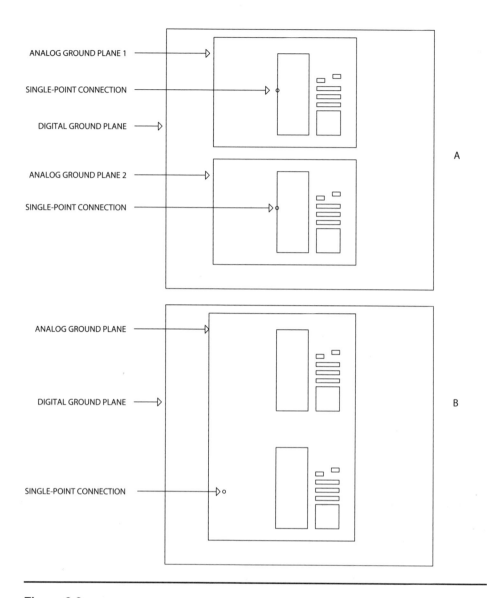

ANALOG GROUND PLANE 1

SINGLE-POINT CONNECTION

DIGITAL GROUND PLANE

ANALOG GROUND PLANE 2

SINGLE-POINT CONNECTION

A

ANALOG GROUND PLANE

DIGITAL GROUND PLANE

B

SINGLE-POINT CONNECTION

Figure 9.6
Multiple analog devices on a single PCB.

suitable for analog components. They are often noisy, and you don't always get the voltages you need. Many computer systems, such as PC/104, operate with 5 V only, or with 5 V and 12 V only.

In some cases, you can fix a noisy supply by adding LC filters, as shown in Figure 9.7A. The inductor and capacitor must be selected to filter out the power-supply switching frequency, which is usually in the tens of kilohertz. In some

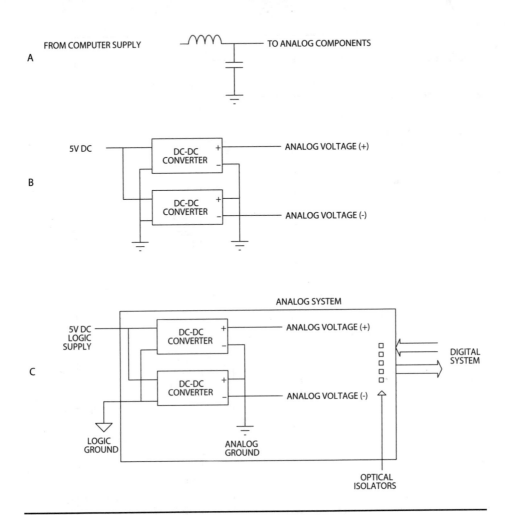

Figure 9.7
DC-DC converters in analog circuits.

applications you need different voltages than the voltage supplied on the bus to which you're interfacing. An analog input that has to accept ±12 V inputs but is operating from a 5 V only system is a typical example. Figure 9.7B shows how DC-DC converters can be used to produce additional voltages. Because the DC-DC converter is a switching supply, you may need to filter these outputs.

It is also possible to completely isolate the analog subsystem from the digital system to which it interfaces. Figure 9.7C shows the use of DC-DC converters with isolated outputs and an analog ground that is separate from the digital ground. This system might include a precision analog front-end and an ADC to convert the analog signals to digital. Optical isolators are used to communicate between

Analog Interfacing to Embedded Microprocessor Systems

the analog and digital systems, making noise management easier and avoiding the possibility of ground loops between the two systems. You can minimize the number of optical isolators needed by using a serial interface such as SPI and using the bidirectional technique described in Chapter 3. Note that when you are testing and debugging such a system, your test equipment should not connect the two grounds together or you may introduce noise problems. An example of this would be the use of a dual-channel oscilloscope with the two probes grounded to the two different grounds.

Statistical Tolerancing

When determining the worst-case range of values in an analog circuit, you can use the specified extreme limits of the parts to guarantee a good design. If you are using 1% resistors, assume that the actual resistor values your manufacturing line receives will span the full range and that a worst-case stackup will occur eventually. This results in the safest design, but it may result in unnecessary complication. For instance, calculating the worst-case tolerance stackup may result in a design that requires manual adjustment.

Most components you use in your design will not have an equal probability of occurring in every value. In most cases, the distribution of values will fit some variation of the normal (bell) curve. If you are using 1% resistors, you will find that most of the resistors you get are closer to the nominal value and very few resistors differ from nominal by 1%. How wide the spread is depends on the process used by the manufacturer.

If you are calculating tolerance stackup for a circuit containing multiple parts, the probability of getting all the values skewed at the ends of their respective ranges is small. The more parts there are, the smaller this probability is. You can estimate the percentage of circuits that will be out of tolerance by taking into account the tolerance ranges and distributions of all the parts in that specific circuit. There are simple statistical methods for determining the resulting spread of values, such as the sum-of-squares method. A more complex analysis such as a Monte Carlo simulation can be performed using statistical software packages.

Statistical tolerancing depends on the parts that go into the tolerance stackup having distributions across their ranges and also depends on the distribution of one part not affecting the distribution of another part. Therefore, to make statistical tolerancing work, the following things must be true:

- The components you are combining must be independent. For instance, if you have two resistors of the same value, it is very possible that, in production, they will come from the same manufacturing batch and therefore may be very close to each other in value. These could not be considered independent parts.

- The components you are tolerancing should have some reasonably normal distribution. For example, suppose that you are using a voltage reference diode and suppose that the manufacturer selects out the ones that are very close to the nominal value for sale at a higher price under a different part number. The parts you will be left with will not be normally distributed, but will be skewed toward the ends of the tolerance band.

When you have finished the calculations, you will have an estimate for the range of values that will be produced in your circuit as a result of the range of component values that go into it. You can calculate what percentage of the parts will fall outside the acceptable limits. Then you have to make a decision.

- If you are building an inexpensive board, you may be able to throw away any boards that are outside specification. This, of course, implies a way to measure the assembled circuits so you know when one is outside spec.
- If you are building an expensive board costing hundreds or thousands of dollars, it may not be feasible to throw away any bad boards. In that case, you have to decide whether statistical tolerancing is worth the cost. For example, you may have to choose between reworking 4% of your boards and having a manual adjustment on all of them. Which is cheaper in terms of manufacturing and support costs?

In making these decisions, true worst-case tolerancing is always the safest approach. However, statistical methods often give acceptable results at lower cost.

Supply-Based References

This book has used as examples supply-based references such as an internal microprocessor ADC that has the +5 V supply as a reference voltage. For consistency, this chapter has done the same thing in many cases. However, in a real-world high-precision application, it is rare to find a logic supply used as a reference. In most systems, the logic supply is noisy and is not regulated well enough to serve as a reference for ADCs or opamps. Again, it was used here so that the examples would be consistent with those found elsewhere in the book.

Analog Interfacing to Embedded Microprocessor Systems

Summary

To summarize, in a high-precision application you need to consider the effects of all the following factors:

- Opamp open-loop gain
- Opamp input offset voltage
- Opamp input resistance
- Opamp frequency/gain roll-off
- Temperature effects in resistors
- Temperature effects in voltage references
- Grounding
- PCB layout
- The possibility of isolating the high-precision part of the system

Standard Interfaces   *10*

Most embedded systems interface to sensors and output devices directly. However, there are a couple of standard interfaces used in industrial applications. Devices meeting these specifications are usually attached to an industrial computer (industrial PC) or a programmable logic controller (PLC). They are briefly covered here, because the embedded designer may run into them somewhere along the way.

IEEE 1451.2

The IEEE 1451.2 is an open standard that provides a standard interface for sensors and actuators. IEEE 1451.2 defines the electrical and interface protocol. IEEE 1451 sensors and actuators contain an embedded microprocessor on a module called a Smart Transducer Interface Module (STIM). The STIM microprocessor handles the physical interface to the sensors and the standard interface to the controlling system. Each STIM can contain up to 255 sensors or actuators.

Electrical

IEEE 1451 is a 10-wire, synchronous, serial interface. Signals include +5 V, ground, data-in and data-out lines, a clock, an interrupt, and other signals. IEEE 1451 STIMs are hot swappable, meaning they can be inserted and removed with power applied. Each IEEE 1451 STIM can support multiple transducers or actuators.

Transducer Electronic Data Sheets

IEEE 1451 specifies that each STIM have a transducer electronic data sheet (TEDS) This tells the controlling system certain parameters about the transducers on the module, including upper and lower range limits, warm-up time, calibration information, and timing information. The specification also includes additional TEDS parameters that are optional, some that are sensor specific, and some that are reserved for future extensions to the standard.

Standard Units

Information passed from an IEEE 1451 STIM must be in standard units. The actual sensor may be measuring temperature, voltage, current pressure, velocity, or any other real-world parameter. Whatever is being measured is converted to a standard unit before it is transmitted to the controlling processor via the IEEE 1451 interface. The IEEE 1451 standard permits sensors to support the following units:

- Length (in meters)
- Mass (in kilograms)
- Time (in seconds)
- Current (in amps)
- Temperature (degrees kelvin)
- Amount of substance (mole)
- Luminous intensity (candela)
- Plane angle (radians)
- Solid angle (meters^2)

Whatever unit the sensor measures in must be converted to these standard units. A sensor may be measuring speed in miles per hour or furlongs per fortnight, but it must be converted by the STIM microprocessor to meters per second before transmission over the IEEE 1451 interface.

When the controlling processor reads sensor data from an IEEE 1451 sensor, what gets transmitted is a string of exponents, one for each of these values. The velocity-measuring example just given would output a positive exponent for meters and a negative exponent for seconds, making a meters/second result. All the other exponents would be 0 (anything to the 0 power, except 0, is 1). The standard also provides for digital data from a sensor or to an actuator.

Although this method complicates the software in the STIM microprocessor, it provides a standard interface for the controlling processor. In theory, any IEEE 1451 STIM can be attached to any IEEE 1451 controller and it will work.

4–20 ma Current Loop

The 4–20 ma standard (Figure 10.1) uses the same pair of wires to power a remote sensor and to read the result. The controlling microprocessor, usually an industrial PC or other industrial computer, provides a voltage on a pair of

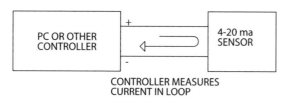

CONTROLLER MEASURES
CURRENT IN LOOP

Figure 10.1
4–20 ma current loop.

wires. The controller also senses the current in the wires. The sensor converts whatever it is measuring (temperature, velocity, etc.) to a current value. The sensor draws 4 ma at one end of its measurement range, and 20 ma at full scale.

Because the 4–20 ma loop is differential, the system is suitable for sensors that are removed from the controller by quite a distance. Any common-mode noise is ignored by the current measurement circuit. One drawback to this method is the need for a pair of wires and sensing circuitry for every sensor in the system.

Fieldbus

Fieldbus is a digital, serial, two-way communications system that interconnects measurement and control equipment such as sensors, actuators, and controllers. Conceptually, Fieldbus provides a means to replace point-to-point connectivity of 4–20 ma sensors with a mutidrop connection that can communicate with multiple sensors over a single communication path (Figure 10.2). The Fieldbus specification describes a layered model, including the physical connection layer, a data link layer, and application layers.

Fieldbus uses twisted-pair wiring. A single pair of wires provides both power and data communication. Fieldbus devices draw power from the wiring, just as 4–20 ma devices do. Data transmission is performed by changing the current drawn by the transmitting device; the current swing between 0 and 1 is 20 ma. The data rate is 31250 bits per second using Manchester encoding. Manchester encoding always has a transition in the middle of the bit; one of the advantages of Manchester encoding is that the average DC value of the signal pair is zero because the bits are always high for 50% of the bit period and low for 50% of the period. The relatively low data rate permits very long cabling runs, which is important in large factory and plant control environments. Figure 10.2 shows Manchester encoding for one and zero bits, and for a bit string of 0110.

Fieldbus communication uses a combination of polling and token passing. Bus masters poll devices on the bus for information, and a Fieldbus device can

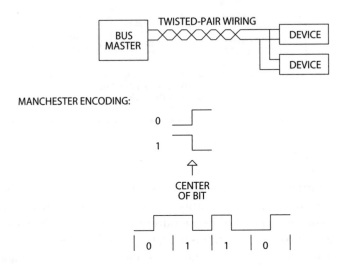

Figure 10.2
Fieldbus.

transmit only when polled. If the bus has multiple masters, control of the bus is managed by a "token" that is "owned" by one master at a time. When a master is finished using the bus, it sends a message to the next master, handing off control of the bus to that master.

Available Fieldbus peripherals match those available in 4–20 ma format, and include such devices as pressure sensors, temperature sensors, flow measurement sensors, and controllable valves.

Analog Interfacing to Embedded Microprocessor Systems

Analog Toolbox   11

This chapter contains some miscellaneous topics and topics that pull together multiple concepts from preceding chapters.

Microcontroller Supply and Reference

Chapter 2 mentioned the effect that supply voltage can have when used as a reference for microcontroller-based analog inputs. In many cases, you can minimize these effects by referencing your analog inputs to the supply voltage. Figure 11.1A shows a thermistor connected to an analog input and using a pull-up to a precision reference voltage. At first glance, it might appear that this is a very accurate design because the precision reference gives a repeatable voltage versus temperature at the analog input. The problem with this design is that the microcontroller is measuring the temperature using the supply voltage as a reference, so the overall accuracy is only as good as the micro-controller supply voltage.

Figure 11.1B shows the same circuit, but with the thermistor referenced to the microcontroller supply. This provides a more repeatable result. If the thermistor is 10 K and R1 is 10 K, for example, the analog input to the microcontroller will always sense half the supply voltage regardless of what the supply voltage actually is. This method will work only if the analog input can be made to follow the supply voltage. This essentially means that the output being measured by the microcontroller is referenced to the supply. Note that just powering the sensor or sensor circuit from the microcontroller supply may not be sufficient. If the sensor circuit has its own internal reference that controls the output value, it will produce the same output regardless of variations in the supply voltage.

An alternative compensation method, for cases in which the input is independ-ent of the microcontroller supply voltage, is shown in Figure 11.1C. In this

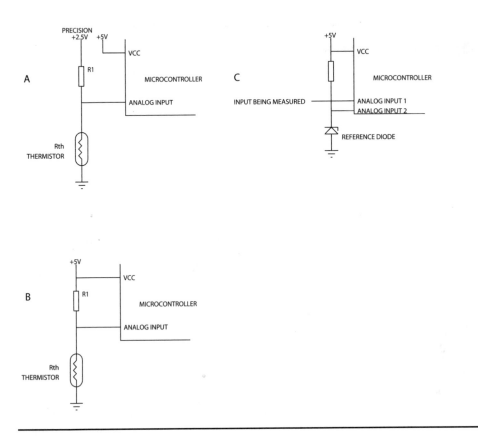

Figure 11.1
Microcontroller supply reference.

figure, a second analog input is used to measure the value of a precision reference diode. Of course, the microcontroller must have at least two analog inputs to take advantage of this technique. In operation, the microcontroller would use the reference diode to determine the error caused by the supply voltage. For example, if the reference diode is 2.5 V and the supply voltage is 5 V, the reference diode will produce a value of 80_{16} (128 decimal) when the voltage is converted (assume the internal ADCs are 8 bits). If the supply is 4.8 V, the reference diode will convert to a value of 85_{16} (133 decimal). The microcontroller can use this value to correct the values from the independent input. In this case, the values read from that input will be multiplied by 128/133, or 0.96, to get the correct reading. Note, though, that the overall accuracy is only as good as the combined accuracy of the reference diode and whatever reference the external input is using. Finally, to make use of this technique, the microcontroller must have sufficient throughput to make the required calculations and memory to hold the math algorithms; this may be a problem on some small microcontrollers.

Analog Interfacing to Embedded Microprocessor Systems

Resistor Networks

Some applications need better repeatability than you can get with standard 1% resistors, but don't need the level of precision (and cost) of going to 0.1% resistors. Sometimes you can gain an advantage by using resistor networks. Resistor networks are typically specified with the same resistance tolerances as discrete resistors: 0.1%, 1%, and 5%. However, the matching between resistors within the same network is often twice as good as the absolute resistance accuracy. If your circuit uses multiple resistors of the same value, you can often get better accuracy by using a resistor network rather than discrete parts. Note, though, that this works only for resistors in the same package; it doesn't work across packages.

Figure 11.2 shows a simple voltage divider. This circuit might be used to bring an analog input that swings between 0 and 8 V down to the 0 to 5 V range used by a microcontroller analog input. In the figure, both resistors are 10 K. Ideally, the output voltage would be half the input voltage. However, if the resistors are 1% discrete parts, the output voltage may not be exactly half the input.

Say that R1 is high by 1% and equals 10,100 ohms, and R2 is low by 1% and equals 9900 ohms. The output is given by the following equation:

$$\text{INPUT} \times \frac{\text{R2}}{\text{R1} + \text{R1}} = \text{INPUT} \times 0.495$$

which is incorrect by 1%, the tolerance of the resistors.

Now, say that R1 and R2 are resistors that are in the same resistor network package. The specified resistance is 1%, but the part-to-part variation is 0.5%. If R1 is high by 1%, it will be 10,100 ohms, as before. However, because parts within the

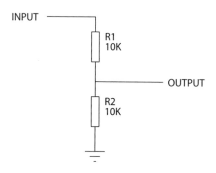

Figure 11.2
Resistor voltage divider.

network package can only vary by 0.5%, R2 cannot be less than 10,049.5. As a result, the output will be

$$INPUT \times \frac{R2}{R1 + R1} = INPUT \times 0.4987$$

which is within 0.25% of the ideal value.

Multiple Input Control

In some cases a system will have multiple inputs. For example, you might be controlling a telescope that is taking pictures of clouds. For some reason (perhaps to protect sensitive optics coatings), you don't want to aim the telescope at the sun (Figure 11.3). In this case, one of the inputs would be the position of the sun, probably determined by the date and time of day. You would also have as inputs the telescope's current position and the desired position.

This is a good example of a two-input problem, because the position of the sun is not fixed. You can't just use a table to look up the move path because the position of the sun varies. To move the telescope without crossing the path of the sun, you can take two approaches.

The first approach is to calculate the direct path, determine that it crosses the sun's path, then calculate a new path that just misses the sun. This is illustrated in Figure 11.3A and 11.3B. This calculation may be complicated and time-consuming, especially on a microcontroller or other system with limited capability.

A simpler approach is to calculate the position of the sun and then calculate a path that remains as far as possible from the sun. One way to do this is to divide the telescope range into a grid of, say, 8 or 16 regions. When calculating the move path, any region overlapped by the sun is avoided. A typical example is shown in Figure 11.3C. Figure 11.3D shows how the move area can be subdivided into 16 regions.

Another alternative would be to find a sunless path to the perimeter of the motion circle, and then determine which way to move around the circle to avoid the sun. In the example shown, either direction would work, but if the sun were on the perimeter of the motion circle, the direction would have to be determined.

You could make the path decision table driven by having two move paths from any region to any other region. One path would be a straight line and the other path would avoid any region in common with the first path. In this way, you could

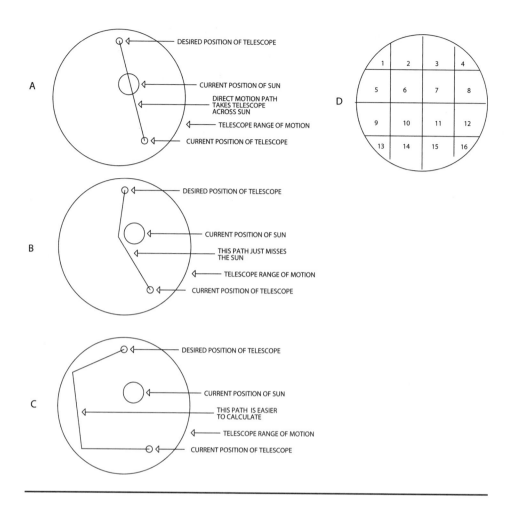

Figure 11.3
Telescope pointing example.

determine a safe path by checking the straight line move for "interference" from the sun. If the straight line path goes through a region containing the sun, just pick the other path. Once in the target region, calculate a straight line move to the desired point. This method has the advantage of minimizing calculation requirements for simple processors.

The foregoing assumes that the system requirements don't include taking photos of any region containing the sun. If you did have to take photos right next to the sun, you could make the regions smaller or you could have multiple paths from any region to any other, arriving at the destination from different directions.

Although the telescope example is very specific, the general principles are applicable to many similar multiple input problems, such as

- Multihead fluid pipetting systems in which the pipettes can interfere with each other
- A heating system in which the maximum safe heater power depends on a fluid level
- A stepper motor with resonance points that depend on the load
- A valve control system in which valve closing/opening speed depends on fluid viscosity and flow rate—variable closing/opening time might be required to avoid "water hammer" or similar effects
- A heater or cooler system in which the intent is to quickly get the target to a specific temperature and where the amount of heating or cooling applied depends on the size and initial temperature of the target

Another example of multiple input systems is the need to adjust system parameters based on an input. In Chapter 5, a heater example was mentioned. In this example, the proportional (or PID) control had an offset. This offset had to be adjusted for varying loads and ambient conditions. A large load or very cold ambient temperature might need a larger offset to maintain the temperature. In a case like this, additional sensors may be needed to measure these parameters. The system could calculate parameters such as the offset and/or gain, or a set of tables could be used to select the values based on the values of the additional input parameters.

AC Control

Some designs require control of AC power to turn on lights, motors, heaters, or other AC devices. The simplest method of controlling such devices is with solid-state relays (SSRs), as shown in Figure 11.4. An SSR consists of an optoisolator driving an SCR or triac. The internal optoisolator is selected by the manufacturer to ensure that it will be capable of driving the SCR or triac. Some SSRs have heatsink plates on the back that need to be bolted to a metal chassis or heatsink to avoid overheating the SSR.

In many cases you need to perform *zero crossing switching*. This consists of switching the load only when the AC signal crosses zero (Figure 11.5). If the AC signal is switched when the voltage is not zero, then the load will see a sudden jump in the applied voltage instead of a smooth sine wave. This can damage some loads. In addition, the fast rising edge causes considerable EMI. Finally, in some cases, the load will draw excessive current if the AC voltage is suddenly applied and the value of the voltage isn't zero. You can get solid-state relays that have zero crossing built in. These parts include circuitry that turns on the SCR or triac only when the AC voltage is zero.

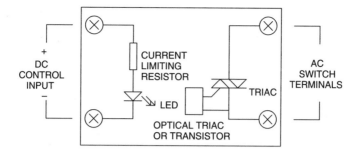

Figure 11.4
SSR.

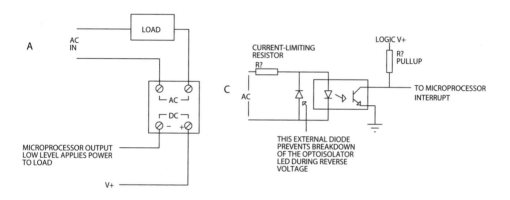

Figure 11.5
SSR control.

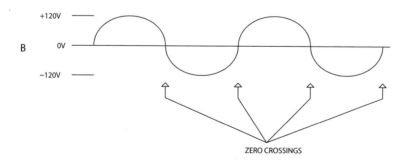

In some cases, you need to perform the zero crossing detection in software. Figure 11.5C shows a way to do this; an optoisolator is connected, with a current limiting resistor, across the AC line. Each time the AC voltage goes through zero, the optoisolator turns off and an interrupt is generated to the microprocessor. All switching of external AC loads is performed in the ISR. Typically, to get fast response, the software outside the ISR will set flags or semaphores to determine what AC outputs should be turned on. The ISR reads the flags and switches the appropriate outputs on; the ISR does not do whatever processing is required to determine what should be off or on, it just switches the outputs. This provides minimum latency between the interrupt and the output switch.

Note the external diode across the optoisolator LED. This diode conducts during the negative half of the AC cycle, preventing excessive reverse voltage across the optoisolator LED.

Voltage Monitors and Supervisory Circuits

A number of ICs are available that provide voltage monitoring functions for microprocessor circuits. An example is the Texas Instruments TL7770. The TL7770 has two voltage comparators that can monitor either of two voltage inputs. Generally, these devices work by asserting a microprocessor reset when the supply voltage reaches some predefined value (1 V for the TL7770), and then remove the reset when the monitored voltage has been above a preset threshold for some predefined period of time. This ensures that the microprocessor is held in reset until the supply voltages are stable.

Although many supervisory ICs are intended for monitoring multiple microprocessor supplies, they can be used to monitor other voltages as well. Typically, one input would be used to monitor the microprocessor supply and the other would be used to monitor a higher voltage such as that used to drive a motor. In some cases, you will need to use resistive voltage dividers to bring the voltage you want to monitor within the range of the supervisory IC.

Driving Bipolar Transistors

A bipolar transistor is often used as an output driver for a microprocessor. Figure 11.6A illustrates how a transistor can be used. When the microcontroller output pin is high, it sources current into the transistor base and the transistor turns on.

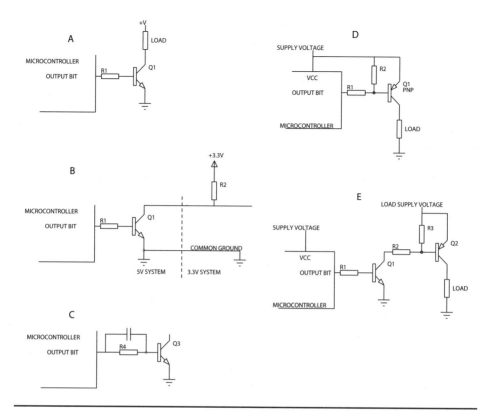

Figure 11.6
Driving bipolar transistors.

When the output is low, the transistor turns off. The requirements for driving a bipolar transistor from the output of a microcontroller are

- Voltage output from the microcontroller must be high enough to turn the transistor on, typically greater than 0.8 V.
- Current into the base of the transistor must be high enough to saturate the transistor.
- Current into the base of the transistor must be limited to a value that will avoid damage to the transistor.
- Low-output voltage of the microcontroller output must be low enough to ensure that the transistor turns off. This is typically not a problem unless the output must sink significant current.

  The current into the base of the transistor is calculated as

$$\frac{\text{Logic high voltage} - \text{transistor } V_{be}}{\text{Base resistor}}$$

(In the figure, R1 is the base resistor.) The logic high voltage is the value of the output voltage for the logic used. It may vary with the load, so a logic output that nominally swings to the supply may deliver less voltage if it cannot supply adequate current. The transistor base-emitter voltage, Vbe, is typically 0.6 V to 0.8 V.

Whether the transistor can pull its collector close enough to ground to function as a logic output depends on the load and the base drive. The maximum collector current is approximately equal to the base current times the current gain of the transistor, up to the point at which the transistor saturates. A signal transistor might have a gain of 100, so a few ma of base current can switch a few hundred ma of collector current. A large power transistor may only have a gain of 10 or 20, so it is difficult to drive them directly from the microcontroller outputs—there isn't enough gain to ensure that the transistor is saturated when driving a high-current load. Consequently, driving very high current loads typically requires a signal transistor driving the base of a larger power transistor.

The simplest approach to using bipolar transistors is to set the base current at half or less of the maximum rated base current. If this does not provide sufficient collector current for your application, or if you calculate the required base current and find that it exceeds what the microcontroller can produce, then you are trying to switch too much current. Use another type of driver.

Finally, remember that the gain of transistors tends to vary quite a bit from one lot to the next, so don't build a circuit that depends on very high gain transistors unless you are willing to sort them in production.

Logic Level Translation

Bipolar transistors provide a convenient means to pass signals between two systems at different supply voltages. Figure 11.6B shows a transistor used to connect a 5 V microcontroller and a 3.3 V external system. The collector of the transistor is pulled up on the 3.3 V system through a resistor.

Switching Speed

One problem with driving bipolar transistors directly from the output of a microcontroller (or other logic) is speed. When the transistor is saturated, the base-emitter junction exhibits a characteristic known as *stored charge*. This, in effect, acts as a capacitor, making the transistor slow to turn off when the logic input goes low. In addition, the output of the transistor circuit (the collector) does not have an active pull-up to force the output high. Instead, a resistor pulls the output high when the transistor turns off. Consequently, the risetime of the output is dependent on the transistor switching speed and the capacitance in the collector circuit. If the transistor is connected to another board via a long cable, this capacitance can be significant.

The turn-on and turn-off speed of the transistor can be improved with the addition of a capacitor across the base resistor, as shown in Figure 11.6C. The capacitor is a low impedance when the logic output is changing states, rapidly charging or discharging the base circuit. A typical value for this capacitor is 220 pf, although larger values may be needed for large transistors.

The collector risetime can be reduced by reducing the value of the pull-up resistor. However, smaller resistor values increase supply current drain and transistor dissipation. Also, a smaller pull-up resistor means more base current is needed to ensure that the transistor will be saturated. These techniques will make a transistor circuit switch faster, but a discrete transistor design will never be as fast as a driver or interface IC designed for a specific application. Bipolar transistors find primary use in controlling currents or voltages beyond the capability of the microcontroller/microprocessor itself.

High-Side Switches

In some cases, you need to pull an output up instead of clamping it to ground. Figure 11.6D shows a PNP transistor used in this way. The PNP is wired with the emitter connected to the positive supply voltage (the NPN had the emitter grounded), so pulling the base toward ground turns the transistor on. The resistor between the base and emitter of the transistor ensures that the base goes all the way to the supply, turning the transistor completely off, in case the microcontroller output doesn't quite swing all the way.

The same considerations apply as for the NPN transistor in terms of the base current. The base current in this case is at maximum when the microcontroller output is low.

In some cases, you need to supply current from a higher supply voltage than the microcontroller is using. For instance, a 5 V or 3.3 V microcontroller may need to switch the 12 V supply to a motor. Figure 11.6E shows how a PNP and NPN can be used together for this. The NPN transistor isolates the microcontroller from the high voltage on the base of the PNP transistor.

Driving MOSFETs

Like bipolar transistors, MOSFETs also provide a means to control voltages and currents outside the range of the microcontroller. The simplest MOSFET drive is shown in Figure 11.7A. Here, a microcontroller output directly drives the MOSFET gate. When the microcontroller output is high, the MOSFET is turned on and

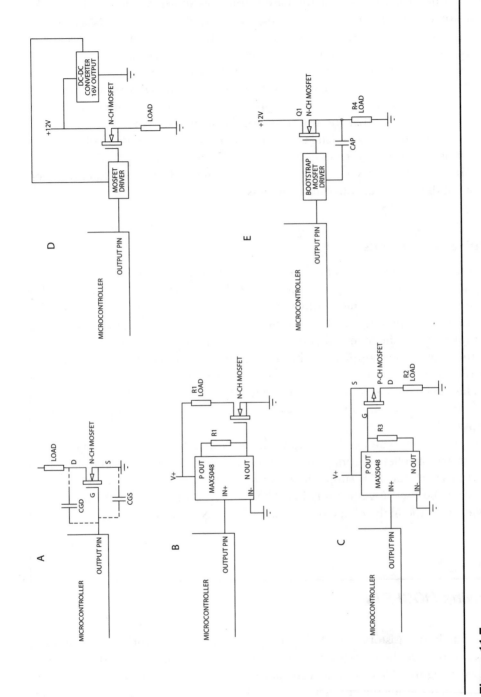

Figure 11.7
Driving MOSFET transistors.

sinks current. When the microcontroller output is low, the MOSFET is turned off. The key points to remember in driving a MOSFET in this way are

- The output voltage of the microcontroller must be greater than the MOSFET gate-to-source threshold voltage or the MOSFET will not turn on. This is more of a problem with 3 V logic than with 5 V logic, but either logic voltage requires the use of a MOSFET with a logic-level threshold voltage. If necessary, a pull-up resistor can be added to the logic signal to ensure that it goes all the way to the supply voltage.
- The MOSFET has significant gate-to-source and gate-to-drain capacitance, shown as Cgs and Cgd in the figure. Generally, the larger the MOSFET, the greater this capacitance is. If the MOSFET is driving a signal that can have large voltage spikes, such as an inductive load, sufficient voltage can be coupled back into the microcontroller to damage the outputs.
- The MOSFET turn-on time is limited by the speed at which the gate-to-source voltage rises. This in turn is determined by how quickly the microcontroller can charge up the gate-source capacitance. Many microcontroller outputs have very limited output current capability. If the MOSFET turn-on time is too long and the switching frequency is high, the MOSFET will dissipate excessive power as it transitions from cutoff to saturation.
- If a pull-up resistor is needed to ensure adequate turn-on voltage, the turn-on time of the MOSFET will be limited to the risetime of the pull-up resistor in combination with the gate-source capacitance of the MOSFET. Because the current sinking capability of the microcontroller output limits the size of the pull-up resistor, the switching speed of the MOSFET is also limited by the same current sink capability.

Many of these problems can be eliminated by using a MOSFET driver IC, as shown in Figure 11.7B. In this circuit, a Maxim MAX5048 is used to drive the MOSFET. The MAX5048 provides logic level inputs and can operate on supply voltages up to 12.6 V. The MAX5048 has separate sourcing (P-channel) and sinking (N-channel) outputs. In the figure, resistor R1 is not needed. If R1 were not used, the P output and N output would be tied together and to the gate of the FET. R1 in series with the P output limits the risetime of the gate, and thereby the turn-on time of the FET. If the gate of the FET is connected to the P output instead of to the N output, then R1 will limit the fall time of the gate and thereby the turn-off time of the FET.

High-Side Switching

In some cases, you want to source current instead of sinking current. The simplest way to do this is with a P-channel MOSFET, as shown in Figure 11.7C. In this circuit, the MAX5048 is used to drive the P-channel output transistor. Note that the P-channel MOSFET has the source connected to the positive supply and the gate must be driven toward ground to turn the transistor on.

The problem with P-channel MOSFETs is that they tend to be more expensive than equivalent N-channel MOSFETs and they usually have a higher ON resistance, causing the transistor to dissipate more power when turned on. In some applications, the gate-to-source capacitance can couple the load voltage into the MOSFET gate, turning it on when it should be off. This typically occurs with inductive loads or when there is another transistor pulling the load to ground when the P-channel MOSFET is off. For these reasons, N-channel MOSFETs are usually preferred for high-side switching applications.

The primary difficulty in using an N-channel MOSFET for high-side switching is the gate drive voltage. To turn the N-channel MOSFET on, the gate must be driven higher than the source; because the source is connected to the load in a high side application, this means the gate must be driven higher than the positive supply voltage.

In most cases, the MOSFET is used to drive the load from the highest voltage available in the system, so there is no higher voltage available to drive the MOSFET gate. You have two choices in this case: you can use a bootstrap MOSFET driver or you can add a DC-DC converter.

The DC-DC converter is the simplest solution, as shown in Figure 11.7D. You add a DC-DC converter to the board and use a MOSFET driver IC. The output of the DC-DC converter must not exceed the maximum gate-source voltage, or the MOSFET may be damaged. In the figure, a DC-DC converter with a 16 V output produces the gate drive voltage for a driver IC. The gate of the MOSFET will switch between ground and 16 V, and the load will switch between ground and 12 V. Note that the gate drive voltage cannot exceed the gate-to-source breakdown voltage, which is typically 18 V for a MOSFET.

A boostrap MOSFET driver IC can also drive a high-side MOSFET, as shown in Figure 11.7E. A bootstrap driver uses a capacitor (external to the IC) that is charged up to the supply voltage when the load is low. If the circuit is being used to drive a high-side switch, with no low-side driver, the capacitor charges through the load. If the circuit is being used to drive a pair of MOSFETs, one providing high-side drive and one providing low-side drive, the capacitor charges through the low-side MOSFET when it is turned on.

When the high-side driver is turned on, the bootstrap capacitor is switched so that it drives the gate of the MOSFET above the supply voltage to turn it on. Typically, the bootstrap capacitor is much larger than the gate-source capacitance of the MOSFET, so the voltage across the capacitor does not drop very far when driving the MOSFET gate. However, once the high-side MOSFET is turned on, there is no longer a charging path for the bootstrap capacitor, so it will eventually discharge. For this reason, bootstrap circuits are normally used in applications in which the MOSFET is continuously switching. If you need to turn the MOSFET on and leave it on, you will need a DC-DC converter or some similar method.

Reading Negative Voltages

Sometimes you need to read and convert a negative voltage with an ADC that operates only from ground and a positive supply. Sometimes the only way to accomplish this is to use an opamp, powered from both positive and negative supplies, to shift the signal to a range the ADC can use.

Figure 11.8 shows a simple resistor voltage divider that will accomplish the same thing, with some limitations. In the figure, the input is a sine signal that swings between -2 V and $+2$ V, being read by a microcontroller that operates from $+5$ V and ground. Using a voltage divider (R1 and R2) brings the signal within the 0–5 V range of the microcontroller ADC input. With the values used in the figure, the signal swing is 1.5 V to 3.5 V. There are a few limitations on this technique:

- The voltage divider essentially acts as a resistive pull-up to the supply voltage. This may affect the input signal.
- The voltage swing is reduced; in the figure, a 4 V P-P signal is reduced to 2 V P-P at the microcontroller ADC input.
- Large resistors may be needed to avoid loading the input signal source. Large resistors, coupled with the input capacitance of the microcontroller, limit the speed.
- If the input can occasionally go negative enough to bring the microcontroller input below ground, the microcontroller may be destroyed. The maximum

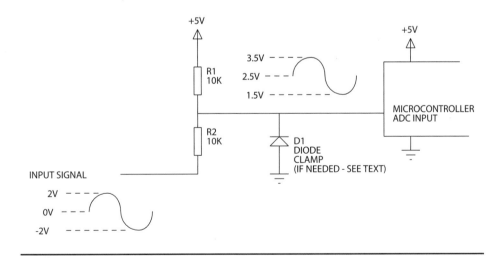

Figure 11.8
Resistive divider for reading negative input signals.

signal excursion must be known, or a diode, as shown in the figure, must be used to clamp the signal to ground.

- The actual voltage produced at the microcontroller input is dependent on both the input signal voltage and the supply voltage. Variations in the supply voltage will affect the ADC reading.

Example Control System

To illustrate some of the principles described in previous chapters, an example control system was developed. This concept system is easy to build and is useful for experimenting with control concepts. Figure 11.9 shows a block diagram of the system. The control system is simulated with an inexpensive lamp coupled to an infrared phototransistor. The lamp and phototransistor are held in place with a length of heatshrink or other opaque tubing.

A PWM circuit is used to control the current through the lamp. The prototype used for the examples here operated at about 14 kHz. An analog control could also be used, with a DAC followed by an opamp capable of delivering sufficient

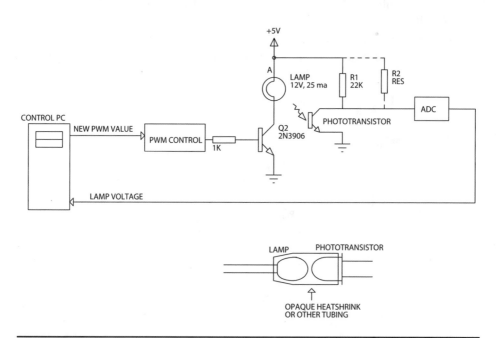

Figure 11.9
Simulation system block diagram.

Analog Interfacing to Embedded Microprocessor Systems

current to the bulb. The ADC was an 8-bit converter, with an output value of 0 representing 0 V and a value of 255 representing 5 V.

The system is controlled by a PC, although the same arrangement could be controlled by a microcontroller or single-board computer. Using a PC is less precise than using a more hardware-oriented approach, because the sampling rate in a PC will vary with operating system activity. However, it is close enough to make a useful experimentation tool. For the examples used here, the code was written in Python. The actual Python code is shown in Appendix D.

This simple arrangement provides a good simulation of a control system. The lamp filament is, in effect, a heater. The lamp filament does not heat up instantly and the phototransistor is relatively slow, so the combination has many of the characteristics of a real heater or motor arrangement.

In Figure 11.9, R2 is shown with dashed connections. R2 is installed in parallel with R1 to simulate an external load, as will be described later.

Note that this is a reversed control system—a higher control value results in a lower ADC value because a hotter filament results in more phototransistor current.

Figure 11.10A shows the step response of the system. This waveform was created by starting with a PWM value of 1 (just barely turning the lamp on) and then changing to a PWM value of 250 (almost 100% on) and sampling the resulting voltage from the phototransistor once per millisecond. Note that the lamp has a short delay before it starts heating, then a rapid heating period, then a slower curve as it approaches its final temperature. This data was plotted using Microsoft Excel.

Figure 11.10B shows the reverse of the positive step. Here, the PWM value was set to 250 and the output was allowed to settle for one second. The PWM was then turned off and the output was measured once per millisecond. The result is an exponential curve as the lamp filament cools. This asymmetrical characteristic of the system is typical of many real-world environments.

Figure 11.10C shows the characterization of the system with respect to the control value. This curve was made by applying 16 equally spaced control values from 1 to 241, allowing the output to settle, and measuring the ADC result.

On-Off (Bang-Bang) Control

An on-off control is illustrated in Figure 11.11A. The setpoint for this example was 100, corresponding to about 1.95 V at the phototransistor collector. Note the oscillation around the setpoint—it ranges from 98 to 112, a range of 0.3 volts, or 15% of the setpoint value. The oscillation is not centered around the setpoint, but is skewed toward the high values. This occurs because the control

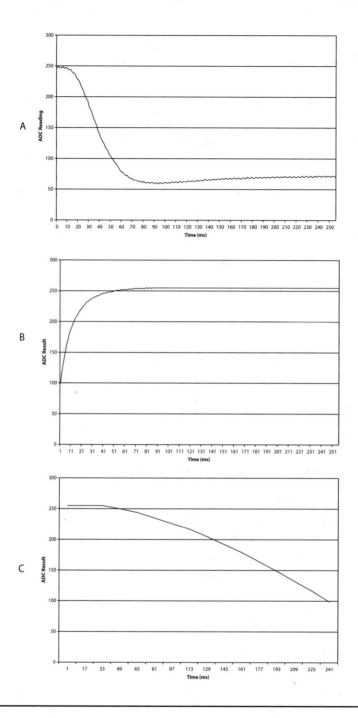

Figure 11.10
Simulation system characterization.

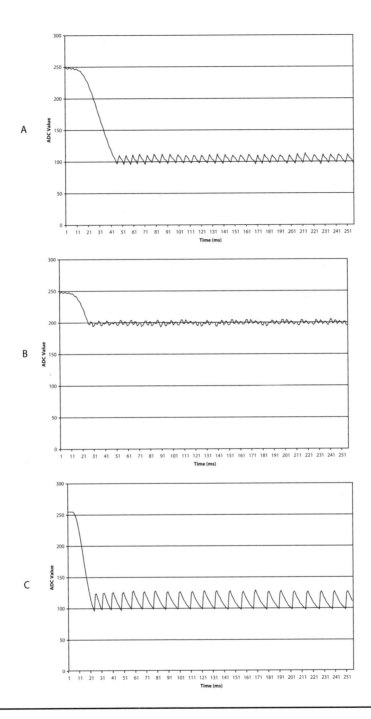

Figure 11.11
On-off control examples.

response is not symmetrical—the filament cools down more quickly than it heats up.

Figure 11.11B shows an on-off control with a setpoint of 150. There is less oscillation at this setpoint; a control system that is not linear across its range will exhibit characteristics like this. Figure 11.11C shows an on-off control with a setpoint of 100 and a sampling interval of 4 ms. Note the size of the oscillation; the sampling interval has a significant effect on the result.

Figure 11.12 shows an on-off control starting with the PWM full on and using a setpoint of 150. Unlike the case that started with the PWM off, there is significant overshoot past the setpoint; the lamp filament cools down more easily than it heats up, so there is more momentum in that direction.

Proportional Control

Figure 11.13A shows a proportional control with a setpoint of 150 (about 2.9 volts) and a gain of 2. Using the input-to-output characterization curve, an offset of 200 was selected for this setpoint. The equation for the control value is

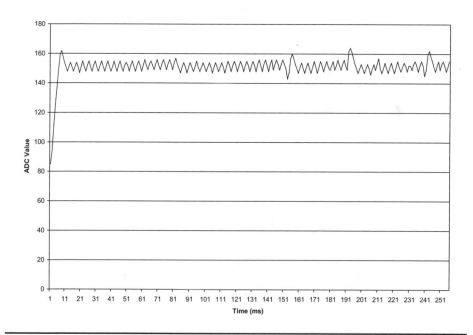

Figure 11.12
On-off control, starting with PWM 100% on.

Analog Interfacing to Embedded Microprocessor Systems

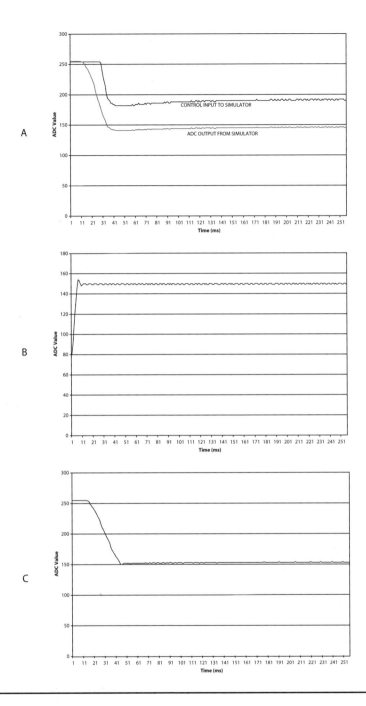

Figure 11.13
Proportional control.

$$\text{Control output} = 200 + (\text{ADC value} - \text{setpoint}) \times \text{Gain}$$
$$\text{If control output} > 254, \text{control output} = 254.$$
$$\text{If control output} < 1, \text{control output} = 1.$$

The last two statements limit the control value to the 8-bit range of the system.

At a gain of 2, the system stabilizes with an output around 145. Figure 11.13B shows a proportional control, but starting at the top of the range (100% PWM) and using a gain of 20. This time the result makes it to the setpoint of 150, but with significant oscillation. Note the overshoot as the signal passes through 150; like the on-off example, this is caused by the asymmetrical nature of the heater and the additional gain. If the gain is reduced, the overshoot can be eliminated, but the result ends up below the setpoint (150). Although a graph is not shown for this condition, at a gain of 10, the waveform overshoots just slightly and then settles down to oscillate between 149 and 150.

Figure 11.13C shows a proportional system with a gain of 10, setpoint of 150, and an offset of 100. The lower offset results in a final result between 157 and 158. As you can see, the gain and offset both affect the final result in a proportional system. However, the proportional control is still better than open-loop control, because an open-loop control value of 100 results in an ADC value of 222 (see the characterization chart).

Figure 11.14 shows the proportional system with a setpoint of 150, gain of 10, and a load of 47 K (R2) in parallel with the 22 K collector resistor (R1). There is a small overshoot as the output passes 150, then the output settles down to oscillate between 152 and 153. Note that the addition of a load caused a permanent offset in the output—the proportional system was unable to completely compensate for the effects of the added load.

PID

Figure 11.15A shows a simple PID control. The parameters are

- Proportional gain = 2
- Derivative gain = 2
- Integral gain = 2
- Setpoint = 150

To prevent integral windup, the integral is held at zero until the ADC result is within 10% of the setpoint. As you can see, there is a little overshoot and then the output settles down to values of 150 and 151. Figure 11.15B shows the integral and derivative terms. Note that changes (edges) in the integral waveform

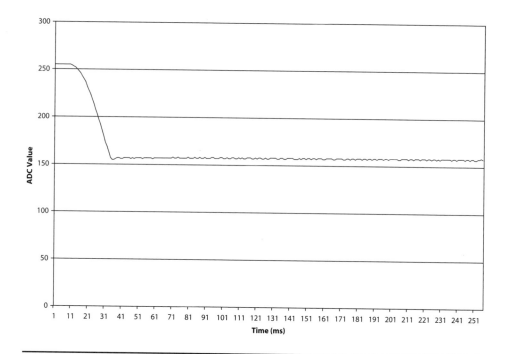

Figure 11.14
Proportional control with load.

correspond to a positive and negative transition in the derivative waveform, because the derivative is measuring the amount that the error changed from the previous sample.

Figure 11.16A shows what happens if the derivative gain is set to 40; a high-frequency oscillation occurs, although it is centered on the setpoint. In Figure 11.16B, the derivative gain is set to 2 again, and the integral gain is set to 40. This condition causes an oscillation between about 135 and 172, and at a lower frequency than the oscillation caused by the large derivative value. This is typical of PID control systems—excessive derivative gain and excessive integral gain both cause oscillation, but the oscillation caused by the integral gain is at a lower frequency.

Figure 11.17A shows the following conditions:

- Proportional gain = 4
- Derivative gain = 2
- Integral gain = 2
- Setpoint = 150

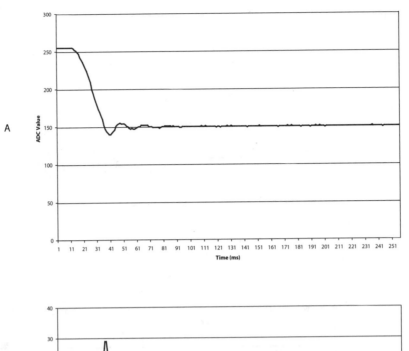

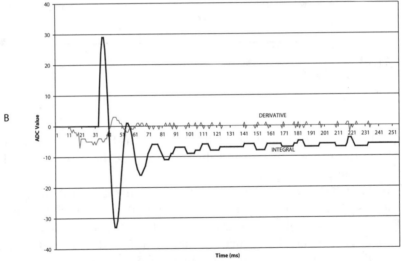

Figure 11.15
PID control with integral and derivative waveforms.

The result is a very smooth waveform with good control at the setpoint. The waveform in Figure 11.17B uses the same parameters, but adds a 47 K resistor (R2) in parallel with the 22 K resistor R1. The important thing to note here is that the final value still reaches the setpoint, although there is a "knee" in the waveform around sample 37.

Analog Interfacing to Embedded Microprocessor Systems

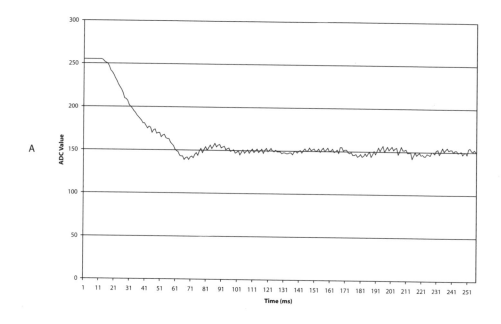

A

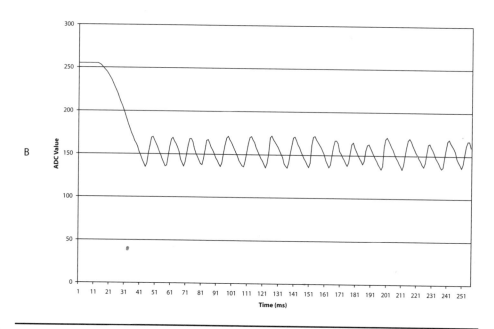

B

Figure 11.16
PID control with large derivative and integral values.

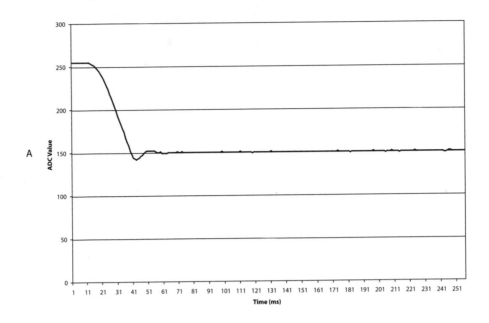

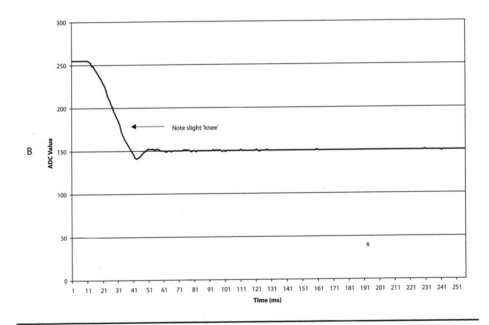

Figure 11.17
PID control with load.

Proportional-Integral Control

Figure 11.18 shows a proportional-integral control only, with proportional gain = 4 and integral gain = 0.1. The waveform overshoots to 140, which is past the value of 145 that was reached with the proportional-only control, but the integral eventually brings the result up to the target value of 150.

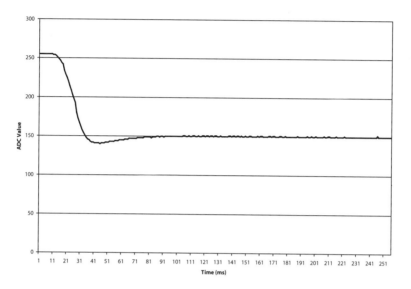

Figure 11.18
Proportional-integral control.

Appendix A
Opamp Basics

The opamp is a very high-gain amplifier with two inputs and an output. One input is called the inverting input (V_-), and the other input is called the noninverting input (V_+). The formula for the output (Vo) is given by:

$$Vo = Av(V_+ - V_-)$$

where Av is the gain of the opamp (usually very high—over 100,000) and V_- and V_+ are the voltages at the inverting and noninverting input pins.

Opamp Configurations

Figure A.1 shows four opamp configurations: a buffer, inverting amplifier, noninverting amplifier, and differential amplifier. We analyze these in the following sections.

Buffer

For the buffer configuration, the output (Vo) is connected to the inverting input (V_-), and the input signal is applied to the noninverting input (V_+). We can write the basic opamp equations like this:

$$Vo = Av(V_+ - V_-)$$

where Av is the open loop gain of the opamp. Because Vo is connected to V_-:

$$Vo = V_-$$

The input voltage, V1, is applied to the noninverting input, V_+, so we can rewrite the basic opamp equation like this:

275

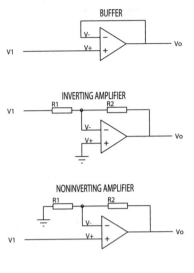

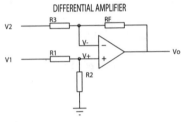

Figure A.1
Opamp configurations.

$$Vo = Av(V_+ - V_-); \quad Vo = Av(V1 - Vo)$$

Solving for Vo we get

$$Vo = \frac{Av\ V1}{1 + Av}$$

Dividing by Av, we get

$$Vo = \frac{V1}{\dfrac{1}{Av} + 1}$$

If Av is very large, the $\dfrac{1}{Av}$ term approaches zero, leaving $Vo = V1$.

Inverting Amplifier

Starting with the basic opamp equation:

$$Vo = Av(V_+ - V_-)$$

In this case, the noninverting pin is grounded, so V_+ is zero. V_- is at the junction of a voltage divider made up of R1 and R2. So we can write an equation for V_- as

$$V_- = \frac{(Vo - V1)R1}{R2 + R1} + V1$$

Substituting this into the basic opamp equation:

$$Vo = Av\left(-\frac{(Vo - V1)R1}{R2 + R1} + V1\right)$$

Solving for Vo, we get:

$$Vo = \frac{-Av \times V1 \times R2}{R2 + R1 + AvR2}$$

Dividing the right side by Av/Av:

$$Vo = \frac{-V1 \times R2}{\dfrac{R2}{Av} + \dfrac{R1}{Av} + R1}$$

If Av is very large, the $\dfrac{R2}{Av}$ and $\dfrac{R1}{Av}$ terms are very small, leaving $Vo = \dfrac{-V1 \times R2}{R1}$ $-R2/R1$ is the gain of the inverting configuration.

Noninverting Configuration

The formula for the noninverting configuration is

$$Vo = Av(V_+ - V_-)$$

The V_+ pin is connected to the input, V1. The V_- pin is a voltage divider with Vo and ground:

$$V_- = \frac{Vo \times R1}{R2 + R1}$$

Substituting these values into the basic opamp equation:

$$Vo = Av\left(V1 - \frac{Vo \times R1}{R1 + R2}\right)$$

Expanding:

$$Vo(R1 + R2) = (Av \times V1 \times R1) + (Av \times V1 \times R2) - (Av \times Vo \times R1)$$

Solving for Vo:

$$Vo = \frac{Av \times V1 \times R1}{R1 + R2 + (Av \times R1)} + \frac{Av \times V1 \times R2}{R1 + R2 + (Av \times R1)}$$

Dividing both terms on the right by Av/Av:

$$Vo = \frac{V1 \times R1}{\dfrac{R1}{Av} + \dfrac{R2}{Av} + R1} + \frac{V1 \times R2}{\dfrac{R1}{Av} + \dfrac{R2}{Av} + R1}$$

If Av is very large, we are left with

$$Vo = V1 + \frac{V1 \times R2}{R1} \quad \text{or} \quad Vo = V1\left(1 + \frac{R2}{R1}\right)$$

Differential Amplifier

The differential amplifier is a combination of the inverting and noninverting configurations. V_+ and V_- are both voltage dividers, so we can write the equations for them like this:

$$V_- = \frac{(Vo - V2)R3}{Rf + R3} + V2 \qquad V_+ = \frac{V1 \times R2}{R1 + R2}$$

Substituting into the basic opamp equation:

$$Vo = Av\left(\frac{V1 \times R2}{R1 + R2} - \frac{(Vo - V2)R3}{Rf + R3} + V2\right)$$

Expanding and solving for Vo:

$$Vo = Av\frac{(V1RfR2 + V1R2R3) - (V2RfRL + V2RfR2)}{R1Rf + R2R3 + R2Rf + R2\,R3 + AvR3R1 + AvR2R3}$$

Dividing the right fraction by Av/Av and allowing Av to be very large:

$$Vo = \frac{V1R2Rf + V1R2R3 - (V2Rf\,RL + V2RfR2)}{R1R3 + R2R3}$$

$$= \frac{V1 \times R2}{R1 + R2}\left(1 + \frac{Rf}{R3}\right) - V2\frac{Rf}{R3}$$

If R2 = RF and R1 = R3, then we get

$$Vo = (V1 - V2)\frac{Rf}{R3}$$

So the differential amplifier multiplies the difference between the inputs by the gain, Rf/R3. If a voltage divider was not used on the noninverting input, and V_+ was connected to the V1 input, the output would be

$$Vo = V1\left(1 + \frac{Rf}{R3}\right) - V2\frac{Rf}{R3}$$

Without the voltage divider on the noninverting input, the gain for V1 is greater than the gain for V2. With the voltage divider, if V1 = V2, Vo will be 0. Without the divider, this is not the case.

General Opamp Design Equations

In general, an opamp that is operating in the linear range (where the output is not saturated) will have some kind of feedback from the output to the inverting input, or some kind of inverted feedback from the output to the noninverting input. This is the case for most opamp applications. Because the feedback path allows the output to control one of the inputs, you can make the following simplification:

$$V_+ = V_-$$

Note that this applies only when the opamp output is not saturated. We can analyze the foregoing examples using this relationship to simplify the process.

Inverting Amplifier

V_- is a voltage divider between Vo and the input, V1. Because $V_+ = 0$, we can write the equations like this:

$$V_- = V_+ = 0 = \frac{(Vo - V1)R1}{R1 + R2} + V1$$

Rearranging and solving for Vo:

$$Vo = -V1 \frac{R2}{R1}$$

Noninverting Amplifier

$$V_- = V_+ = V1 = \frac{Vo \times R1}{R1 + R2}; \qquad Vo = V1\left(1 + \frac{R2}{R1}\right)$$

Differential Amplifier

$$V_+ = \frac{V1 \times R2}{R1 + R2}; \qquad V_- = \frac{(Vo - V2)R3}{Rf + R3} + V2$$

$$V_- = V_-; \qquad \frac{V1 \times R2}{R1 + R2} = \frac{(Vo - V2)R3}{Rf + R3}$$

Expanding and solving for Vo, we get:

$$Vo = V1 \frac{R2}{R1 + R2}\left(1 + \frac{Rf}{R3}\right) - V2 \frac{Rf}{R3}$$

We get the same result in all cases, but using the $V_+ = V_-$ relationship is usually easier.

Nonresistive Elements

So far, we have looked only at resistors in the opamp circuit. It is possible to use other elements such as capacitors and inductors to produce frequency-dependent circuits. The equations work the same way, with the following cautions:

- You must substitute impedances, using complex numbers, to calculate the output.
- The frequency characteristics and roll-off of the opamp must be taken into consideration.
- Be sure that the inputs of the opamp are not driven beyond their specified limits or the equations will no longer apply. Because of energy storage, such as flyback voltage in an inductor, you may get voltages with capacitor/inductor circuits that would not be possible with a resistive-only circuit.
- Similarly, you can't cause the output to go beyond its limits, either in voltage or speed.

Reversing the Inputs

In some applications, you need to reverse the inputs of the opamp. Figure A.2 shows a case like this. Here, an opamp drives an NPN transistor (Q1) through a current-limiting resistor, R1. The transistor collector drives a resistive load. You might use a circuit like this if the load draws more current than the opamp can sink.

In this circuit, the junction of Q1 and the load is connected to the noninverting input of the opamp, and the input is connected to the inverting input. This might look like the opamp is operating open loop, but it really isn't. The function of the inverting and noninverting inputs is switched because Q1 acts as an inverting amplifier. In this case, the opamp acts as a follower, with the junction of Q1 and the load following the input voltage.

Instead of a transistor, you could have another opamp, connected as an inverting amplifier, in the feedback path and the result would be the same. The point is that to make an opamp linear, you can use the noninverting input as the feedback pin and some kind of signal inversion between that and the output. Some opamps have both inverting and noninverting outputs, which can simplify the design of circuits like this.

Comparators

Figure A.3 shows an opamp connected as a comparator. An input signal is applied to the inverting input, and a fixed reference voltage is applied to the noninverting input. Say that

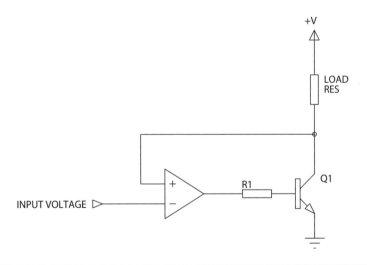

Figure A.2
Reversing opamp inputs.

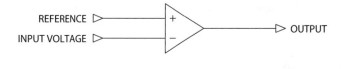

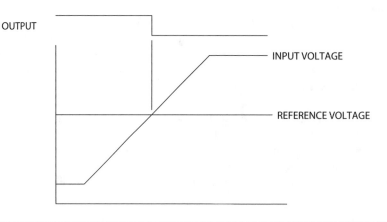

Figure A.3
Comparator operation.

the opamp supply voltages are +5 V and ground, and that the reference voltage is 2.5 V and the input voltage is 1 V. The general equation for the output of an opamp is

$$Vo = Av(V_+ - V_-)$$

If our opamp has a voltage gain of 100,000, then the output will be

$$100000(2.5 - 1) \text{ or } 150000 \text{ volts.}$$

Of course, the opamp cannot produce an output voltage anywhere close to that value, so the output pin goes to the positive supply (+5 V), or as close as it can get, considering the saturation voltage of the output.

Now suppose the input changes to 4 V. Doing the same calculation results in an output voltage of $-150,000$ volts. Again, the opamp goes as far as it can, which is the negative supply voltage, 0 V.

The function of a comparator is to make the output high when the inverting input is less than the noninverting input, and to make the output low when the inverting input is greater than the noninverting input. Comparators are typically used to sense when an input voltage is greater than or less than a fixed threshold, providing a digital (high/low) indication of that condition.

Although an opamp can be used as a comparator, it is more typical to use a comparator IC. These parts are essentially opamps, but they are optimized for use as comparators. They typically have lower gain than an opamp, but much greater speed. They often have open-collector outputs, so the output voltage swing can be different from the positive supply voltage. For instance, the comparator may operate from +12 V and ground, but the open-collector output may be pulled to +5 V or +3.3 V with a resistor, making a logic-compatible digital output.

Hysteresis

What happens to the comparator output if the two inputs are very close together? Figure A.4 illustrates this condition. As the input rises slowly through the reference voltage, the difference between the inputs becomes small enough that the gain of the comparator cannot drive the output to the rail. As a result, the device becomes linear and the output ramps down instead of switching quickly.

Another problem, also shown in Figure A.4, is the effect of a slowly changing input with noise. When the difference between the input and the reference is small, low-amplitude noise on the input can cause the output to switch several times between the high and low states. If the comparator output is an interrupt input to a microprocessor, this can cause real problems.

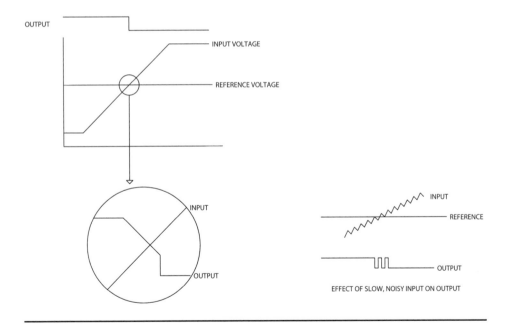

Figure A.4
Comparator with slowly changing input.

One way to avoid the problems associated with slowly changing inputs is to add hysteresis to the circuit. Figure A.5 shows the same comparator circuit from Figure A.4 with hysteresis added. A resistor, R2, is connected to the noninverting input and the output. A second resistor is connected between the reference voltage and the noninverting input. Say that the comparator operates with a supply voltage of 5 V and ground. The input voltage starts at 1 V, as before, with a reference voltage of 2.5 V. The output will be high, so the voltage on the V_+ pin will be determined by the voltage divider created by R1 and R2. This voltage is:

$$V_+ = \frac{(V_o - V_r) \times R1}{R1 + R2} + V_r$$

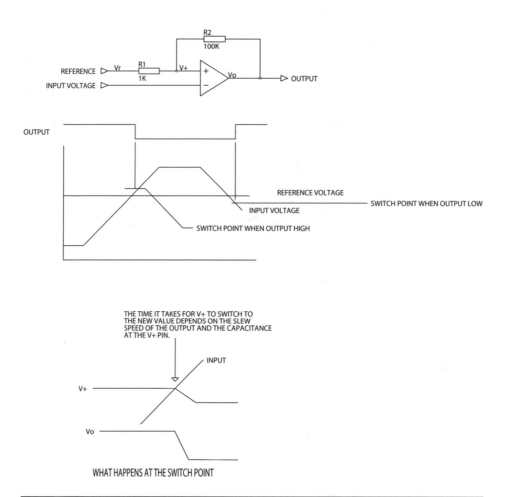

Figure A.5
Comparator with hysteresis.

For Vo high (5 V), Vr = 2.5 V, R1 = 1 K, and R2 = 100 K, V_+ = 2.5247 V. So the output will not switch until the input reaches 2.5247 V. Once the input reaches this value, the output starts to change state. Since V_+ is dependent on V_o, it will change values as V_o changes. When V_o reaches its final value (0 V), V_+ will have a new value. R1 and R2 are still voltage dividers between V_o and V_+, but now V_o is 0 V. So if we calculate the new value for V_+, we get 2.475 V. The input has to cross through this value to get the output to switch back high. However, we got this value because the input reached the original value of 2.5247 V, so the input would have to swing 0.049 V (2.5247 − 2.475) to make the output switch. This circuit has a hysteresis of 0.049 V. Any noise on the input with an amplitude smaller than this will not affect the output.

The advantages of hysteresis are:

- Faster switching. Once the output starts to change state, the V_+ input is "pulled" through the region where the limited gain makes the device linear. This change in V_+ accelerates the change in Vo, which in turn changes V_+, and so on.
- Better noise immunity. Noise on the input has to exceed the hysteresis value before it will affect the output.
- Circuit performance in the linear region is less dependent on device-to-device variations in the gain of the comparator IC.

Hysteresis does have some drawbacks. Because the comparator output does not switch instantly, there is still some time when the response of the comparator is linear and when noise on the inputs can affect the outputs. This time is dependent on the speed of the comparator (propagation delay and output slew rate) and the capacitance on the non-inverting input. In general, though, hysteresis significantly reduces the amount of time the comparator spends in the linear region. Another drawback to hysteresis is that the switch-point is no longer fixed, but varies with V_o and with the tolerances of resistors R1 and R2.

Some comparators have built-in hysteresis of a few millivolts. However, using external resistors permits the hysteresis levels to be set as required by the application.

Instrumentation Amplifiers

One problem with normal opamps is that the input impedance of a practical circuit is limited. Although the input impedance of the opamp itself is very high, the input impedance of a closed-loop circuit such as a differential amplifier is limited by the resistors. For instance, the input impedance of an inverting amplifier circuit is equal to the value of the input resistor. In some applications, high-input impedance is needed, while retaining the noise-rejecting differential amplification of the differential amplifier. The instrumentation amplifier provides this capability. Figure A.6 shows an instrumentation amplifier circuit using three opamps. The input impedance of the instrumentation amplifier is equal to the input impedance of the two input opamps.

Instrumentation amplifiers do not need to be built from discrete opamps and resistors, but are available as discrete ICs. For example, the AD624 from Analog Devices is available in a 16-pin package. The AD624 can be programmed for a gain of 1, 100, 200, 500, or 1000

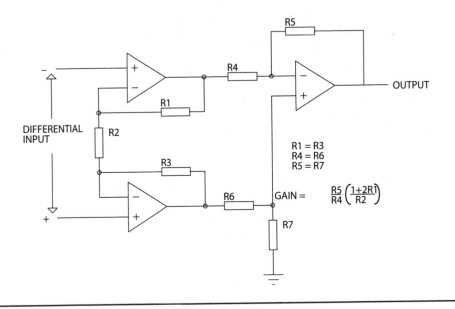

Figure A.6
Instrumentation amplifier.

by connecting various pins on the package together. An integrated instrumentation amplifier uses laser-trimmed resistors, providing very good matching and excellent accuracy.

Appendix B
Pulse Width Modulation

Pulse width modulation (PWM) is a means of providing digital control of the current in a device such as a motor, heater, or even an audio speaker. PWM replaces analog techniques to provide more efficiency in computer-controlled systems.

Why PWM?

A typical analog driver looks like the one in Figure B.1. A power device such as a high-current opamp provides driving current to a heater. In this case, the heater has a resistance of 18 ohms, so the current at 12 V is 667 ma. An input voltage determines the voltage across the heater and therefore the amount of heat generated. Presumably, the control electronics is able to measure the temperature of the system and adjust the input voltage accordingly, but that is not important to this discussion.

To drive a heater like this with a power opamp, you would need a power supply voltage of around 16 V, because the opamp output can't go all the way to the supply voltage. Let's say that the supply voltage is 16 V and the input voltage is 6 V. The output voltage will also be 6 V, so the current through the heater is V/R, or 6 V/15 Ω, or 400 ma. This is a power dissipation of (P = I × E) 6 × 0.4, or 2.4 watts.

The opamp, operating with a supply voltage of 16 V, has to supply the 400 ma current to the heater. But since the supply is 16 V and the heater voltage is 6 V, the remaining voltage (16 V − 6 V = 10 V) is dropped across the opamp output stage. This means the opamp is dissipating 10 V × 400 ma or 4 watts. Unless it has a good heatsink, it may get hotter than the heater.

The total dissipation in this circuit is the sum of the opamp dissipation plus the heater dissipation. This is 2.4 watts plus 4 watts or 6 watts. (You can also find this by multiplying the power-supply voltage by the total power-supply current: 16 V × 400 ma = 6.4 W). The following table shows the power dissipated for various input/heater voltages:

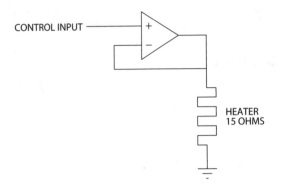

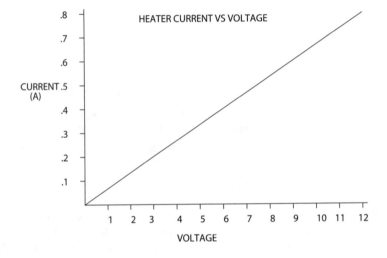

Figure B.1
Heater with analog driver.

Input Voltage	Current	Heater Dissipation	Opamp Dissipation	Total Dissipation
2	133 ma	0.267 w	1.87 w	2.14 w
3	200 ma	0.6 w	2.6 w	3.2 w
4	270 ma	1.067 w	3.2 w	4.27 w
5	333 ma	1.667 w	3.67 w	5.34 w
6	400 ma	2.4 w	4 w	6.4 w
7	466 ma	3.267 w	4.2 w	7.47 w
8	533 ma	4.27 w	4.27 w	8.54 w
9	600 ma	5.4 w	4.2 w	9.6 w
10	667 ma	6.667 w	4 w	10.67 w
11	733 ma	8.067 w	3.67 w	11.74 w
12	800 ma	9.6 w	3.2 w	12.8 w

Figure B.2 graphs the dissipation of the opamp and the heater as a function of input (heater) voltage. The power dissipated for both devices is the product of the heater current and the voltage across the device. In the case of the opamp, the power is dissipated in the output transistors that drive the heater. The worst-case power dissipation for the opamp occurs when the output is at half the supply voltage (8 V). Even though the heater in this application never dissipates more than 9.6 W, the power supply must be capable of delivering at least 12.8 W.

A PWM-based control method is illustrated in Figure B.3. This circuit uses the same 16 V supply as the analog circuit, but the control electronics turns the heater on and off by switching the control transistor on and off (a bipolar transistor is shown; a MOSFET also could be used). The timing diagram shows how the PWM circuit works. In the first interval shown, the transistor collector is low, so the heater is on for 66% of the PWM interval. The heater is off for 33% of the PWM interval. The heater current during the ON time is $16\,V/15\,\Omega$, or 1.0667 amps. However, the heater will respond to the time average of the current flowing through it, so the equivalent current for the purpose of generating heat is $1.0667\,amps \times 66\%$ (the ON time), or 0.711 amps.

In the second part of the timing diagram, the PWM is ON for 33% of the interval and off for 66%. The heater current during the ON time is still 1.0667 amps, but the time-averaged current is $1.0667 \times 33\%$, or 0.355 amps. To achieve a particular time-averaged current, we can use the following equations:

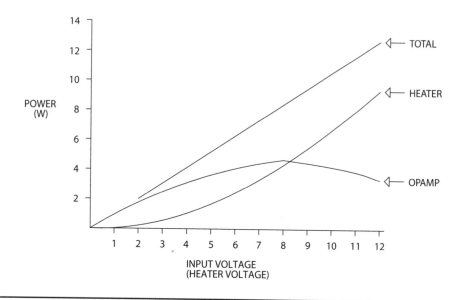

Figure B.2
Power dissipation in heater and analog driver.

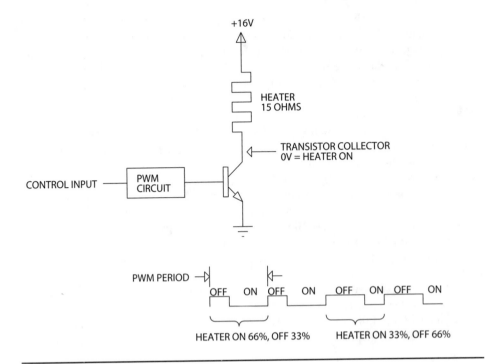

Figure B.3
Heater with PWM driver.

$$I_{on} = V_s/R$$
$$I_t = I_{on} \times T_{on}$$
$$P_{av} = V_s \times I_{on} \times T_{on}$$

where

- I_{on} is the heater current during the ON time
- V_s is the supply voltage
- R is the heater resistance
- I_t is the time-averaged current
- T_{on} is the ON time, expressed as a decimal ($33\% = 0.33$)
- Pav is the average dissipation

We can make a table of the ON time percentages required to get the same time-averaged current as the original analog driver used to get a specific amount of heat.

290

Original Input Voltage	Original Current	Original Heater Dissipation	Percent ON Time for Same Dissipation
2	133 ma	0.267 W	1.5%
3	200 ma	0.6 W	3.5%
4	270 ma	1.067 W	6.25%
5	333 ma	1.667 W	9.7%
6	400 ma	2.4 W	14%
7	466 ma	3.267 W	19%
8	533 ma	4.27 W	25%
9	600 ma	5.4 W	31.6%
10	667 ma	6.667 W	39%
11	733 ma	8.067 W	47%
12	800 ma	9.6 W	56%

The function of the PWM control circuitry is to turn the input voltage into a duty cycle. This specific example never uses a PWM ON time greater than 56%. This is because the power supply is 16 V, the same as the analog example, and our application never needs more than 9.6 W. If we had a 100% ON time, the dissipation would be 17 watts.

The total dissipation in a theoretical PWM circuit is exactly the same as the dissipation in the load. This is because the control transistor, when OFF, dissipates no power because the current through it is 0. When ON, the transistor dissipates no power because the voltage drop across it is 0. In either case $E \times I = 0$. A real transistor has very close to zero current when OFF, but doesn't quite have zero volts across it when ON.

We'll take a look at real parts later. For now, we will treat the transistor as ideal. Because the power dissipated in a PWM circuit is all dissipated in the load (the heater, in this case), the power supply needs to supply only what is actually needed—nothing is wasted in the driver. In our example, this means we only need a 9.6 W power supply, instead of the 12.8 W supply needed for the analog drive circuit we looked at originally.

Both the analog and PWM examples used a 16 V power supply. We could use a different voltage, say, 18 V. In this case, the dissipation in the opamp and total dissipation would be greater for any given input voltage. The heater dissipation would be the same, however, because the opamp holds the heater voltage at the input voltage, regardless of what the supply voltage is. As long as the supply voltage is high enough that the opamp output can follow the input, the power dissipated in the heater is independent of the supply voltage. This means we could use an unregulated supply for the analog driver. The unregulated supply would have significant ripple at the power-line frequency, but the opamp would compensate for that.

The PWM driver, on the other hand, is very dependent on supply voltage. If the supply voltage is raised to 18 V, the PWM duty cycle has to be lower to get the same average heater dissipation. Consequently, to achieve the same accuracy as the opamp circuit, the PWM circuit would need one of the following:

- A well-regulated power supply, so the dissipation at any given PWM duty cycle is known
- A means to measure the supply voltage and compensate for variations
- A means to measure the output (heat and/or dissipation) and adjust the duty cycle accordingly

In a real application, there is typically some feedback from whatever is being controlled (heater temperature, motor speed, etc.), so the software can adjust the duty cycle to compensate for power-supply variations without knowing the actual power-supply value. In this case, the power-supply voltage variation becomes another variable in the system, just like a varying load. In some applications, it may be necessary to measure the supply. A heater without feedback, for instance, might use a 50% duty cycle to get 50 °C temperature, or a 75% duty cycle to get 75 °C. If there is no feedback to indicate the actual current flowing through the load when the transistor is ON, then the software may need to measure the supply voltage with an ADC and adjust the duty cycle to compensate for supply variations.

To make PWM work, the PWM frequency has to be high enough so that the load responds to the average current flowing through it. For a large heater that is controlling the temperature of, say, an engine block, you might get by with a PWM frequency less than 100 Hz. For a high-speed DC motor, you might need a PWM frequency of 50 kHz.

Real Parts

Now we'll take a look at a real transistor. A real power transistor, when ON, has a saturation voltage across the collector-emitter. This can be as high as a couple of volts. A MOSFET transistor has an ON resistance that results in a voltage drop. In both cases, the voltage drop across the transistor is dependent on the current.

Say that our example PWM transistor has a voltage drop of 1 V. For this discussion, we'll pretend that the drop is independent of current. The result of this voltage drop is that the transistor dissipates some power when ON. In addition, less voltage is available across the heater. In this case, when the transistor is ON, the 1 V collector-emitter voltage (1 V) is subtracted from the supply voltage (16 V), leaving 15 V across the heater. Consequently, the heater now has a current of 15 V/15 Ω, or 1 amp, when the transistor is ON. The lower voltage available to the heater has exactly the same effect on the PWM duty cycle as a lower supply voltage would; a slightly longer PWM ON percentage is required to achieve the same average heater dissipation.

When the transistor is turned on, it dissipates one watt (1 amp × 1 volt). Just like the heater, the transistor temperature will respond to the time-average of the power. When the heater is ON 33% of the time, the average transistor dissipation will be 0.33 W, and when the heater is ON 66% of the time, the average transistor dissipation will be 0.66 W.

Frequency Limitations

A real transistor dissipates power when it is on. It also dissipates power when it is switching. Figure B.4 illustrates this. The digital control signal that turns the transistor ON or OFF is nearly instantaneous (as far as the transistor is concerned). However, the transistor itself

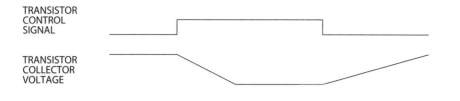

Figure B.4
PWM switching dissipation.

takes some time to turn ON, and when the control input changes state, the transistor takes some time to turn OFF. During the turn-on and turn-off times, the transistor dissipates power, just like an analog driver does. This limits the maximum PWM frequency that can be used. The higher the PWM frequency is, the higher the percentage of time that the transistor spends in the intermediate state, where it dissipates the most power. If the PWM frequency is high enough, the transistor will never turn completely OFF or ON, and will dissipate significant power.

Resolution Limitations

A PWM system is typically implemented with a digital counter that generates the PWM frequency. A second counter or logic that decodes the frequency counter is used to determine the period. For example, a PWM signal might be generated using an 8-bit counter, which can divide the clock by 256. If the input is 1 MHz, then the output will be 1 MHz/256, or 3906.25 Hz.

Because this theoretical clock has 256 discrete periods, then the smallest step size we can have in the PWM output is 1/256. If the PWM output is set to be ON when the counter is in states 0 through 99 and OFF for states 100 through 255, then we have a duty cycle of 100/256, or 39.06%. If we change this to ON for states 0–100 and OFF for states 101–255, then the new duty cycle is 101/256, or 39.4%. The change is 0.39%, or 1/256.

This characteristic limits the precision with which a PWM-based controller can adjust its output. A linear system has nearly infinite control accuracy. Like any digital system, a PWM controller has a limited resolution. Of course, an analog controller whose input comes from a microprocessor-controlled DAC has the same limitation. But the number of bits of resolution has to be taken into account when designing a PWM-based controller.

One way around the resolution problem is to modulate the output. If our example system is ON for states 0–99 for one PWM cycle, and ON for states 0–100 on the next PWM cycle, then the average is half of the PWM resolution. By using 0–99 for two cycles and 0–100 for one, you can get three times the original resolution. But, as you would expect, there are a couple of catches:

- The microprocessor (or whatever is controlling the PWM output) has to change the output duty cycle on every PWM cycle. The duty cycle can't just be set to a particular value and left that way until a change is needed. This can significantly increase the processing demand on the microprocessor.

- The PWM frequency has to be selected so that the load does not respond to the individual PWM pulses, but only to the average. If the PWM output is modulated on a cycle-by-cycle basis, the PWM frequency must be selected so that the load does not respond to the modulation frequency. Otherwise, a ripple will be seen in the load response.

In some microcontrollers, the PWM frequency and duty cycle can be varied. The period is typically varied by adjusting the rollover point of the period timer. This also affects resolution. If you are using the same 8-bit PWM timer just discussed, using the full 256 counts provides a 3906 Hz PWM clock. If you need a faster clock, you can program the period timer to roll over at 100 counts. This will provide a 10 KHz PWM clock. However, the best resolution now available for changes in PWM output is 1% instead of 0.39%. This is an important consideration when selecting PWM hardware. If you need a specific frequency of operation, you need to calculate the available resolution using that frequency, not using the maximum timer count. Or, you may have to adjust the microprocessor clock to provide the correct frequency and resolution.

Power-Supply Considerations

When using PWM, the average current drawn from the power supply is equal to the average used by the load. In the heater example we've already looked at, the maximum power used is 9.6 W, and the average current is 800 ma. However, the current when the heater is on is 1.0667 amps. The power supply must be capable of delivering this current for the heater to work properly. In most cases, this can be accomplished with a sufficient amount of capacitance on the power-supply output. If the board with the PWM controller is powered from a supply that is some distance away, the resistance of the cabling may cause ripple at the PWM frequency on the power supply. In such a case, it may be necessary to have additional capacitance, not at the power supply, but at the board with the PWM circuit.

PWM and EMI

One disadvantage to using PWM is the additional EMI that is produced. In the heater example, the linear controller used a current that varied with the control voltage, but was constant if the control voltage did not change. The PWM controller will produce a heater current of 1.0667 amps every time the switching transistor turns on. Regardless of the average heater power, there will be a 1.0667 amp current spike at the PWM frequency. If the wiring to the system has significant resistance or inductance, this will result in a supply voltage variation that follows the PWM waveform. For this reason, PWM systems should use large wires or wide PCB traces, or some method of minimizing the impedance of the power supply connections. Where there are low-level sensors, such as thermistor or thermocouple signals, use separate grounds for those devices so that the voltage drop caused by the PWM signal does not affect the readings.

In addition to the current and voltage excursion caused by the PWM switch, the inductance in the system will ring when the transistor turns on. This will produce radiation at the resonant frequency(s) of the wiring. To minimize the ringing, it is often desirable to control the turn-on edge of the PWM switch. There are MOSFET drivers that limit the edge rate of the signal going to the gate for exactly this reason. In a simpler system without a MOSFET driver, you can limit the switching time by adding a small resistor (100 ohms to 1 K) in series with the MOSFET gate lead. This resistor, in combination with the MOSFET capacitance, produces a slower edge. The tradeoff is increased MOSFET power dissipation because the transistor spends more time in the linear region. Using the resistor also gives less repeatable results because the actual switching time is based on the transistor capacitance, which can vary from one device to the next.

Audio Applications

PWM techniques were originally developed to improve efficiency and reduce heating in control applications. However, PWM has been applied to audio amplifiers as well. A block diagram of an audio PWM amplifier is shown in Figure B.5. An audio amplifier using PWM is referred to as a *class D amplifier*. The Philips TDA8920 is a typical class D power amplifier IC, with two 50 W audio amplifiers operating at up to 90% efficiency. Class D audio amplifiers typically switch at hundreds of kHz to avoid influencing the audio output with the PWM frequency. The advantages of PWM for audio applications are the same as for any other application: better driver efficiency, smaller power supplies, and less heating.

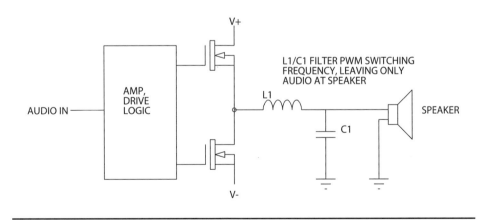

Figure B.5
PWM audio amplifier.

PWM Hardware

Figure B.6 shows how a typical microcontroller-based PWM might be implemented. An 8-bit down-counter is loaded with the value in an 8-bit register (the period register). The counter starts counting at this value and counts down toward zero. A second register, the duty cycle register, contains another 8-bit value. When the count equals the value in the duty cycle register (determined by the 8-bit comparator), the PWM output goes high. The PWM output stays high until the count value is less than the duty cycle value. This happens when the counter rolls over from 00 to FF. The counter rollover output detects this condition and reloads the counter with the value in the period register again.

Note that a real microcontroller would have considerable additional logic to ensure that the PWM output would not have spurious pulses on it when the counter changes value, and to synchronize everything with the clock. In addition, registers would be provided for other functions, such as starting and stopping the timer and selecting PWM versus normal mode.

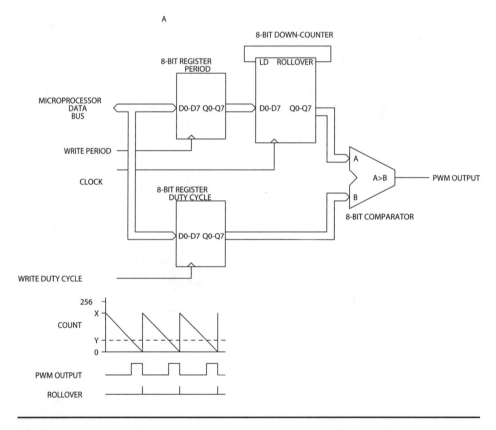

Figure B.6
PWM Hardware.

The circuit shown could be used to implement a PWM output with a period up to 256 clocks and a duty cycle from 1/256 to 100%. Figure B.6 also shows how the timing works. The counter value is shown as a continuous line, although it of course decrements in steps. The value X on the graph is the value in the period register, which is where the counter starts counting when it is reloaded. The value Y on the graph represents the value in the duty cycle register. Note that if the duty cycle value is greater than the period value, the PWM output will never go high. This sort of scenario is possible on many microcontrollers with PWM outputs.

This particular hardware configuration was selected to make the explanation easy. There are a number of variations on this, including up-counters instead of down-counters, and timers that count in both directions, setting the PWM output when counting up past the duty cycle value and resetting when counting down past the duty cycle value. Some microcontrollers can only provide a few fixed periods, based on specific divisors of the system clock.

PWM Software

Although hardware configurations may vary, most hardware PWM controllers have certain things in common:

- A register to set the duty cycle
- A register to set the period (sometimes very limited)
- A way to start and stop the timer
- A way to enable interrupts from the timer
- A way to set the PWM clock source and/or frequency

In general, the software procedure to set up PWM is to initialize all the registers, start the timer, and enable the timer interrupt (if necessary). Once the timer is running, the software must update the duty cycle (and, if appropriate, the period) as system requirements dictate.

In some cases, the PWM timer generates an interrupt to the microprocessor. When the interrupt occurs, the software updates the period and/or duty cycle. On some microcontrollers, the PWM timer does not allow you to select a 0% or 100% duty cycle. This may happen, for example, if you are using the full 256-count period; there may be no value you can put into the duty cycle register that will not result in a pulse on the output. In that situation, 0% output is not possible.

In a case like that, you may have to stop the timer and directly manipulate the output bit to get either the 0% or 100% duty cycle. In most microcontrollers, the PWM outputs are shared with bit-oriented I/O ports, so such manipulation is possible. However, because time interrupts will not occur while the timer is stopped, another method must be used to ensure that updates occur. One method, if the microcontroller supports it, is to let the PWM timer continue to run and generate interrupts, but to disable the PWM output.

Appendix C
Useful URLs

Semiconductors

www.analog.com; Analog devices
www.atmel.com; Atmel
www.burr-brown.com; Burr-Brown
www.clarostat.com; Clarostat—optical and Hall effect sensors
www.dalsa.com; Dalsa—CCDs
www.fairchild-ic.com; Fairchild
www.honeywell.com; Honeywell—Hall effect sensors
www.maxim-ic.com; Maxim
www.microchip.com; Microchip
www.mot-sps.com; Motorola semiconductors
www.nsc.com; National Semiconductor
www.pmdcorp.com; Performance Motion Devices—motor control ICs
www.sel.sony.com/semi; Sony semiconductors—CCDs
www.ti.com; Texas Instruments
www.xicor.com; Xicor

Motors

www.bodine-electric.com; Bodine Electric—DC, brushless, stepper
www.eadmotors.com; Eastern Air Devices—DC, brushless, stepper
www.maxonmotor.com; Maxon motors—DC
www.micromo.com; Microchip
www.orientalmotor.com; Oriental Motors—DC, brushless
www.pacsci.com; Pacific Scientific—DC, brushless, stepper

Other

www.guardian-electric.com; Guardian relays/solenoids
www.liteon.com; Liteon optoelectronics
www.omron.com; Omron relays
www.optoswitch.com; Clarostat optoelectronics
www.qtopto.com; QT optoelectronics

Appendix D
Python Code for Chapter 11;
Excel Data for Chapter 4

Following is the Python code used to generate the various waveforms in Chapter 11 using the light bulb/phototransistor simulator. External routines PWM and ADCREAD write values to the PWM controller and read data from the ADC that is connected to the phototransistor collector. All code uses the Python "time" module to implement delays. The hardware communicates with the host PC using a 115,200 baud serial link, so an open-source serial module also was used. To avoid confusion, those details are left out of these examples, which include only the portions of the code necessary to illustrate the control mechanism.

All of these examples print the waveform array to a console window. This was copied and pasted into Microsoft Word so it could be edited into a column format (the values in the Python output were separated by commas) and the resulting column of data was then pasted into Excel for plotting.

If you are unfamiliar with Python, you can find information on the Internet at www.python.org. All these code fragments take 256 samples and write the ADC input values to an array called "waveform". A real application, of course, would run continuously.

Code for step test:

```
PWM(254)                 # PWM full on

count = 0                # Loop counter

time = clock( )
while count < 256:
while clock( ) – time < .001: pass    # Delay 1 ms
    time = clock( )
    adc = ADCREAD( ).                 # Read ADC
    waveform.append(ord(adc))         # Append result to waveform array
    count + = 1
```

```
PWM(1)                    # Turn PWM off
print waveform            # Print waveform to console
```

Code to produce negative step:

```
PWM(250)                  # full on
#   Let output stabilize for 1.5 sec.
time = clock( )
while clock( ) − time < 1.5: pass     # delay 1 sec


count = 0                 # Loop counter
time = clock( )
PWM(1)                    # full off

while count < 256:
   time = clock( )
   while clock ( ) − time < .001: pass     # Delay 1 ms
   adc = ADCREAD( )                        # Read ADC
   waveform.append(ord(adc))               # Append result to waveform array
   count + = 1


#   Print result.
print waveform
```

Code for on/off (bang-bang) control:

```
setpoint = 100
count = 0                 # Loop counter
waveform = [ ]            # Waveform result array
control = [ ]             # Control output array

#   Note: To test control starting with PWM full on,
#   uncomment the following two Python statements.
#   These turn the output full on and wait 1 sec:
#   PWM (250)
#   while clock( ) − starttime < 1: pass

time = clock( )

#   Note: To illustrate effect of sampling rate on the result,
#   change the delay value from .001 to something else. .004
#   gives a 4 ms sample rate.
while count < 256:
   while clock( ) − time < .001: pass     # Delay 1 ms
   time = clock( )
   adc = ADCREAD( )                        # Read ADC
```

```
    adcint = ord (adc)                      # Convert result to integer
    waveform.append (adcint)


    #  If result < setpoint, turn PWM off.
    #  if result > setpoint, turn PWM on full.
    if adcint < setpoint:
      PWM (1)
      control.append (0)
    else:                                    # (adcint >= setpoint)
      PWM (250)
    control.append (1)


    count + = 1

#  Test done, turn PWM off.
PWM (1)

#  Print result.
print waveform




Proportional control:

setpoint = 150
offset = 200
gain = 10

count = 0
waveform = [ ]
control = [ ]

#  Note: To test control starting with PWM full on,
#  uncomment the following two Python statements.
#  These turn the output full on and wait 1 sec:
#  PWM (254)
#  while clock ( ) – starttime < 1: pass

time = clock( )

while count < 256:
    while clock( ) – time < .001: pass      #  Wait 1 ms
    time = clock( )
    adc = ADCREAD( )                         #  Read ADC result
    adcint = ord (adc)                       #  Convert result to integer
    waveform.append (adcint)                 #  Save input value in array
```

```
#   In the following code, use adc value – setpoint
#   because control is negative (bigger PWM value = smaller
#   adc result)
#   Limit result to range 1–254.
output = offset + (adcint – setpoint)*gain
if output < 1 : output = 1
if output > 254 : output = 254


    PWM (output)
control.append (output)          # Save control value in array


    count += 1


#   Test done, turn PWM off.
PWM (1)


#   Print result.
print waveform


PID control example:

setpoint = 150
offset = 200


#   PID loop gains
#   Note that integral and derivative are both calculated over a single
#   sample interval. If a different sampling interval is used, then
#   the same gain values will produce different results.
GI = 2                           #  Integral gain
GD = 2                           #  Derivative gain
GP = 4                           #  Proportional gain


derivative = 0
integral = 0


count = 0
waveform = [ ]                   # Array to save ADC results
control = [ ]                    # Array to save control output results
I = [ ]                          # Array to save calculated integral values
D = [ ]                          # Array to save calculated derivative values


preverr = 0                      # initialize value of prev error
                                 # Used in calculating derivative


#   Note: To test control starting with PWM full on,
#   uncomment the following two Python statements.
```

```
#   These turn the output full on and wait 1 sec:
#   PWM(254)
#   while clock( ) – starttime < 1: pass

time = clock( )

while count < 256:
    while clock( ) – time < .001: pass     #   Delay 1 ms
    time = clock( )
    adc = ADCREAD( )                        #   Read ADC result
    adcint = ord(adc)                       #   Convert result to integer
    waveform.append(adcint)                 #   Save input value in array

    #   Calculate error. Note that adc–setpoint is used
    #   instead of setpoint – adc. This is because
    #   control is reversed – big control value = little output
    error = adcint – setpoint

    #   Calculate derivative as current error – prev error
    derivative = error – preverr
    preverr = error                         #   For next pass through loop
    D.append (derivative)

    #   If error less than 10% of setpoint, calculate integral as
    #   integral + error. If error greater than 10% of setpoint,
    #   set integral to 0. This limits integral windup.
    if error < setpoint/10 : integral = integral + error
    else: integral = 0
    I.append(integral)

    #   Calculate new output value, limiting result to range 1–254.
    output = offset + (error*GP) + (derivative*GD) + (integral*GI)
    if output < 1 : output = 1
    if output > 254 : output = 254

    PWM(output)
    control.append(output)

    count + = 1

#   Test done, turn PWM off.
PWM (1)

#   Print result.
print waveform
```

Table 4.1 was generated using a Microsoft Excel spreadsheet. The spreadsheet was configured as follows:

- Column A: 1000 rows containing: Rand( ) (generates 1000 random numbers)
- Column B: 1000 rows containing: Value + Ax
- Column C: 1000 rows containing: TRUNC(Bx, 0)
- Column D: 1000 rows containing: IF(Cx = 3, 1, 0) (Puts 1 in the cell if Cx = 3, 0 in the cell if Cx = 4)

To calculate the result for 100 samples, the first 100 values in column C were added together and the result divided by 100. For 1000 samples, all the values in column C were added together and divided by 1000.

Note: In all cases, the "x" in the cells corresponds to the row number. For example, cell C4 contains: TRUNC(B4,0).

"Value" in column B was the value of the event being measured: 2.25, 2.5, and 2.8 in Table 4.1.

Glossary

ADC (analog-to-digital converter): A circuit that converts an analog value, usually voltage, to a digital value.

CDS (correlated double sampling): A method of compensating for noise in a CCD system by subtracting two samples. The first sample is taken immediately after reset, when the CCD output voltage is at the reset level, and the second sample is taken when the CCD charge output is present.

Closed-loop gain: The gain of a circuit with feedback components added. For an opamp circuit, this means that the feedback loop to one of the inputs is closed with resistors or other components. Closed-loop gain may be an integer number, or it may be an equation that is dependent on frequency, time, or other factors. Closed-loop gain can apply to a simple one-IC opamp circuit or to a complex system that includes a microprocessor in the feedback loop. Closed-loop gain in any real system has limitations such as supply voltage or the capability of the output driving components.

Codec: Depending on usage, codec is short for compressor/decompressor and refers to a device, system, or software that compresses or decompresses data. An example would be an IC that converts to and from the JPEG image-compression format. In the telecom industry, codec is short for coder/decoder and is a device that converts from digital to analog and back.

Cross Conduction (see Shoot-through): A condition that occurs when an incorrect pair of transistors turns on in an H-bridge. This condition usually results in low impedance between the two supply voltages.

DAC (digital-to-analog converter): A circuit that converts a digital value to an analog value.

Dynamic range: The range of values that a system must measure or control. Conceptually, the maximum value divided by the smallest increment.

EMC (electromagnetic compatibility): Generally refers to compatibility with the various electromagnetic interference standards, such as those issued by the FCC (Federal Communications Commission) in the United States or by the IEC in the European community.

EMI (electromagnetic interference): A general term for any kind of interference in an electronic circuit that is caused by any electromagnetic effect. EMI includes RF, ESD, and magnetic interference effects.

Encoder: On a motor, an encoder attaches to the motor shaft and produces output signals that indicate motor position. The encoder may produce a series of pulses indicating a certain degree of rotation or an absolute indication of shaft position.

ESD (electrostatic discharge): An arc that is created when electricity flows between two charged objects. The spark you get when you walk across a carpet on a dry day and touch a doorknob.

Hall effect: Discovered by Dr. Edwin Hall in 1879. It refers to the voltage that appears across a conductor if it is placed in a magnetic field while a current is passed through it.

Hall effect sensor: A semiconductor sensor that measures magnetic fields using the Hall effect.

Index: In a shaft-position encoder, an output that indicates when the shaft has reached a predetermined position, usually occurring once per revolution.

Integration time (CCD): The amount of time that light is allowed to fall (charge is allowed to accumulate) on a CCD array before readout.

LVDT (linear variable differential transformer): A linear position sensor that uses a movable core and balanced coils.

Open-loop gain: The gain of a circuit (typically an opamp) with no feedback components added. The open-loop gain of an opamp is high, usually in the tens or hundreds of thousands.

Peltier cooler: A solid-state cooler using the Peltier effect.

PID (Proportional/Integral/Derivative) control: A control method that determines the new output of a system by using the difference between the desired value and the actual value (proportional term), the rate of change (derivative term), and the accumulation of the error over time (integral term).

PWM (pulse-width modulation): A means of controlling the current through a device by applying an on-off waveform with a current that is higher than the desired current. The device responds to the time average of the current through it, so the ratio of on to off time in the waveform determines the effective current value.

Reference voltage: In an ADC or DAC circuit, the voltage that establishes the conversion range. In a comparator circuit, the voltage at one input that is compared to the other input to determine if the output is high or low.

RTD (resistance temperature detector): A conductor that is used to measure temperature by measuring resistance change.

Sample and hold (S/H): A circuit that stores a voltage value so it can be measured. Typically used with an ADC to stabilize the input value during measurement.

Shoot-through (see Cross conduction): A condition that occurs when an incorrect pair of transistors turns on in an H-bridge. This condition usually results in low impedance between the two supply voltages.

Strain gauge: A sensor that measures mechanical strain, such as weight, by measuring the resistance change in a conductor due to the change in cross-sectional area.

Thermistor: A resistive component that changes resistance with temperature.

Thermocouple: A temperature sensor that measures the voltage generated at the junction of two dissimilar metals.

Torque: The amount of force a motor can apply to its shaft. The formula for torque is:

$$\text{Force} \times \text{Moment Arm} = \text{Torque}$$

Torque is measured in foot-pounds, inch-pounds, ounce-inches, or Newton-meters (metric).

8.85 inch-pounds = 1 Newton-meter

1 foot-pound = 12 inch-pounds

16 ounce-inches = 1 inch-pound

1 Newton = 1 kilogram-meter per second squared

VRS (variable reluctance sensor): A sensor that uses a magnet and a coil to sense rotation of a toothed wheel. The teeth on the wheel produce changes in the magnetic field from the magnet, inducing an AC voltage on the coil.

V-F (voltage-to-frequency) converter: A circuit that generates an output frequency that varies with an input voltage.

Index

1 LSB, 35
2-channel arrays, 74
2's complement outputs, 30
4–20ma current loop, 244–245
4N35 optoisolator, 68
6N136 optoisolator, 68
8031 family, 39
80186 processor bus contention,
    33–34

A

Absolute encoders, 198
AC power control, 252, 254
Acceleration sensors. *See* motion/
    acceleration sensors
Accumulation of errors, 35, 122
Accuracy, extending with limited
    resolution, 102–106
Acquisition time, 28
AD594/595, 58
ADCs (analog-to-digital converters),
    13–15, 307
  2's complement outputs, 30
  accuracy of reference, 43
  CCDs (charge coupled devices), 81
  comparing types of, 25–26
  controlling multiple sensors, 65–67
  dual-slope (integrating) ADCs, 20–21
  flash ADCs, 19
  half-flash converter, 24–25
  Hall effect sensors, 83
  high-resolution, 234–235
  I^2 bus, 38–39
  input levels, 29
  interfacing to fast processor, 36
  internal microcontroller, 42–43
  internal reference voltage, 29

internal S/H (sample-and-hold) circuit,
    29–30
  interrupt rates, 44
  lower-voltage, single-supply operation,
    29
  low-pass filter ahead of, 27
  microprocessor interfacing, 30–35
  multichannel, 41–42
  output coding, 30
  output values in BCD, 30
  output word, 16
  parallel interfaces, 30–32
  proprietary interfaces, 39
  reference bypassing, 29
  reference voltage, 16
  resistor ladder or string, 24
  resolution, 16–17
  serial interfaces, 36–41
  S/H (sample-and-hold circuit), 26–30
  sigma-delta converter, 21–24
  single-slope converter, 21
  SMBus, 39, 41
  SPI/Microwire, 36, 38
  successive approximation converter,
    19–20
  tracking ADCs, 17, 19
  types, 17–25
Agilent HCTL-1100 controller IC, 203–204
Aliasing, 11–12
Analog Devices AD570, 29
Analog Devices AD872, 29
Analog Devices AD5203, 166
Analog Devices AD5220, 163–165
Analog Devices AD7801, 162–163
Analog Devices AD7823, 38
Analog Devices AD7824, 41–42
Analog Devices ADV7120, 163
Analog Devices ADXL202, 86

Analog Devices Web site, 299
Analog Hall effect sensors, 82
Analog multiplexers, 168–169
Analog signal transmitted over electrically
    noisy wire, 100
Analog switches, 166–168
Applications, high-precision, 225–227
Area CCDs (charge coupled devices), 78–79
Arrays, 74–77
Asynchronous V-F converters, 99
Atmel AT90S4434, 42
Atmel ATtiny parts, 44
Atmel AVR devices, 44
Atmel Web site, 299

B

Back EMF, 209
Bandpass filter, 97
Bandwidth, 5
Bang-bang control. *See* On-off control
BestSoft Web site, 138
Bipolar Hall effect switches, 83
Bipolar stepper motors, 173, 179–180
Bipolar transistors, 254–257
Bodine Electric Web site, 299
Brushless DC motors
    compared to other types of motors, 206
    digital drive, 194–195
    drive electronics providing commutation,
        193–195
    electronic commutation, 206
    Hall-effect sensor, 195
    operation of, 193
    sensorless, 195–196
    sinusoidal drive, 193–195
Burr-Brown Web site, 299
Bus architecture, 7–8
Bus contention, 33–34
Bus cycle without wait states, 35

C

Calibrating system with known target,
    80–81
Calibration
    calculating with software, 3
    compensation for, 2–3
    EEPROM containing, 3
    human element, 5
    measurement, 2–5
    microcontroller performing, 3–4
    storing, 3

Camcorders and Area CCDs, 78
Capacitors
    LSB errors, 34–35
    supplying current to coil, 148
    time required to charge up, 34
    V-F (voltage-to-frequency converters),
        98–99
Capture counter, 91–93
CCD array, 73–74
CCDs (charge coupled devices), 71
    ADCs (analog-to-digital converters), 81
    area, 78–79
    basics, 72
    calibrating system with known target,
        80–81
    CDS (correlated double sampling), 79–80
    clock and reset inputs, 81
    color, 75
    color processing, 78
    dark reference, 79
    driving, 81
    electrostatic potential, 72
    exposure control, 72
    functions, 72
    integration, 72
    integration time, 72
    lighting variations, 80
    linear, 73–75
    nonuniformity, 80–81
    normalizing output, 80
    operation, 72
    reducing noise, 79–80
    sense node, 72
    trilinear, 75–78
    voltage requirements, 81
CDS (correlated double sampling), 79–80,
    307
Chopper circuit, 186
Chopper control, 186–187
Chopper oscillator, 186–187
Chromel-alumel (Type K) thermocouples,
    57
Circuits
    electrical isolation between, 67
    high-side injection, 97
Clarostat Optoelectronics Web site, 300
Clarostat Web site, 299
Class D amplifier, 295
Clock resolution, 100–102
Clocked interfaces, 35–36
Closed-loop gain, 307
Codecs, 43, 307
Color and Trilinear CCDs (charge coupled
    devices), 75–78

Combined logic analyzer/DSO, 135–136
Commercial software for tuning PID loops, 138
Comparators, 17, 19–21, 23
    Hall effect sensors, 83
    hysteresis, 283–285
    opamp, 281–283
    open heater condition, 149, 151
    optical sensors, 62–63
    V-F (voltage-to-frequency converters), 98–99
Components
    safety ground, 216–217
    tolerance stackup, 55–56
Continuous-duty solenoids, 145
Control design, 143
Control loops, measuring and analyzing, 134–143
Control systems
    combined logic analyzer/DSO, 135–136
    debugging problems, 134
    hardware monitoring, 134–143
    inaccuracy, 126
    logic analyzer, 134
    monitoring, 134–135
    motor control, 127–133
    on-off control, 109–112
    overshoot, 112
    PID controls, 116–127
    predictive controls, 133–134
    proportional controls, 112–115
Controls, open-loop, 107
Coolers
    fans, 155–157
    solid-state (Peltier), 155
Copper-constant (Type T)
    thermocouples, 57
Counters
    incremented by frequency input, 94
    motor control, 128
    overflowing, 102
Cross-conduction, 180–184, 307
CTR (current transfer ratio), 61
Current chopping, 148

D

DACs (digital-to-analog converters), 13–15, 17, 162–163, 307
Dale thermistor, 48
Dalsa Web site, 299
Darlington transistor outputs, 61
Data access time, 32

dB (decibels), 1
D.C. (dissipation constant), 50
DC motors
    ability to brake, 192–193
    analog driver, 191
    brushless, 193–197
    compared to other types of motors, 206
    control circuits, 191
    controller ICs, 199–204
    current control, 191
    driving, 191
    dynamic braking, 192–193
    encoders, 197–198
    H-bridge driving, 190–193
    higher loading, 191
    light loading, 191
    power-up issues, 207–209
    software controllers, 204–205
    speed, 209
    synchronization, 190
    torque, 206
Deadtime, 126
Derivative term and PID controls, 126
Differential amp, 22
Differential amplifier equation, 280
Digital potentiometers, 163–166
Discrete optical sensors, 69–71
Discrete parts, 69
DMA controller reading ADC at regular intervals, 44
Driving
    bipolar transistors, 254–257
    CCDs (charge coupled devices), 81
Droop rate, 28
DSO (digital storage oscilloscope), 135–136
DSP filtering in software, 97
Dual-function pins on microcontrollers, 44–46
Dual-slope (integrating) ADCs, 20–21
Dynamic braking, 192–193
Dynamic range, 1–2, 307

E

Eastern Air Devices Web site, 299
EEPROM, containing calibration data, 3
Electrical and IEEE 1451.2 standard, 243
EMC (electromagnetic compatibility), 8
EMI (electromagnetic interference), 308
    ground loops, 215–220
    interference, 215
    PWM (pulse width modulation), 294
    susceptibility, 215

Encoders, 197–198, 206, 308
Errors, 112–113
  accumulation of, 122
  motor control, 128
  proportional controls, 115
ESD (electrostatic discharge), 220, 308
  protection, 221–223
  self-induced, 221
Ethernet between systems, 216
Events
  accurate measurement short, 103–104
  duration longer than clock period, 104
  duration not changing, 105
  ISR interrupt, 106
  measuring nonsynchronized to
      measurement clock, 104
  period increases, 105
  repeatability, 105
  repetitive, 104, 106
Example control system, 262
  on-off (bang-bang) control, 263, 266
  PID controls, 268–272
  proportional controls, 266–268
  proportional-integral control, 273
Excel data for Chapter 4, 306

F

Failed LED, 66–67
Fairchild TMC1103, 81
Fairchild Web site, 299
Fans
  built-in tachs, 157
  controlling speed, 155
  electronic controllers, 155
  monitoring, 155–156
  MOSFET transistors, 155
  optical (or Hall effect) sensor output, 156
  set/reset flip-flop, 156
Feedthrough, 28
Ferrite beads, 223
Fieldbus, 245–246
FIFOs (first in, first out memory), 77
Filtering
  noisy input, 140–141
  slotted switches, 63
  V-F converters, 100
Flash ADCs (analog-to-digital converters),
    19, 24
Floating-point math, 103
Frequency
  detecting changes quickly, 95
  high-precision applications, 229

input range, 97
measurements, 91
measuring *versus* period, 94–95
sampling clock, 100–102
Frequency mixer, 96–97
Frequency shifts, 96–98
Full power bandwidth, 28

G

Geartooth Hall effect sensors, 83
Ground loops, 215
  damaging electronics, 216
  measurement errors, 216
  motor current, 218–220
  self-induced current errors, 220
Grounding and high-precision
    applications, 234–235
Guardian Relays/Solenoids Web site, 300

H

Half-flash converters, 24–25
Half-stepping stepper motors, 175–177
Hall, Edwin, 82
Hall effect, 82–83, 308
Hall effect potentiometer, 83
Hall effect sensors, 82–83, 195, 308
Hall effect switches, 82–83
Hanson Motors Web site, 299
Hardware
  peripherals, 8–9
  PWM (pulse width modulation), 296–297
  requirements, 9–11
  system adaptions to lower costs, 9–11
  throughput requirements support, 6
H-bridge circuits, 179
  braking capability, 192
  cross-conduction, 180
  enabling and disabling, 187
  power-up conditions, 182–183
Heaters
  detecting open heater condition, 149,
      151
  driven by transistor, 149
  open sensor, 151–152
  RTD heaters, 152, 154–155
High-precision applications
  frequency characteristics, 229
  grounding, 234–235
  input offset voltage, 227–228
  input resistance, 228–229
  noise, 234–235

opamps causing errors, 225–227
printed circuit board layout, 236–239
statistical tolerancing, 239–240
supply-based references, 240
temperature effects in general, 233–234
temperature effects in resistors, 230–231
voltage references, 231–233
High-side injection, 97
High-side switches, 257
High-side switching, 259–260
Hold capacitor, 27–28
Honeywell Web site, 299
Hybrid stepper motors, 171–173
Hysteresis, 283–285

I

I^2 bus, 38–39
IEEE 1451.2 standard
electrical, 243
standard units, 244
TEDS (transducer electronic data sheets),
243–244
Index, 308
Inertia, 117
Input
dynamic range, 1–2
frequency greater than measurement
capability, 12
frequency range, 97
multiple controls, 250–252
offset voltage, 227–228
resistance and high-precision
applications, 228–229
voltage and V-F (voltage-to-frequency
converters), 99
Instrumentation amplifiers, 285–286
Integral terms
pseudocode example, 139–140
saturation, 124–125
Integrals, 121–122
Integration, 72
Integration time, 72, 308
Integrator, 20–21
Interfaces
shared, 9
system design, 11
throughput requirements, 6
Interference, 215
Internal microcontroller ADCs, 42–43
Internal reference voltage, 29
Internal S/H (sample-and-hold circuit),
29–30

Interrupt rates, 44
Interrupts
repetitive events, 106
throughput requirements, 6
Inverting amplifier equation, 279–280
Iron-constantan (Type J) thermocouples, 57
ISR (interrupt service routine), 6, 92

K

Kodak KLI series, 76
Kodak KLI-2113, 77

L

L297 stepper-controller IC, 189
L6201 IC, 185, 192
L/C low-pass filter, 97
LEDs
current-limiting resistor in series, 157
driving multiple, 160–162
driving with constant current, 158–159
hooking in parallel with one limiting
resistor, 160–161
input voltage, 159
optoisolator outputs, 160
unregulated supply, 157–158
Linear arrays, 74
color filters, 75
nonuniformity, 80
Linear CCDs (charge coupled devices), 73–75
Line-scan CCDs (charge coupled devices).
See linear CCDs
Liteon Optoelectronics Web site, 300
LM231, 99
LM335, voltage proportional to
temperature, 58
LM336 reference, 231–233
LM336A-2.5 reference diode, 231
LM628/9 controller IC, 199–204
LM1820 IC, 185
LMD18200 H-bridge, 192, 207
Low-pass filter, 97–98
LVDTs (linear variable differential
transformers), 84–85, 308

M

Magnetic sensors
Hall effect sensors, 82–83
LVDTs (linear variable differential
transformers), 84–85
VRSs (variable reluctance sensors), 85–86

MAX 350, 169
MAX6576, 101–102
MAX6576 temperature sensor, 101
MAX6577, 91
Maxim MAX151
    adding data bus buffer before
        processor, 34
    bus cycle extended with wait states, 35
    bus relinquish time, 32–34
    -BUSY output, 32
    clocked interfaces, 35–36
    coupling of bus control signals, 34
    data access time, 32
    delay between conversions, 34
    internal S/H (sample-and-hold circuit),
        30
    interrupt rates, 44
    microprocessor interface, 32
    minimizing effect of coupling, 34
    parallel interface, 30
    ROM mode, 30–32
    sampling mode, 34
    Slow Memory Mode, 30
Maxim MAX191, 29
Maxim MAX349, 169
Maxim MAX1101, 39, 81
Maxim MAX1242, 36, 38, 43
Maxim MAX1617, 58
Maxim MAX5048, 259
Maxim MAX6225 reference, 233
Maxim MAX6576, 91
Maxim Web site, 299
Maxon Motors Web site, 299
MC2100 series controller IC, 203
MC2300 series controller IC, 203
Measurement
    1 °C accuracy, 2
    calibration, 2–5
    clock accuracy, 105
    frequency, 91
    input frequency greater than capacity, 12
    number of bits of precision required, 1–2
    time-based, 91
    tolerances, 2
Measuring
    analyzing control loops and, 134–143
    motor parameters, 136–138
    period versus frequency, 94–95
Mechanical potentiometers, 164–166
Microchip 16C7x parts, 51
Microchip PIC devices, 44
Microchip PIC16C series, 205
Microchip PIC167C7xx family, 42
Microchip Web site, 299

Microcontrollers
    binary values, 143
    division, 143
    dual-function pins on, 44–46
    input capture capability, 102
    multiplication, 143
    negative values, 143
    on-chip hardware to implement
        synchronous serial I/O, 39
    performing calibration, 3–4
    proprietary serial interfaces, 39
    with PWM outputs, 148
    supply and reference, 247–248
    timers incremented with external
        signal, 93
Microprocessor interface, 32
Microprocessor-based systems, 1, 108–109
Microprocessors
    buffer, 34
    connecting switch to, 87
    deadtime, 126
    extending accuracy with limited
        resolution, 102–106
    gain function, 108
    interfacing, 30–35
    interfacing to solenoids and relays,
        145–146
    internal wait-state generators, 32
    interrupt latency issues, 93
    measuring temperature using
        thermistor, 48, 50
    NMI (non-maskable interrupt) input, 93
    RDY or -WAIT signal, 32
    sampling output of sensors, 108
    sampling rate, 108–109
    slow memory mode, 32
    without capture capability, 93
Microsoft Excel, random number function,
    104
Microstepping stepper motors, 177–179
MIDI (Musical Instrument Digital
    Interface) optical isolation, 67
Mixer, complicated design of, 98
Mixing and time-based measurement,
    96–98
Monitoring control systems, 134–135
Monochrome images, 78
MOSFETs, 109, 146
    driving, 257–260
    gate-to-source and gate-to-drain
        capacitance, 259
    high-side switching, 259–260
    not turning on, 259
    turn-on time, 259

Motion/acceleration sensors, 86–89, 87–89
Motor control
    checking count of internal free-running
        counter, 130
    checking velocity, 130
    constant speed, 129–131
    control loop, 129
    counters, 128
    error, 128
    fixed-count sampling method, 130–131
    indicating desired position, 128–129
    positioning, 131, 133
    slotted switch, 129
    software considerations, 133
    timeout to detect stalled, 131
Motorola Semiconductors Web site, 299
Motors
    current and ground loops, 218–220
    DC motors, 190–205
    measuring parameters, 136–137
    rotor, 173–174
    stepper motors, 171–189
    torque, 208–209
    tuning parameters, 136
MPC (model predictive control), 134
Multichannel ADCs, 41–42
Multi-output arrays, 74
Multiple input control, 250–252
Multiple optical sensors, 65–67
Multiplexers, 168–169

N

National LM34 and LM35 sensors, 58
National LM74, 58
National LM75, 58–59
National Semiconductor LM4546, 43
National Semiconductor Web site, 299
National TP3054 telecom-type codec, 43
N-channel MOSFET, 260
Negative feedback and control, 107–108
Negative voltages, reading, 261–262
NMI (non-maskable interrupt) input, 93
NMPC (nonlinear model predictive
    control), 134
Noise and high-precision applications,
    234–235
Noninverting amplifier equation, 280
Nonuniformity CCDs (charge coupled
    devices), 80–81
NPN transistor, 145–146
NTC (negative temperature coefficient), 47
NTC thermistors, 48, 151–152

O

Offset voltage and high-precision
    applications, 227
Omron Relays Web site, 300
On-chip ADCs (analog-to-digital
    converters), 42
On-chip hardware to implement
    synchronous serial I/O
    microcontrollers, 39
One-phase-on drive, 175
On-off (bang-bang) control, 263, 266
    coupling, 110
    dead band, 111–112
    optimum conditions, 111
    oscillation, 113, 115
    overshoot, 113, 115
    thermal mass, 110
    time lag, 110
Opamps
    buffer configuration, 275–277
    calculating output voltage, 53
    causing errors, 225–227
    comparators, 281–283
    design equations, 279–280
    deviations from ideal, 108
    differential amplifier configuration,
        278–279
    differential amplifier equation, 280
    equation, 225–227
    frequency limitations, 108
    input impedance, 228
    input resistance, 228–229
    instrumentation amplifiers, 285–286
    inverting amplifier equation, 279–280
    negative feedback, 107–108
    noninverting amplifier equation, 280
    noninverting configuration, 277–278
    nonresistive elements, 280
    reversing inputs, 281
Open heater condition, 149, 151
Open sensors, 64–65, 151–152
Open-loop controls, 107
Open-loop gain, 308
Operating system requirements and
    throughput, 7
Optical encoders, 197
Optical isolators, 67–68
Optical sensors
    comparator, 62–63
    connecting output to ADC, 62
    discrete, 69–71
    failed LED, 66–67
    interfacing to microprocessor, 69

Optical sensors (*continued*)
  IR problems, 63–64
  mechanical instability, 64
  multiple, 65–67
  open sensors, 64–65
  optical isolators, 67–68
  reflective sensors, 59–63
  slotted switches, 59
Optocouplers, 67–68, 182
Optoisolators, 67–68
  driving multiple, 160–162
  isolating bidirectional signal between two
      systems, 69–71
  LEDs, 160
  transistor and logic outputs, 160
  triac outputs, 160
Oriental Motors Web site, 299
Oscillators, crystal-controlled, 234–235
Out-of-bounds controls, 141–142
Output
  coding, 30
  dynamic range, 1–2
  offset, 28
  voltage, 13–15
Output word and ADCs, 16
Oversampling, 21–22

P

Pacific Scientific Web site, 299
Parallel interfaces and ADCs, 30–32
PC/104 Plus bus, 7–8
PCB grounding, 236
P-channel MOSFET, 259–260
Peltier cooler, 308
Performance Motion Devices Web site, 299
Periods
  measuring *versus* frequency, 94–95
  sampling clock, 100–102
Peripherals, 8–9, 39
Permanent-magnet stepper motors, 171
Phillips TDA5140, 197
PIC15C6x series, 91
Pick/hold circuit and solenoids, 147–148
PID analysis package, 138
PID (proportional, integral, derivative)
    controls, 116, 308
  amount of change in one time interval,
      126
  antiwindup for integral term, 139–140
  block diagram, 116
  deadtime, 126
  derivative term, 126
  derivatives, 117–120

difficulty of making measurements, 124
discontinuous inputs, 127
drawbacks, 133
effectiveness, 133
filtering noisy input, 140–141
formula for calculating output, 116–117
handling specific inputs, 127
inertia, 117
integral and derivative gains, 123
integrals, 121–122, 126
light load *versus* a heavy load, 117
motor control, 127–133
offset, 117, 133
oscillation, 120
overshoot, 119–120
practical considerations, 123–124
preventing out-of-bounds average
      output, 141–142
preventing out-of-bounds control
      output, 141
proportional gain and derivative, 120
pseudocode examples, 138–143
saturation, 124–125
software considerations, 125–126
special requirements, 127
summarized, 122–123
terms, 117
time delays, 126
tuning, 123–124
velocity setpoint, 131, 133
PID loop
  measuring effects of changes, 136
  pseudocode examples, 138–140
PMDC (Permanent magnet DC) motor DC
      Motors, 190
PN junction, 58
Positioning motor control, 131, 133
Potentiometers
  mechanical, 166
Potentiometers, digital and mechanical,
      163–166
Power supplies and printed circuit board
      layout, 236–239
Printed circuit board layout
  PCB grounding, 236
  power supplies, 236–239
Processing requirements and throughput, 7
Processor
  avoiding excess speed, 7–8
  clock-synchronized bus, 35
  cost, 7–8
  EMC (electromatic compatibility), 8
  hardware divide instruction, 10
  throughput, 6–7

Products and EMC regulations, 8
Proportional controls, 266–268
    adjusting control signal, 113, 115
    adjusting gain and offset, 115
    conditional problems, 115
    equation, 113
    error, 112–113, 115
    handling varying loads better, 118
    known load, 115
    negative output capability, 113
    oscillation around setpoint, 113
    overshoot, 113
    reaching setpoint without oscillating, 115
    without offset, 115
Proportional-integral control, 273
Proprietary serial interfaces, 39, 41
Pulse-duty solenoids, 145
PWM (pulse width modulation), 308
    audio applications, 295
    EMI, 294
    hardware, 296–297
    power-supply considerations, 294
    resolution limitations, 293–294
    software, 297
Python code for Chapter 11, 301–305

Q

QT optoelectronics reflective sensors, 61
QT optoelectronics Web site, 300
Quad digital potentiometer, 166
Quadrature encoder, 198

R

Random number function, 104
Range, 100–102
Reading negative voltages, 261–262
Reference voltage, 16, 42–43, 308
References
    bypassing, 29
    reducing input, 17
Reflective sensors
    adding hardware and/or software to
        detect unusual conditions, 64
    CTR (current transfer ratio), 61–62
    focal length, 59
    gain, 61–63
    IR problems, 63–64
    mechanical instability, 64
    mechanical jitter, 64
    sensing objects of differing types, 64
    speed, 61

Refrigerators and temperature, 105–160
Relays, 145
    chopping current, 148
    clamping, 147
    DC current drawn by, 147–148
    diode camp usage, 146–147
    extra set of contacts on, 148
    flyback voltage, 146–147
    interfacing to, 145–147
Repetitive events, 104, 106
Resistance
    RTD heaters, 152, 154
    temperature, 2
Resistor ladder, 24
Resistor networks, 249–250
Resistor voltage divider, 261
Resistors
    dissipating power, 148
    standard values, 54
    temperature effects, 230–231
Resolution
    ADCs (analog-to-digital converters),
        16–17
    extending with limited, 102–106
    improving, 16–17
Resonance and stepper motors, 173–175,
    188
ROM mode, 36
Rotor and stepper motors, 173–174
RTD (resistance temperature detectors),
    56, 308
RTD heaters
    drawbacks, 154
    driving, 152, 154
    measure-when-off circuit, 154
    measure-when-on circuit, 154
    measuring temperature of heating
        element, 154–155
    measuring temperature with heater off,
        154
    resistance, 152, 154
    sense resistor, 152, 154
    temperature measurement dependent
        on supply voltage, 154
    thermistors, 152
    tolerance, 154

S

Safety and failed sensors, 64–65
Sample rate, 11–12
Sampling clock, higher frequency, 96
Saturation, 124–125

Scaling output for temperature sensors and thermistors, 51–55
Seebeck, Thomas, 57
Self-heating, 50
Self-induced current errors, 220
Self-induced ESD (electrostatic discharge), 221
Semiconductor strain gauges, 90
Sense resistor
  RTD heaters, 152, 154
  stepper motors, 184
SENSEFETS, 154
Sensors
  magnetic, 82–86
  motion/acceleration, 86–89
  open, 151–152
  operating from different reference, 99–100
  optical, 59–71
  saturation, 125
  temperature, 47–59
Serial interfaces
  ADCs (analog-to-digital converters), 36–41
  I^2 bus, 38–39
  proprietary, 41
  SMBus, 39, 41
  SPI/Microwire, 36, 38
  TP3054, 43
Setpoint, settling small distance from, 121–122
Set/reset flip-flop, 156
S/H (sample-and-hold circuits), 308
  acquisition time, 28
  CDS (correlated double sampling), 79–80
  finite input impedance, 28
  full power bandwidth, 28
  hold capacitor, 27–28
  internal, 29–30
  maintaining output in hold mode, 28
  output offset, 28
  waveform, 27
Shared interfaces, 9
Shoot-through, 180–184, 308
Sigma-delta converter
  accuracy, 24
  comparator, 23
  complexity of digital filter, 24
  differential amp, 22
  high resolution, 24
  input range, 24
  speed, 24

Single-channel arrays, 74
Single-slope converter, 21
Sinusoidal input signal, 11
Slotted switches, 59
  CTR (current transfer ratio), 61
  current transfer ratio, 61
  Darlington transistor outputs, 61
  filtering, 63
  gain, 61–63
  IR problems, 63–64
  motor control, 129
  speed, 61
Slow Memory mode, 36
SMBus, 39, 41
Smith, Otto, 126
Smith Predictor, 126
Software
  artificially limiting integral buildup, 125–126
  motor control considerations, 133
  PID considerations, 125–126
  PWM (pulse width modulation), 297
  registers of limited size, 125
Software controllers and DC motors, 204–205
Solenoids
  clamping, 147
  DC current drawn by, 147–148
  driven by transistor, 149
  flyback voltage, 146–147
  interfacing to, 145–147
  pick/hold circuit, 147–148
Solid state temperature sensors, 58–59
Solid-state acceleration sensors, 86
Solid-state (Peltier) coolers, 155
Solid-state sensor, detecting open, 151–152
Sony ILX series, 76
Sony ILX724
Sony Semiconductors Web site, 299
Specialized DACs (digital-to-analog converters), 163
SPI/Microwire, 36, 38
SPI/Microwire interface, 58
SSRs (solid-state relays), 252
Stall torque, 209
Standard interfaces
  4–20ma current loop, 244–245
  Fieldbus, 245–246
  IEEE 1451.2, 243–244
Statistical tolerancing, 239–240
Stepper DC motors, 206
Stepper motors
  analog driver, 191
  bipolar *versus* unipolar windings, 173

chopper control, 186–187
constant current drive, 188
control method, 188
cross-conduction, 180–184
current sensing, 184
driving, 179–180
firmware, 211–213
half-stepping, 175–177, 188
hybrid, 171–173
interrupt routine logic, 213
linear drive, 188–189
main loop logic, 211
microstepping, 177–179, 188
motor current logic, 212·
motor drive ICs, 185
one-phase-on drive, 175
permanent-magnet, 171
ramping down, 212
real-world application, 209–213
resonance, 173–175, 188
rotor, 173–174
sense resistor, 184
speed and current update logic, 212
state update logic, 212
sudden loss of torque, 174–175
switch debounce logic, 212
torque, 186–187
variable-reluctance, 171
Stored charge, 256
Strain gauges, 89–90, 309
Successive approximation ADCs, 42
changing signals, 26–27
reference bypassing, 29
resistor ladder, 24
Successive approximation converter, 19–20
Successive approximation register, 19–20
Summarized PID, 122–123
Supply-based references, 240
Surface-mount (SOT-23) device, 91
Surface-mount packaging, 83
Surveillance cameras and area CCDs, 78
Susceptibility, 215
Switches
analog, 166–169
bounce, 87–88
contact resistance, 88–89
detecting press of, 87–88
motion/acceleration sensors, 87–89
types, 87
Synchronous V-F converters, 99
System design
aliasing, 11–12
avoiding speed, 7–8
bandwidth, 5

calibration, 2–5
dynamic range, 1–2
hardware requirements, 9–11
interfaces, 11
peripheral hardware, 8–9
processor throughput, 6–7
sample rate, 11–12
shared interfaces, 9
task priorities, 9
word width, 11
Systems
capable of division, 105
Ethernet between, 216
inertia, 117
microprocessor-based, 108–109

T

Task priorities, 9
TEDS (transducer electronic data sheets),
243–244
Temperature, 47
converting to time-based output, 93
general effects, 233–234
refrigerators, 105–160
relating output of sensor to, 3
resistance, 2
thermistor measurement of, 48, 50
Temperature control loop, 149
Temperature sensors
converting temperature to time-based
output, 93
PN junction, 58
RTD (resistance temperature detectors),
56
scaling output, 51–55
solid state, 58–59
thermistors, 47–51
thermocouples, 57–58
tolerance stackup, 55–56
Temperature-sensitive resistor, 47
Texas Instruments Web site, 299
Thermal mass and on-off control, 110
Thermistors, 109, 309
characteristics, 47
D.C. (dissipation constant), 50
generating heat, 50
limiting repeatability, 48
measuring temperature, 48, 50
NTC (negative temperature coefficient),
47
placement and performance, 111
resistance, 47–48, 51

Thermistors (*continued*)
  RTD heaters, 152
  scaling output, 51–55
  self-heating, 50
  sensitivity, 47
  tables, 48
  thermal mass, 110
  tolerance, 48, 56
Thermocouple signal conditioner, 58
Thermocouples, 57–58, 151–152, 309
Throughput requirements, 6–7
TI VSP 2000, 81
Time delays and PID controls, 126
Time-based measurement
  capture counter, 91–93
  clock resolution, 100–102
  extending accuracy with limited
    resolution, 102–106
  interrupt latency issues, 93
  mixing, 96–98
  period *versus* frequency, 94–95
  range, 100–102
  V-F (voltage-to-frequency converters),
    98–100
Timers, 93, 103
TMP03, 93
TMP04, 93
Tolerance, 2, 154
Tolerance stackup, 55–56, 239–240
Torque, 208–209, 309
Tracking ADC (analog-to-digital
    converter), 17, 19, 24
Transistors, 292–293
Tranzorbs, 147
Trilinear arrays, 76–77
Trilinear CCDs (charge coupled devices)
  linear CCD arrays, 78
  skewed data, 77–78
  three-element array, 75–76
Tuning PID loops, 138
Two-channel encoders, 198

U

Unipolar Hall effect switches, 83
Unipolar stepper motors, 173

V

Van DeGraff generator, 221
Variable-reluctance stepper motors,
    171
V-F (voltage-to-frequency converters),
    98–100, 309
Voltage, 254
Voltage divider, 261–262
Voltage precision, 2
Voltage references
  high-precision applications, 231–233
  tolerance, 56
VRSs (variable reluctance sensors), 85–86,
    309
VST 3000 series, 81

W

Wintune Web site, 138
Word width, 11

X

Xicor Web site, 299

Z

Zener diodes, 147, 223
Zero crossing switching, 252–254
Ziegler/Nichols method, 123–124